Human
Geography
in the Making

Series Editor:

ALEXANDER B. MURPHY

Department of Geography,
University of Oregon, USA

SERIES PREFACE

To understand the rapidly changing world in which we live, the study of geography is essential. Yet the nature and importance of a geographic perspective can easily be misconstrued if geography is seen simply as a set of changing patterns and arrangements. Like the world around it, the discipline of geography itself has undergone sweeping changes in recent decades as its practitioners have confronted and developed new concepts, theories, and perspectives. Placing the contributions of geographic research within the context of these changes is critical to an appreciation of geography's present and future.

The *Human Geography in the Making* series was developed with these considerations in mind. Inspired initially by the influential 'Progress Reports' in the journal *Progress in Human Geography*, the series offers book-length overviews of geographic subdisciplines that are widely taught in colleges and universities at the upper division and graduate levels. The goal of each of the books is to acquaint readers with the major issues and conceptual problems that have dominated a particular subdiscipline over the past two to three decades, to discuss and assess current themes that are shaping the evolution of the subdiscipline, and to highlight the most promising areas for future research.

There is a widely recognized gap between topically focused textbooks and narrowly defined scholarly studies. The books in this series move into this gap. Through analyses of the intellectual currents that have shaped key subdisciplines of geography, these books provide telling insights into the conceptual and empirical issues currently influencing research and teaching. Geographic understanding requires an appreciation of how and why ideas have evolved, and where they may be going. The distinguished contributors to this series have much to say about these matters, offering ideas and interpretations of importance to students and professional geographers alike.

Alexander B. Murphy
Series Editor
Professor of Geography
University of Oregon

TITLES IN THE SERIES

Making Political Ecology
(Roderick P Neumann, Florida International University, USA)

Making Political Geography
(John Agnew, UCLA, USA)

Making Population Geography
(Adrian Bailey, University of Leeds)

Making Development Geography

VICTORIA A. LAWSON
Department of Geography
University of Washington, USA

Hodder Arnold

A MEMBER OF THE HODDER HEADLINE GROUP

Distributed in the United States of America by
Oxford University Press Inc., New York

Orders: please contact Bookpoint Ltd, 130 Milton Park, Abingdon, Oxon OX14 4SB. Telephone: (44) 01235 827720. Fax: (44) 01235 400454. Lines are open from 9.00–6.00, Monday to Saturday, with a 24 hour message answering service. You can also order through our website www.hoddereducation.co.uk

If you have any comments to make about this, or any of our other titles, please send them to educationenquiries@hodder.co.uk

British Library Cataloguing in Publication Data
A catalogue record for this book is available from the British Library

ISBN-10: 0 340 809647
ISBN-13: 978 0 340 809648

Impression number   1 2 3 4 5 6 7 8 9 10
Year   2009 2008 2007 2006 2005 2004

Typeset in 10 on 14.5pt Gill Sans by Phoenix Photosetting, Chatham, Kent
Printed in Malta for Hodder Arnold, an imprint of Hodder Education, a member of the Hodder Headline Group, 338 Euston Road, London NW1 3BH

CONTENTS

Preface
CANCER STORIES – EXPLANATION AND ACTION IN DEVELOPMENT

...it [development] frustrates present satisfaction (in Latin enough-ness), so that one always longs for something better that lies in the 'not yet' (Illich 1997: 104)

Development defies definition and, at once, motivates and paralyses its students. When I taught my class on critical development theory in the autumn of 2002, my goal was to move students beyond the expectation that we can provide quick and easy solutions to the dilemmas of development. That autumn was also when my partner began his struggle with leukaemia. I spent those months alternating between the hospital and the classroom and this proved surprisingly instructive. Some striking parallels emerged between my struggles to understand cancer and my students' efforts to understand and analyse their role in development.

Many of my students were being exposed to a critical reading of mainstream development theory for the first time. At the hospital, my partner and I experienced what I suppose many do: a stunned sense of our world out of control, of uncertainty and of a lack of answers. We put our hopes and his life in their good faith efforts to find the right treatment. We found ourselves amazed at the paradox of a technologically sophisticated, well-endowed research hospital groping for a diagnosis, then suggesting a treatment that 'might' offer hope, and so on. In my classroom, students were horrified by the state of inequality and suffering in our world; they were stunned to learn that so much of mainstream development seems to exacerbate precisely the poverty and inequality that it purports to solve. The students became frustrated that despite 50 years of research, technological advancement and investment, development was still failing to deliver social justice and a more sustainable and fully democratic future for the world's societies.

I found myself nonplussed (or even downright aggravated) with my students' sense of frustration and impatience with critical development theory. Some of them wanted straightforward answers and actions that would 'solve' development dilemmas. Then it occurred to me that these same students would never take a 10-week course in medical school and expect to come up with a cure for cancer at the end of the quarter. The questions swirling around development are equally complex and much like medicine; the answers for social science are very hard to find. Social systems are open, unpredictable, untestable and multiply determined (by political, economic, cultural forces), and social scientists do not have the chance to close the system through experimentation. Of course, these expectations that we have 'solutions' to cancer and to development failures at our fingertips emerge from the normative bent of mainstream science and social engineering. We are socialised to expect that problems are defined and then solved, regardless of time and place. This is the allure of science (social, natural and medical) – we in the academy construct expectations that we know, understand and can solve 'the problem'.

However, development actors (and doctors) address incredibly complex questions, under very difficult circumstances and attempt to understand how these processes work. Just because this work is difficult and frustrating, we do not give up on finding cures for devastating diseases. I found myself urging my students that, in a similar way, we must not give up on interrogating development processes and our own roles within them, just because the answers are elusive or difficult to swallow. Living with cancer means living with uncertainty and ambiguity. Living with a critical understanding of the failures of development, and the complicity of the West in sustaining these injustices, means living with uncertainty, ambiguity and complexity in understanding our role and our contributions to change – but we go forward nonetheless, seeking to build greater understanding.

This book provides students with a critical geographical approach to understanding the post-Second World War history of Anglo development debates. I have organised the book to foreground four critical geographical tools for advancing development studies. First, geographers view development knowledge as always situated in cultural, historical and geographical contexts which link language, power and material life. Second, geographers analyse the relationships between the places and scales foregrounded in development thinking and the kinds of processes, actors and institutions deemed relevant to that version of development. Third, critical development geographers attend to the ways in which development processes play out empirically in specific times and places as a corrective to overly abstract theorisations (on the right or the left). Finally, critical development geographers are committed to an accountable analysis of development discourses, institutions and practices that takes seriously the agency and responsibility of all actors. The challenge for students of this book is to draw on this geographical approach to build their own analytical and political relationship to development, or something beyond it, that might not even be called development at all: social and environmental justice, or perhaps human-friendly or freedom-friendly projects.

Saying thank you always seems entirely inadequate and this was never more true than now. My writing of this book coincided with momentous times in my life. All of us who embark on big projects like this know that we would never finish without the people who sustain us. Wayne Ledford provided laughter, strength, perspective and a 'larger than life' presence in my life. Wayne did not win his battle with leukaemia, but the lessons we learned – about love, dignity, the preciousness of life – sustain me now. Dean Odegard's love and companionship literally pulled me back from the cliff, sustained me in loss and now grounds me in what is truly important in life – the joy of sharing it with a loving soulmate.

I have grown throughout this project thanks to the supportive, constructive and engaged commentary of colleagues who are also my dear friends. I thank Lucy Jarosz for her intellectual generosity and deep friendship over many years, Michael Brown for our wonderful 'book lunches', which were always about both books and life, and Katharyne Mitchell and Matt Sparke for intellectual inspiration and the cherished friendship of family times with Sage and Emma, dinners and violin music. Bill Beyers and Richard Morrill I thank for warm and spirited friendship, as well as inspiration through their own academic citizenship. I have grown through the generosity of friends and colleagues who believe in me, who taught me about feminist thought and development studies and who have supported me in all ways. For all this I thank Lynn Staeheli, Jenny Zorn, Kim England, Sarah Radcliffe, Cindi Katz and Sallie Marston. I also thank Larry Brown, who inspired and challenged me to work in critical development studies.

I would especially like to thank Alexander Murphy for his friendship, which I cherish, as well as his professional support through very tough times and for his editorship of this series. I am very grateful that he invited me to join this outstanding group of authors in human geography. I would also like to thank my anonymous reviewers, and at Hodder Arnold Abigail Woodman, Liz Gooster, Jamilah Ahmed and Tiara Misquitta for their patience and encouragement.

I thank wholeheartedly the superb students who have shaped my work, Jen Devine, Anna McCall-Taylor and Tony Sparks, my brilliant research assistants who have researched and inspired so much of what is here. Students, both graduate and undergraduate, have guided this project in myriad ways – especially my undergraduate development studies classes from 2002, 2004 and 2006, my graduate seminars in 2003 and 2005, and graduate students Patty Price, Linda Becker, Suzanne Teltscher, Rachel Silvey, Clare Newstead, Lise Nelson, Maureen Hickey, Sarah Wright, Kim Van Eyck, Amy Freeman, Anne Bonds, Dominic Corva and Heather Rule Day.

The author/editor and publishers would like to thank the following for permission to use copyright material in this book:

Permission for Figure 1.1, Poor Nations/Rich Nations, was given by Jubilee USA officials; this image appears in their educational materials. I have been unable to track down the original copyright holder, but Vladimir Tikunov, Moscow State University granted permission to use the map, GNP in the world, for Figure 1.2. Figure 1.3, Size of the armed forces, is reproduced by permission of Lenny Behnke, Permissions Coordinating Lead at McGraw-Hill Contemporary Learning Series. Sarah Wright gave permission to use her photographs from Filipino fieldwork in Figures 1.4, Farmer and NGO Street Conference in the Philippines, and 4.3, Filipino Farmers' and Organisers' Rally. Figures 1.8, Regional Economic Agreements worldwide, and 2.1, Regional Social Fora, worldwide, are used by permission of their author, Tony Sparks. Michael Patrick gave permission to reproduce Figure 1.9, Geography of global economic integration. Box 2.2, Population as the Problem, is reprinted and modified with permission from Maureen Hickey (my co-author) and from Blackwell Publishing for an excerpt from our co-authored chapter in Castree, Rogers and Sherman (eds) (2006) *Questioning Geography*. Figure 3.1, Bretton Woods Conference in 1944, is reprinted with permission from Martha Wilson, Bretton Woods Resort Public Relations Manager. Box 3.3, An explanation of comparative advantage, is modified with permission from Alex Singleton of the Adam Smith Institute. I include Table 3.1 by permission of Anna McCall-Taylor. Figure 3.2, Diffusion of primary education, is reprinted with permission from Northwestern University Press for an excerpt from the volume by J. Barry Riddell (1970) *The Spatial Dynamics of Modernization in Sierra Leone: Structure, Diffusion and Response* (page 67, Figure 15). I use Box 4.2, The Clash of Environmentalism and Developmentalism, with permission from Lucy Jarosz, University of Washington.

Victoria A. Lawson, October 2006

For Dean Odegard

DEVELOPMENT AS SITUATED KNOWLEDGE

As most of us are aware, development rarely seems to 'work' – or at least with the consequences intended or the outcomes predicted. Why then, if it is so unworkable, does it not only persist but seem continuously to be expanding its reach and scope? (Crush 1995: 4)

The notion and practice of development have been severely critiqued from both modernist and postmodern perspectives, yet the global development industry flourishes (Blaikie 2000: 1033)

1.1 Introduction

Why write a book on development geography, when there are innumerable critiques of the very idea of development from all points on the political spectrum? Enormous concerns appear to overshadow development in this new millennium, with (anti-)globalisation and the 'war on terror' reworking the relations, and fault lines, between people and places. And yet I remain committed to teaching and working in development because of all that is at stake. In 2002, I spoke with Nelson Reascos, a philosophy professor in Quito, about the problems facing his country. He put it simply, saying that the whole world faces a health crisis. But, he said, we in Ecuador are dying from too little food and you in the United States are dying from too much (Figure 1.1). Nelson highlights the connectedness and contradictions of our global system, where its dynamics simultaneously produce overconsumption and heart disease in the West and food scarcity and malnutrition in the global South.

In my classes we work to understand the paradox of 50 years of development going hand in glove with grotesque inequalities across places. The situation is urgent:

Figure 1.1 Poor Nations, Rich Nations

▪ According to the *Multinational Monitor*, in 2003, '[T]he richest 10 percent of the world's population's income is roughly 117 times higher than the poorest 10 percent, according to calculations performed by economists at the Economics Policy Institute (data from the International Monetary Fund). This is a huge jump from the ratio in 1980, when the income of the richest 10 percent was about 79 times higher than the poorest 10 percent'.

▪ The 200 richest people in the world more than doubled their net worth in the four years from 1994 to 1998, to $1 trillion (UN Development Program 1999).

▪ Paul Krugman comments on poverty in the United States, saying that the 13,000 richest families have as much income as the 20 million poorest (Krugman 2002).

▪ Eight of the world's top 10 billionaires are United States citizens as of 2004 (www.forbes.com).

▪ Tikunov's cartogram of national territories distorted by the size of the gross national product in the early 1990s powerfully illustrates these global inequalities (Figure 1.2).

▪ A recent UNCTAD (2002) Least Developed Countries Report finds that extreme poverty (defined as the $1-a-day international poverty line) has doubled over the past 30 years, to 307 million.

▪ Figure 1.3 illustrates the size of armed forces around the globe; this map presents another key metric of global inequalities of resources and power.

2

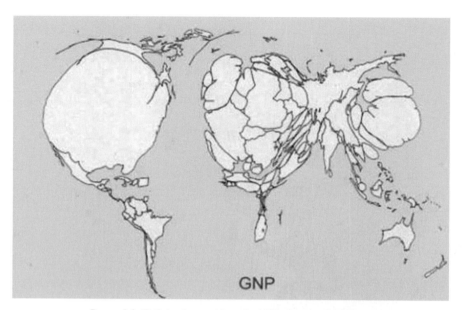

Figure 1.2 GNP in the world, early 1990. Source: Vladimir Tikunov (1995)

Focusing our attention on wealthy countries we find that the USA has the most unequal income distribution in the West. As Paul Krugman (2002: 63) reports, '...the average real annual compensation of the top 100 C.E.O.'s went from $1.3M – 39 times the pay of an average worker – to $37.5M, more than 1000 times the pay of ordinary workers'. And in the state of Washington where I teach, most poor parents work in either services (38 per cent) or retail sales (32 per cent), the two industries with the fastest job growth and the lowest average pay in the state (Columbia Legal Services 1996).

Nelson Reascos's story, and these statistics, point to the crucial importance of North–South relations for understanding development. Development geography is mapped onto the global South to the exclusion of Northern societies. I argue, along with both Marxist-feminist and post-structural researchers (discussed in chapters 4 and 5), that development geography going forward must be framed in terms of material and discursive relations between places and people *across the globe* – examining connections between neoliberal economic and political discourses and actions, as these reshape agricultural policies and farming livelihoods from the United Kingdom to Mexico, for instance. In this book I argue for an explicitly relational and geographical analysis of development (Hart 2001, 2002b). By this I mean analysis that takes into account the interplay of political-economy forces; discursive and cultural constructions of gender,

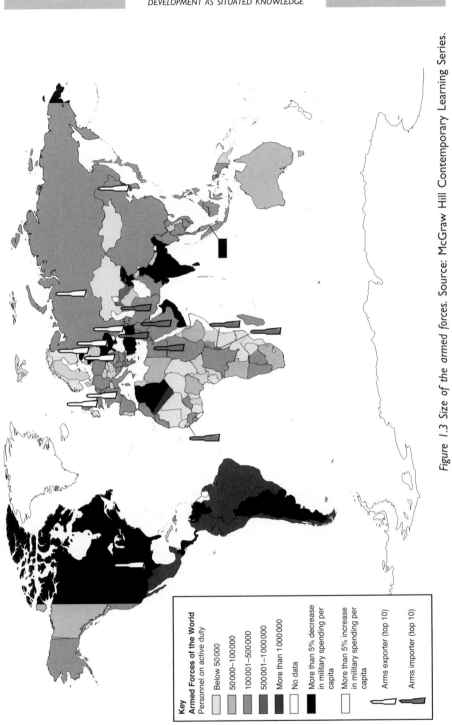

Figure 1.3 Size of the armed forces. Source: McGraw Hill Contemporary Learning Series.

Key
Armed Forces of the World
Personnel on active duty

Below 50000
50000–100000
100001–500000
500001–1000000
More than 1000000
No data

More than 5% decrease in military spending per capita

More than 5% increase in military spending per capita

Arms exporter (top 10)

Arms importer (top 10)

race/ethnicity, development, nationality, and so on; colonial and postcolonial histories; physical geography; and the shifting political and regulatory power of places. Development studies and geography have been framed in such a way that the majority world has been constructed as a poor space in need of saving, while the West has remained invisible. Critical development geography recovers the West as a crucially important site of development studies research. Bebbington (2003: 301) makes a similar call for more work on how development processes are playing out across multiple locations while being simultaneously global processes that are intimately enmeshed with one another.

'Development' itself is a complex, contradictory and powerful term that takes on particular meanings in the context of specific intellectual, institutional and political moments. Particular definitions of development have been invoked to justify and design material and political interventions that have transformed livelihoods, relocated the course of rivers, redrawn national boundaries, reworked governance across a range of scales and even changed people's perceptions of themselves. In this book, we will not search for the 'right' definition of development, but rather, we will look at what these various ideas about development mean. For a particular meaning of 'development' we will ask, whose version of development is this? What political work is it doing? And who does it include and leave out of the development project? As we build these critical and contextual readings of the various 'developments' invoked in geography we will think through how the major schools of development thought produce particular geographies of development and also how geographical research is enriching development studies more broadly.

Development knowledge is produced by diverse actors, including activists, consultants and intellectuals who are located in varied sites, such as international development agencies, universities, social movements, non-governmental organisations (NGOs) and state agencies. These different actors produce distinct ideas about what development is and what it might be going forwards. They also produce development knowledge differently, some through action and activism, others through research or policy-making. Indeed, development knowledge is always produced in the restless interplay between analysis and action, between academics, activists, policy-makers and power brokers. In short, development is a contested term. There are two connected threads of meaning in development theory: development as concrete, material actions and processes; and development as discourse. I introduce both these ideas briefly here and return to them in later chapters. In thinking about development as material change, Gillian Hart suggests that

...'big D' Development [be] defined as a post-second world war project of intervention in the 'third world' that emerged in the context of decolonisation and the
cold war, and 'little d' development or the development of capitalism as a geographically uneven, profoundly contradictory set of historical processes. (Hart 2001: 650)

For Hart, big 'D' Development refers to the intent to develop, focusing on
policy analysis and revision within a range of institutions, such as the World Bank
(WB) and the International Monetary Fund (IMF), and non-governmental organ-
isations (Gore 1984; Farrington, Bebbington, Wellard and Lewis 1993).
Development policies have material effects, such as building infrastructure (dams,
schools, etc.); commercialising agriculture, as with the diffusion of Green
Revolution technologies; and building industrial capacity through Import
Substitution Industrialisation policies. While Hart, and this book, focus on post-
Second World War interventions, efforts to shape development processes have
a much longer history in the work of national governments, missionaries, colonial
authorities, and so on (Cowen and Shenton 1996; Bebbington 2003). Scholars
have also engaged big 'D' Development by critiquing the ways in which discourses
of development,[i] emanating from these sorts of institutions, construct justifica-
tions for, and terrains of, intervention in the global South (Crush 1995; Escobar
1995). Bebbington (2003) usefully points out that Development is not limited to
external interventions by global institutions, but also encompasses many actors
within countries who attempt to shape social and economic development.

The second meaning of material development refers to the unfolding of
economic and social processes within capitalist societies (see Cowen and
Shenton 1996 for an extended discussion). Little 'd' development refers to
unscripted shifts in economies and societies of landscapes of investment, production, consumption patterns, global flows of debt payments, the emergence of
political alliances among workers, feminists, environmentalists, indigenous
people, transnational migrations and the like. Marxist and feminist theorists have
focused on little 'd' development to investigate the multiple articulations of
capitalist social relations within places, histories and cultures. This work poses
questions about state–society relations, patterns of capital accumulation, and the
dynamics producing class, gender and race difference in relation to the internationalisation of capitalist social relations (Corbridge 1986; Watts 1988; Peet
with Hartwick 1999). Within this work, Development institutions and discourses
are a particular, historically specific moment in a process of securing the conditions for global capitalist accumulation (Hart 2001, 2002a). Where relevant to
my argument, I will indicate both senses of development with D/d.

Turning now to development as discourse, some theorists have focused on the ways in which particular meanings of development are constructed in histories and power relations, through which some meanings become very influential and others are sidelined. Discourse refers to ways of knowing, made up of ideas, ideologies, texts, narratives, institutions, and individual and collective practices. Powerful discourses of development are able to set the terms of the debate, about what development is, and what it can be. For example, some scholars from the global South view development economics as a field that defines development in terms of Western histories, values and norms, such that for influential institutions and national governments, development comes to be synonymous with capitalist economic growth (Escobar 1995; Shresthsa 1995; Illich 1997). This powerful discourse about development, which is reinforced through academic work, scientific research and popular cultural productions, becomes so influential (indeed commonsensical) that we can no longer see, or even imagine, other ways of defining development.

For example, consider the following two definitions of development, and think about the confluence of ideas, institutions, resources, values and political power that make one much more influential (perhaps even more thinkable?) than the other. In a conversation with Majhid Rahnema, Ivan Illich (1997: 105) described meaningful development in the following terms: '"Enough" is like a magic carpet; I experience "more" as a burden, a burden that during the twentieth century has become so heavy that we cannot pack it on our shoulders. We must load it into lorries that we have to buy and maintain.' Illich is a philosopher and cleric who has dedicated his life to teaching and organising against Western development interventions and around the possibility of imagining meaningful alternatives.

Compare this with the following quote from the World Bank annual report (1999: 13), which characterises development as '…raising per capita income and consumption are part of that goal, other objectives – reducing poverty, expanding access to health services, and increasing educational levels are also important.' This quote captures the dominant discourse wherein economic growth fundamentally constitutes the essence of development, underscored by decades of economic theory, substantiated by volumes of research carried on in universities, financed by enormous volumes of money pumped into this 'development industry' (cf. Escobar 1995) and housed in powerful institutions which legitimate these ideas. While both quotes provide clear arguments about the meaning of development, they do not have equal legitimacy or influence in the powerful institutions of governments or civil society.

This book provides a critical and (inevitably) selective survey of the meaning and scope of Anglo-American development geography, with a focus on the contexts of development thought, the geographies of development they produce and the subjects included and excluded in particular theorisations of development.[ii] Development geography does not have a long history in the discipline. Rather, it has been an interdisciplinary field of inquiry to which geography has contributed over time, even as the larger field has shaped and shifted the questions and emphases in development geography. The task of this book is to trace influential ideas, key scholars who have shaped development geography and the pressing questions they pose, and to present an argument about the contributions of this sub-field to development debates more broadly. I argue here that development geography became a more coherent and recognisable sub-field quite recently, and I trace the intellectual currents of development geography that contributed to its strengthening within the discipline.

1.2 Moments in the making of development geography

Geographic research on development has been informed by distinct theoretical streams and substantive concerns over recent decades. Tracing its roots from colonial geographies of the late nineteenth century, Marcus Power (2003) discusses the rise of 'tropical regional geography' in the UK and the USA as a precursor to development geography. He charts the uncritical relationship between geographies of 'the tropics' and the maintenance of European empires (both through colonial administration and military means) prior to the Second World War. Even in the early post-war period, Power (2003: 49) points to the '...numerous bulky, regional geographies of the non-western world' that provided encyclopedic information in uncritical service of settlement, economic development and 'progress' in the global South (see for example regional handbooks written for the CIA in the USA and the Naval Intelligence Division in the UK). At mid-century geographers began to address the substantive concerns of development as broader theoretical problems rather than solely as the particulars of specific regional studies.[iii] Chapters two and three provide more historical context for the rise of development geography out of its colonial precursors.

The sub-field of development geography began to emerge in the 1960s and 1970s, but was slow in attaining a coherent identity.[iv] Indeed, it was only in the early 2000s that a development speciality group was formed within the Association of American Geographers and the Institute of British Geographers. Potter (2001) has argued that this sub-field remains underemphasised in British geography, with very little work focused on the poorer nations of the globe. The 800-plus-page *Geography in America at the Dawn of the Twenty-first Century* (Gaile and Wilmott 2003) does not include a stand-alone section on development geography. This absence of a coherent development sub-field results partly from the fact that spatial analyses of development dynamics are still often carried on by geographers identifying another speciality (peasant studies, economic geography, regional work on Africa or Latin America, or working in interdisciplinary areas of development studies centres) rather than development geography per se. Clearly there was important work on development being undertaken by geographers (Alan Gilbert, Stuart Corbridge, David Slater, Michael Watts and James Blaut, among many others), but they found their intellectual homes in other sub-fields of geography. As you read this book, you might ponder why development geography cohered as a sub-field in the 1990s much more than it had done in previous decades.

In this section, I trace out some of the major post-Second World War influences in development geography to illustrate the range of theoretical arguments about development that characterise the field. I begin by tracing two contrasting departmental histories of development geography in the 1980s: at the University of California Berkeley and Ohio State University. These two influential departments contributed distinct theoretical approaches to development geography. Like many interested in development, I was first exposed to questions of social justice and economic and political change through the prism of regional geography, studying Africa at Leicester University (UK) in the 1970s. Upon moving to the Ohio State University (USA) in the early 1980s, I worked with Larry Brown, who emphasised the systematic and theoretical study of development over an explicitly regional approach – and my empirical focus turned to Latin America (since there were no Africanists in Ohio State geography then). The concerns of our development geography were guided by twin forces – the social and economic dynamics playing out in Latin America and the intellectual heritage shaping geographic inquiry at Ohio State University.

Our work focused on urban and industrial change, rural to urban migration and uneven development. Development was for us an interdisciplinary endeavour, drawing on a wide range of authors, including economists, demographers and regional scientists, as well as geographers (such as Friedman, Hirschmann, Todaro and Findley). Our intellectual work was framed by a spatial science approach, using deductive modelling to analyse economic, demographic and urbanisation processes. Development geography at Ohio State was firmly situated in a mainstream focus on economic and regional development, quantitative analysis of spatial inequalities and dynamics of population concentration/decentralisation. My dissertation posed questions about the role of state intervention in shaping uneven agricultural growth in Ecuador in the context of diverse agricultural production regimes (Lawson 1986). Consistent with much work at Ohio State at that time, my approach engaged with secondary data and quantitative analysis, producing a primarily descriptive analysis rather than a critical, theoretical explanation of the processes I documented.

Development geography at UC Berkeley had its provenance in two streams of work that distinguished their development geography from that at Ohio State. The Sauerian cultural tradition focused on the historically cumulative impacts of human-environment interactions on landscape. Much of this work emphasised in-depth fieldwork in Latin America or other global South settings. The second broad influence was Marxian political-economy analyses of capitalist accumulation, social relations of class, the role of the state and production systems and processes pursued by scholars such as Michael Watts and Richard Walker. At Berkeley in the 1980s, students and faculty members interested in development studies also looked outside of geography for intellectual guidance, turning to Marxist and cultural theorists (such as Marx himself, Lenin, Luxemburg, E. P. Thompson, Said and Wolfe). Development studies at Berkeley focused on '...the fate of the peasantry ... in peripheral capitalism and by extension the whole question of food as a wage good in the world economy' (Walker 1989). Combining a Marxist analysis of peasant production with cultural ecology, geographers at Berkeley contributed to the emergence of political ecology within geography, examining ecological dynamics as they are transformed through state interventions and class dynamics of production and reproduction (see Rod Neuman's 2005 volume in this series for a book-length treatment).

These vignettes highlight two points. First, development geography has always been a resolutely interdisciplinary affair, with particular strands of geographic inquiry drawing on very distinct theoretical ideas within the broader realm of development studies. Second, development geography has not had a stable identity over recent decades, but rather has been inspired by very different concepts of development, has posed distinct research questions and employed different theoretical frameworks, depending on the particular institutions, the emphases of influential scholars and the regional contexts they study.

Turning now to the broader scope of the sub-field, during the second half of the twentieth century geographers engaged with both 'big D' and 'little d' development. Geographers have produced research reflecting diverse engagements with, and understandings of, the relations between the tendencies of capitalist accumulation and Development interventions. I set the stage for the following chapters by briefly summarising the intellectual streams that have contributed to the making of development geography. These streams do not flow as a sequential historical progression from one to another, but rather they are ongoing elements that are still part of debates in development geography today.

■ Geographers were latecomers to the interdisciplinary field of mainstream development that includes planners, economists and sociologists, who draw on neoclassical economic theories (see chapter 3). Within this broad field, emphasis has shifted over time from debates about Keynesian state regulation and management of capitalist economic forces to analyses of the spatial effects of neoliberal, 'market-friendly' policies under economic globalisation. In the 1970s and 1980s, some geographers examined spatially differentiated economic growth and the role of state policy in spurring urban/industrial growth through optimal spatial distributions of transportation systems, cities and economic innovations (Rondinelli and Ruddle 1978; Gaile 1980; Brown 1991). Broadly speaking, mainstream development studies take Western modernity, nation-state systems and the desirability of capitalist economic growth as given and seek to understand and improve these dominant systems. Early development geography mirrored these assumptions.

■ Building momentum in the 1970s and 1980s, Marxian development geographers employed historical-materialist analysis to analyse the contradictions of capitalism, class struggle, uneven development and imperialism in the global South ('little d' development). This work examines imperialism, patterns of accumulation and work in agriculture and cities, neo-liberalisation processes and struggles over resources, peasants and the agrarian question across Africa, Latin America and Asia (Watts 1983; Laclau 1979; Wolpe 1980; see chapter 4 for an extended discussion). Feminist political-economy researchers take up all these themes, examining the ways in which these multifaceted processes of accommodation and resistance are gendered and how this shapes capitalist production and reproduction processes (Carney 1992; Lawson 1995).

■ Critical development geography came of age in the 1990s, bringing Marxian political-economy analysis into creative tension with post-structural feminist, antiracist, and postcolonial theory (chapter 5). These researchers emphasise the importance of identity, difference, subjectivity, knowledge and power, in relation to the unfolding of capitalist restructuring ('little d' development). This research highlights the shifting geographies of power circulating through discourses of Development, taking as their starting point the '...unbreakable links between language, power relations, and the materiality of daily life' (Pred and Watts 1992: xvi). This post-structural research makes two new contributions to development geography. First, critical development geography attends to the social and geographical sense of location of subjects in power relations, axes of identity and particular places. This work poses crucial questions about the ways in which modernity is situated and rearticulated in specific times and places, for example, looking at the nature and role of civil society and governance in a globalised world, or at the relations between religious/ethnic identities, territory and politics. Second, this research critically interrogates the ways in which '...spatial images and metaphors have always been used to define what development is and does' (Crush 1995: 14). Within critical development geography, 'development' as a concept is theorised as contextual – taking on meaning in the context of a nexus of power relations comprised of discourses, material and intellectual histories, institutional practices and political milieus. So for example, rather than merely reflecting reality, neoliberal discourse actively constructs development as a global marketplace, peopled by 'rugged individuals', competing with privately held resources.

My own formation as a development geographer has continued to evolve since arriving at the University of Washington in 1986. Inspired by students and colleagues, and through reading a range of feminist and post-structural work, I now teach and work in 'critical development geography'. Published since 1990, a series of books on development (writ broadly) by geographers has helped to frame this field of critical development geography. Key volumes include Allan Pred and Michael Watts' (1992) *Reworking Modernities*, Jonathan Crush's (1995) *The Power of Development*, Richard Peet and Michael Watts' (2004) *Liberation Ecologies*, and John Brohman's (1996) *Popular Development*. The *International Studies of Women and Place* series, edited by Janet Momsen and Janet Monk, also highlighted a range of feminist contributions to development studies and to geography; most particularly, volumes such as *'Viva' Women and Popular Protest in Latin America* (1993) by Sarah Radcliffe and Sallie Westwood, *Different Places, Different Voices* (1993) by Janet Momsen and Vivian Kinnaird, and *Women's Voices from the Rainforest* (1995) by Janet Townsend, *Feminism, Postmodernism, Development* (1995) by Marianne Marchand and Jane Parpart. Marcus Power's (2003) *Rethinking Development Geographies* examines the discursive and geopolitical nature of development, analysing the ways in which political and economic power is exercised through development ideas and policies. My account of the making of development geography in this book is directly informed by this burgeoning body of scholarship. Specifically, through engagements with Marxian political-economy analysis in its creative relations with feminist, antiracist and postcolonial theory, I analyse development as situated knowledge that produces particular geographies and subjects, inclusions and exclusions in its various expressions and articulations of power (this framework is elaborated in chapter 2).

1.3 What do geographers bring to development studies?

In a World Bank publication, researchers at the Inter-American Development Bank pose the question *Is Geography Destiny?* (Gallup, Gaviria and Lora 2003). They claim to have rediscovered geography after decades of indifference in the development community. For them, geography is simply location, climate and terrain. These authors exhibit a startling environmental and geographic determinism when they argue that '...geography affects development through ... physical channels such as the productivity of land, rainfall and temperature and human channels such as the location of populations with respect to coasts or urban centers' (Gallup, Gaviria and Lora 2003: 2). This rendition of geography and development resonates with work by Jeffrey Sachs and John Luke Gallup that was covered in the *Washington Post* in 1998. Sachs and Gallup – luminaries in development thinking – conclude that '...there is not a single landlocked country that can claim a high average income ... [A]nd of the 30 top economies ranked by economic output per capita, only three are tropical – Hong Kong, Singapore and Mauritius' (Pearlstein 1998: C12). These deterministic versions of 'geography' imply that climate, land productivity and location (in the tropics or amount of coastline) actually explain levels of economic development. Of course, all this would be news to the Swiss!\[v\] This geographic determinism directly supports mainstream renditions of why the Majority World 'fails to develop' because of its inherent limitations. Further, these deterministic readings create a 'need' for a revised neoclassicism entailing open markets, deregulation, privatisation, infusions of capital, technology and expertise in order to foster economic growth in places supposedly lacking the necessary endowments. Their focus on this limited notion of geography supports a long-held imaginary that constructs places in the Majority World as inherently lacking the wherewithal to succeed on their own, and therefore the necessity of infusions of resources from the outside to overcome these limitations (Sparke 2006b). In order for Sachs,

Gallup, Gaviria and Lora to write these banal geographies, they must actively ignore the scope and depth of 30 years of development geography.

A central reason for writing this book is to highlight geographical contributions to the intellectual history of development studies. I also argue for a *critical geographical approach to development studies* in which we rethink development and evaluate the development record of the last 50 years. This approach:

■ analyses the intellectual and geographical context of ideas and their practice;
■ attends to the spatial variability or place-dependence of processes;
■ analyses processes operating across multiple, intersecting spatial scales;
■ attends to situated agents who shape D/development;
■ concerns nature–society relationships (see Rod Neumann's volume in this series).[vi]

Typically, development processes are analysed temporally, so that we think about what happens to poverty over time. I argue that rethinking development processes through space (as well as over time) reveals the workings of power in crucial processes such as:

■ the globalisation of late capitalism;
■ systems of gender, race/ethnicity and nationality differences putting people in competition for work across the globe;
■ place-specific political struggles that rework livelihoods, civil society and rights to control property.

Beginning from geographical analysis of these sorts of processes and struggles, this book demonstrates how we are building geographically complex and nuanced approaches to development that focus on social and environmental justice projects that are meaningful in particular places. Despite the fact that geographic critiques of development do not wield the broad influence of Sachs and his colleagues (precisely because we are sceptical of universal knowledge claims), they are nonetheless making a difference in specific sites through collaborations and contributions to grounded struggles (there are numerous examples in the chapters that follow: Paul Routledge, Sarah Radcliffe, Cindi Katz, Tony Bebbington, Sarah Wright, Melissa Wright, Gibson-Graham, Gillian Hart, Kim Van Eyck, Pam Martin, Tom Perrault, Suzanne Teltscher, Lucy Jarosz and many others whose actions I am unaware of).

A series of global and intellectual shifts have motivated a broad reformulation of social science research on the 'global South'. These shifts were summarised at a Social Science Research Council conference on 'Rethinking Social Science Research in the Twenty-first Century', which took place in New York in 2001. Participants argued that our social science research agenda must shift and that development thought and practice in the 2000s are inextricable from globalisation, neo-liberalisation, decentring of the national scale and the reconceptualisation of modernity, development and civil society from diverse political and geo-historical locations. Geographic research is ideally positioned to respond to this move away from an emphasis on area studies to a focus on processes of globalisation and connection.

As Michael Watts argues in the following quote, 11 September 2001 highlights a series of global shifts that also demand a reworking of development studies. That day drew stark attention to the connections between poverty in the West Bank, West Asia, the Indonesian archipelago and political disenfranchisement emerging from Western resistance to alternative concepts of progress, modernity and civil society.

> To pose questions of development alternatives in the contemporary moment is, necessarily to confront the events of September 11th. The indelible images of aircraft plunging into the twin towers and of their horrific vertiginous collapse, has brought the development realities of the West Bank, Egypt, West Asia and the Indonesian archipelago to the American heartland with a terrifying bonus: namely, anti-globalisation... (Watts 2003: 65)

In our post-9/11 world, the ethnocentrism of much Western social science has come into clearer focus: as ill-equipped to analyse the multiple facets of globalisation, ethnic/religious based conflict and alternatives/resistances to Euro-American modernity, nationalism and imperialism. Our geographical approach contributes substantially to the ongoing intellectual reworking of development studies. Here I set out five examples, illustrating the contributions of each aspect of our critical geographical approach for development studies. These ideas are developed more fully in the rest of the book.

1.3.1 The intellectual and geographical context of ideas

Geographers analyse the contexts of development knowledge to reveal the ways in which power flows through ideas and their practice. Post-structural analyses of the intimate connections between knowledge and power (chapter 5) have inspired geographers to analyse the ways in which certain discourses about places and peoples support certain understandings of the world while foreclosing others. Development geographers are situating Western development knowledge in its cultural and historic context to trace the ways in which this version of development has been constructed as superior and globally legitimate – and with what effects.

For example, Sarah Wright (2004) examines struggles over intellectual property rights for rice seeds. She juxtaposes two very different versions of knowledge about rice, one from a small Filipino farming community and the other from corporations, supported by the World Trade Organisation (WTO), who claim intellectual property rights over rice seeds.

Wright examines how rice seed is being defined as a product of Western scientific knowledge that can legitimately be owned and privatised. This move is made possible by claims to universal (claiming legitimate control on a global scale), scientific knowledge that is supported by Western patent and legal structures and the policies of the WTO. She looks at how intellectual property rights over rice are being secured through a series of legal and policy manoeuvres involving national governments, transnational corporations and the WTO. This process of privatised ownership of rice is moving forward at a rapid rate, enshrined in TRIPS (trade-related intellectual property rights). Wright's work traces how entire new 'territories' – creations of the mind, of genes, seeds, life forms, and so on – are being opened up to privatisation. She sees this move as analogous in pace and extent only to the immense amounts of property brought into Western property regimes during the colonial era. Only now, the power move is not across space, but scale, from the interior spaces of the mind to global regimes of intellectual property law.

She then looks at rice seed in a Filipino village, where rice is the basic building block of food, a manifestation of culture, ritual and community harmony, the expression of multigenerational labour, and the physical embodiment of community through food and seed sharing practices. In order for intellectual property claims to succeed in the global arena, the historical and ongoing work of poor Filipino farmers to continually improve and refine seed varieties must be constructed as local, anecdotal and irrelevant. Figure 1.4 depicts a street conference organised by Filipino farmers and NGO activists to contest efforts to privatise rice (and many other plant varieties). Farmers are attempting to protect their practices of seed saving, sharing and developing diverse varieties to sustain their farming lives.

Figure 1.4 Farmer and NGO street conference in the Philippines. Source: Sarah Wright (2003)

By situating both of these claims to rice seed in their cultural, historical and geographical contexts, Wright reveals the connections between knowledge, power and privilege. In Wright's study, Western notions of knowledge as private property are legitimised through the formidable power wielded by Western science, Western states, corporations and global institutions. The globalisation of US/European standards of intellectual property facilitated a scale-jump in which one, located, specific regime of knowledge became globally legitimated and empowered. In the process, transnational corporations establish global-scale royalty regimes that inhibit the free exchange of seeds, privatises knowledge that historically circulated freely to the benefit of poor communities and so disempower poor farmers. These changes, bolstered by a particular construction of powerful knowledge, contribute to the poverty of Filipino farmers.

1.3.2 Spatial variability or place-dependence of processes

Geographers argue that crucial insights emerge from examining the ways in which abstract development theories play out empirically, in specific times and places. As Harvey (1996: 103) puts it, '...the insertion of concepts of space, place, locale, and milieu into any social theory has a *numbing effect* upon that theory's central propositions'. He is referring to the limits of aspatial theories, such as microeconomists' emphasis on perfect competition, which is limited by its encounters with spatial barriers and fixities in the operation of markets, or Marxists' claims for the centrality of class relations, which are numbed by the complexities of households, nationalisms and ethnic identifications. A geographical analysis of poverty, then, directs our attention to the interplay of economic, political and cultural processes in places. This is not an argument for atheoretical empirical analysis of the uniqueness of places. Rather, this geographical work theorises processes (economic development, identity formation, struggles over land, and so on) as conditioned by located structures of social relations and webbed connections with the workings of power in other places. The idea of the place-dependence of processes analyses the uneven workings of power as they are situated in, and connected across, places (Massey 1994, 1999; see chapters 2, 4 and 5). Our geographic research moves beyond theoretical and discursive abstractions, bearing witness to the empirically specific reworkings or consolidations of development discourses and practices.

Take, for example, the policy of developing export processing zones (EPZs) which are widely promoted by international development policy and national governments as a mechanism for attracting foreign investment, new jobs and improving incomes. Melissa Wright (2004) starts from place – Ciudad Juárez – to trace how economic, cultural and political processes in the city, and across the globe, shape the place-specific outcomes of EPZ policies. Wright draws on Marxist-feminist analysis (chapters 4 and 5) to analyse how global economic competition for low-wage jobs contributes to the devaluation of women workers in Mexico's maquiladora factories. She traces how workers are discursively constructed as 'untrainable' and 'intrinsically suited to unskilled, low-wage labor', and how this feeds into discourses of their lesser value in society more broadly. She links this devaluation of women with the lack of official attention to the horrific serial murders of over 200 young women in the city. She reveals how discursive and economic processes work together to marginalise women as factory workers and as citizens, helping to explain violence against women as well as their persistent poverty.

These ideas about women workers emerge from discourses of 'good women', who are constructed primarily as mothers who (as the story goes) will inevitably exit the workforce. In fact, many women are forced to leave these jobs because of the physical deterioration that this repetitive work creates (eyes, hands, wrists and whole bodies eventually give out). Leaving these jobs means financial hardship because many of these women are sole income earners for their households. At the same time, a second discourse of 'oversexed', immoral young women, walking the streets inappropriately at night suggests that they bring sexual violence upon themselves. This discourse also devalues young women, ignoring the fact that many are returning from night shifts at the maquiladora (Figures 1.5, 1.6 and 1.7).

These twin discourses work to absolve city officials and maquiladora owners and managers of financial responsibility: of investing in training programmes for women workers, investing in police, improved street lights, bus services, and so on. At the same time, in the highly competitive, globalised world of manufacturing, this discourse of 'immoral young women' lays blame on the victims themselves for the murders. This, in turn, allows city officials to continue downplaying (essentially ignoring) these horrific crimes and so positioning Ciudad Juárez as a modern city that can compete effectively for international investments.

By starting from the place of the city, Wright's work shows how maquiladora production, global economic competition for low-wage jobs and the cultural devaluation of women all come together in Ciudad Juárez to explain violence against women and their persistent poverty. This research complicates the 'one size fits all places' claims of EPZ programmes that rely solely on the universal economic argument about attracting investment and jobs.

Figure 1.5 Maquiladora plant in Ciudad Juárez. Source: Victoria Lawson

Figure 1.6 Bussing workers from Maquiladora to irregular settlements. Source: Victoria Lawson

Figure 1.7 Irregular settlements in Western Juárez. Source: Victoria Lawson

1.3.3 Processes operating across multiple, intersecting spatial scales

Geographers are investigating the multiple ways in which development processes operate across multiple and intersecting scales, and through this work they are building more nuanced and critical readings of development processes. Dominant development institutions (such as the World Bank, Inter-American Development Bank, International Monetary Fund, World Trade Organisation), since their founding, have operated at the nation-state scale. These powerful institutions primarily disburse loans and grants and define policy directions with agents and institutions of the nation state. This emphasis on the national scale reflects the East-West fixation of the pre-1989 globe, when cold war concerns dominated the development agenda. A central preoccupation of mainstream development was integrating newly independent nation states into capitalist economic and political circuits. This national-scale preoccupation of mainstream development now sits in uneasy juxtaposition with our contemporary world in which new coalitions and new geographies are emerging.

We live in times of globalised economic flows and interconnections, times of political struggle that are challenging national boundaries (from Chechnya to Palestine to the Kurds), times when countries are forging regional economic communities (from the European Union to the Southern African Development Community) and indigenous groups are creating transnational networks of solidarity. In other words, rather than thinking of the national scale as fixed and inevitable, we can see all around us that the scales that matter for economic, political and social change are being actively reworked before our eyes. Marxist-feminist geographers describe this as the political and social construction of scale (more detail in chapters 2 and 4). These scales that matter are being actively produced by the expansion of supranational regionalism, community organising, global networks of indigenous peoples, farmers' movements from Brazil to the Philippines and the USA and so on. Starting from processes of rescaling, geographers are moving in two directions. First, they critique the limits of mainstream development and its inability to address the processes producing economic growth, inequality and poverty. Second, they are posing new questions about the way resources, political influence and people are circulating in our contemporary world.

For example, our world is being reconfigured through supranational regional coalitions such as the European Union, the Association of South East Asian Nations, the North American Free Trade Agreement, the newly emerging (at the time of writing) South Asian Association for Regional Cooperation and the intense negotiations over the Free Trade Area of the Americas. Figure 1.8

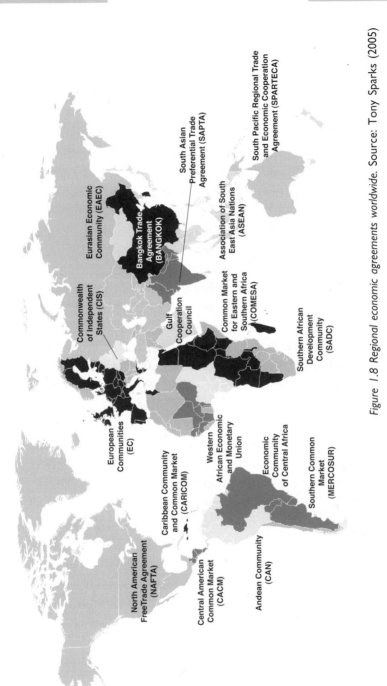

Figure 1.8 Regional economic agreements worldwide. Source: Tony Sparks (2005)

depicts some of the major global economic agreements. These groupings are redefining control over global flows of commodities and investments, and they are competing for regulatory and political power over corporations, migration flows and development dollars. New coalitions and realignments are emerging, shifting from the East–West fixation of the pre-1989 globe to a North–South, rich–poor split of identities and territories organised around economic, environmental and social justice concerns.

Another new geography of trade is emerging in the global South, which the *New York Times* (Rohter 2003) described as an alliance of the '[H]aves, Have-nots and Have-Somes'. At the 2003 ministerial meetings of the World Trade Organisation in Cancún, a new coalition emerged, calling itself the 'Group of 20 Plus' (including nations such as Brazil, India, China, Mexico, Nigeria, South Africa and Indonesia; see Figure 1.9). There are, of course, historical precedents in the Non-Aligned Movement (NAM) of (now) 115 global South countries that emerged from the Bandung Conference in 1955 (as well as the formation of the G-15 post-1989, Sridharan 1998). The NAM was originally organised around taking an independent stance in cold war international relations, opposing neocolonialism and Western domination. The new coalition of the G-20 Plus is distinct in that it brings together large, resource-rich and economically dynamic nations (it now includes countries like China and South Africa), and also in the group's principal focus on gaining influence in international trade negotiations through the World Trade Organisation.

What is notable in terms of the reworking of political and economic power through this new coalition is that they have split off from the poorer and smaller nations of the global South in order for the G-20 Plus to forge its own independent position in trade negotiations. The power of G-20 comes from representing collectively 60 per cent of the world's population, 70 per cent of the world's farmers, the increasing industrial and service components of their economies, as well as all major regions of the global South. This group represents a distinct geographical power block, with large markets and manufacturing bases, that is jostling for political position to demand greater access to the markets of industrialised nations, and pressuring the USA and the EU over farm supports and agricultural export subsidies. In the process, poorer, less powerful nations of the global South are left out of this new configuration of power and negotiation. At the same time, other South–South coalitions are emerging, such as the G-30 and the G-90, and their influence remains unclear at the time of writing. My larger point is that this restless reworking of regional coalitions,

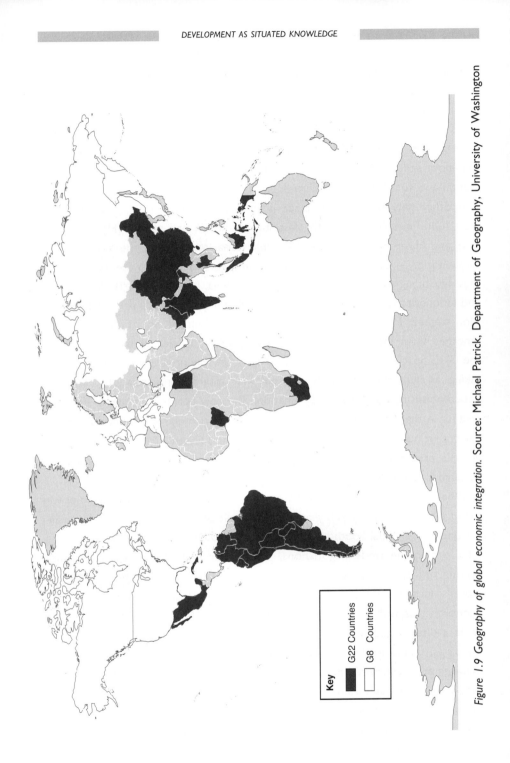

Figure 1.9 Geography of global economic integration. Source: Michael Patrick, Department of Geography, University of Washington

and the geographies of trade and influence they represent, provides just one example of how attention to the politics of scale opens up crucial questions for development studies.

1.3.4 Attention to situated agents who shape D/development

Development is not a hermetically sealed, pre-given project that arrives fully formed in places (Gidwani 2002). People are agents, constrained in certain ways, of course, but who nonetheless engage with development and negotiate its local forms and effects. In Sarah Wright's (2004) work discussed above, despite the powers aligned against them, Filipino farmers are organising through an NGO to participate in a globally networked Farmers' Rights Movement, to resist regulation of their rice farming practices.

Rick Schroeder's book *Shady Practices* (1997) provides another example of how people engage with development processes. Schroeder examines women's struggle against national development policies for environmental and economic sustainability, and men's control over both land and women's unpaid labour. Specifically, in 1970s and 1980s, Gambian women farmers established lucrative communal market gardens. In a short time, women's incomes began to outstrip those of their husbands, changing the balance of power within households. These changing dynamics collided with a shift in development policy – away from gender equity and towards environmental concerns – which threatened women's gardens and their income gains. Male landholders, who suffered as groundnut crops languished, began moving mango and citrus orchards on to the same lowlands used by the women for their gardens.

This shift away from gardens and towards forestry programmes was supported by a shift in development rhetoric, couched in terms of environmental sustainability goals and the ecological superiority of tree crops over all other crops. Schroeder traces how male landowners joined with national forestry personnel in attempts to:

- eliminate women's vegetable gardens
- gain control over fertile river-bottom land
- recapture women's unpaid labour for irrigation of male-controlled tree crops.

Schroeder demonstrates that gendered power and access to key resources such as land and labour are made and remade in specific conjunctures. He provides powerful evidence of the ways in which property rights privilege male control over land and farming resources, and how gendered systems of women's unpaid labour have limited their claims to land rights. Despite these structural conditions of male domination over land and labour, Schroeder traces a much more nuanced story. Women actively resisted these shifts in land use. Women engaged a variety of strategies to maintain control over their gardens, including organising a women's group to advocate for rights to land; allying with NGOs supportive of women's economic activities; extreme pruning or removal of men's trees; minimal watering of fruit trees, girdling trees to kill them, and so on. Schroeder reveals the complexities of ecological and cultural struggles as they are worked out by people in places.

1.3.5 Concern for nature–society relationships

As the above vignette demonstrates, some geographers contribute to development studies by moving away from a dominant focus on economies towards a focus on places as ecological sites of integrated natural/social systems that frame the possibilities of development as well as its failures. Rod Neumann's (2005) volume in this series, *Making Political Ecology*, explores intersections between environmental problems, political, social and biophysical processes, and how these are shifted through development (see especially chapter 4). Neumann takes development to be '...the continuous unfolding of capitalist modernity in particular places at particular times' (2005: 13) and examines the contributions of political ecology to understanding development dynamics in their relationships to environmental changes in specific places. Specifically, he reviews research exploring the intersections of ecological processes, property rights, land tenure arrangements, cultural struggles and political-economic shifts.

1.4 Overview of the book

As you will see throughout this book, development geographers engage development research through multiple strands and distinct agendas. The 'development industry' has been one important focus. Some geographers have engaged with policy analysis and revision within institutions of development. Emphasising the spatially uneven character of economic growth, geographers have argued against urban bias, and for engaging people and communities in development processes, for integrated rural development and for secondary city strategies, in order to reduce the spatial concentration of economic growth in large urban centres (see Gore 1984 for a summary). Others have critiqued the institutions, practices and discourses of the development industry, examining the spatial imagery they invoke, the ways in which development vocabulary constructs terrains of intervention, and their erasure of other places and subjects (discussed in Crush 1995). Another stream of geographical work focuses on the multiple unfoldings of capitalist economic and political processes across the globe. This work has interrogated the material[vii] and discursive production of uneven development, environmental transformation, the complex challenges of social justice, political representation and human rights (Watts 1993; Schuurman 2000a, 2000b; Hart 2002b, 2003).

Despite these different emphases within development geography, it is this attention to the spatiality of development processes and discourses that is geography's fundamental contribution to the broader field of development studies. Harvey summarises nicely the importance of geography:

> [T]he world must be depicted, analysed, and understood not as we would like it to be but as it really is, the material manifestation of human hopes and fears mediated by powerful and conflicting processes of social reproduction (Harvey 1996: 102).

Geographers analyse the ways in which the historical, social and political processes of development are actively constituted in places or through the invocation of spatial constructs such as territories, borders and scales. In this way, geography challenges much development theory by pointing out that D/development does not exist as a thing or an end point. Rather, it is a series of historically specific relations between places, social groups, cultures, spheres of production and consumption. D/development is viewed both as a politically powerful discourse and as relentlessly material, entailing substantial transformations of society as a result of these power relations. Through D/development, livelihoods are transformed, people and communities are moved, social relations are reworked.

Beginning from geographers' insistence on spatiality and context, I analyse D/development in this book as 'situated knowledge' (Haraway 1988; Dixon and Jones 1998; elaborated in chapter 2). This approach challenges mainstream development knowledge that claims to be universal, apolitical and scientific, while simultaneously exerting power over and erasing other knowledges and practices of alternative developments. Our situated, geographical approach to the making of development examines the social, discursive, political and historical processes that produce particular meanings of the term 'development' over time and space. This book examines contemporary shifts in the field of development geography in relation to broader geopolitical and global economic processes, and examines the philosophical and theoretical debates and influential ideas that are moving the field forwards. This book has two broad goals. The first is to review three influential strains of development thought – mainstream, Marxist-feminist and post-structural theories – and identify central questions, places, scales and subjects that are valorised and silenced in each of these approaches to development. My second goal is to discuss the nature and significance of the field of 'critical development geography' that has emerged at the intersection of Marxist, feminist and post-structural theory.

In chapter 2 I introduce my overall framework, employed in subsequent chapters to discuss three key moments in development thought: mainstream, Marxist-feminist and post-structural approaches. I begin by arguing that development is situated knowledge, and that geo-historical, political and institutional contexts influence the ways in which development debates and enactments of development are produced/shaped. I look at the ways in which particular constructions of development knowledge conceptualise the people in development and authorise inclusions and exclusions of certain sorts of subjects (on the basis of class position, gender, race/ethnicity, nationality, and so on). I then examine how issues of authority, inclusion and exclusion are worked out spatially – in the ways that discourses and practices of D/development link or separate places, move across scales and operate in relation to boundaries. Different theoretical approaches produce very different geographies of development, and by explicitly analysing how power is constituted through these diverse geographies, we can reveal and explain the paradoxes of D/development.

Chapter 3 examines mainstream development, from modernisation theories of the 1960s to early twenty-first-century neoliberalism. I begin by situating mainstream development thought in its intellectual (Enlightenment) and geopolitical (cold war) context. I trace the shifts in intellectual and policy debate since the mid-twentieth century, as mainstream development has shifted from supporting protectionist and developmentalist states in the global South, towards a free-market approach to growth that argues for reductions in the state's role in both the market and social programmes. I argue that geography played a minimal and latecomer role in mainstream development thought, and I review the economic theories that are hegemonic in mainstream development institutions and that were imported into early development geography. I then read mainstream development through the lens of our critical geographical approach. This geographical re-evaluation of mainstream thought reveals the dominance (and limits) of spatial separatist thinking – in which space is assumed to have independent effects that can be isolated and manipulated to meet policy goals. I also discuss the privileging of the national scale in mainstream development and the ways in which this shapes who has access to development resources and influence. Finally, I map out the ways in which mainstream theory conceptualises the subjects of development: as the rugged individuals and plucky entrepreneurs of neoclassical economic and liberal political thought.

Chapter 4 explores the contributions of Marxist and Marxist-feminist theory to the emergence of critical development geography. The late 1960s had a cataclysmic effect on many who lived through them, and many pioneers of Marxist geography situate their work in those tumultuous political times. The chapter begins with the impact of what Michael Watts decribes as '1968 and all that' (2001a), and then turns to consider the theoretical debates swirling in Marxist and Marxist-feminist geography. In contrast to our minor intellectual role in mainstream development, geographers contribute significantly to Marxist-feminist debates around development. As a result, this chapter is more tightly focused on intellectual traces within geography. I suggest that geographical studies of imperialism, development and peasant studies contributed substantially to bringing Marxist theory into geography (despite a tendency to attribute this role to urban research in the West). I articulate geographical contributions to radical development studies through an examination of how we push beyond the impasse of economism and determinism in Marxist development studies. Geographers contribute through investigations of how capitalist processes restlessly reconfigure space, place and scale. I then turn to Marxist-feminist extensions of the Marxian emphasis on social relations of production and economy, through a serious engagement with social relations of gender and the sites in which these are worked out. The final section turns to a discussion of how these theorists conceptualise the subjects of development: as collective subjects understood primarily in terms of class and gender identities.

In chapter 5 I examine the seismic shifts in theory and method arising from post-development and postcolonial or, more broadly, post-structural thought. I first examine the intellectual 'space' opened up by these 'posts'. Specifically, they attend to oppressive and unequal power relations, the historical and geographical contexts of privilege and marginalisation, a concern with 'discourse' (the structures of knowledge and power that construct and structure the social realms of everyday life and scientific knowledge) and a conceptual pluralism in which identities and subjectivities are understood as multiply constituted and fluid. I argue that 'post' thought has produced an identifiable field of critical development geography, and I explore the reciprocal impacts of 'post' thought on development geography and the ways in which geographers are contributing to the interdisciplinary field of post-structural development theory.

Finally, chapter 6 articulates contemporary critical development geography as the (uneasy, but productive!) marriage of Marxist and post-structural theoretical insights to produce a 'post-Marxism' that integrates materialist and discursive analyses of development. This post-Marxism deals with the cultural construction of difference, subjectivity and identity, analysing the ways in which the reworking of meanings and practices are central to capitalist restructuring and political transformations. I argue for 'critical spatiality' as part and parcel of re-imagined development studies. This critical, relational approach to learning 'transnational literacy' provides a way forwards for our theory and practice, in which we learn to work with difference while maintaining a commitment to transformative politics. This critical, relational approach can build an accountably positioned development geography that breaks down North–South dualisms, focuses on relations between places and includes Western sites and people as subjects of development studies.

The field of development studies is characterised by links, interconnections, continuities and breaks between approaches. This book should not be read as a simple teleology of development thought (although some approaches are themselves teleological), but rather a complex, intersecting field of theory, discourse, politics, methodologies and practices that are at once historically rooted and intensely contemporary. Geographers have long played a maverick role, in different ways, insisting on the situatedness of development and the spatiality of development processes. As you will see in the chapters that follow, each body of theory explains the dynamics and actors involved in these issues of governance, economic growth, social redistribution and well-being in quite different ways.

Notes

[i]Geographers use the term 'discourse' to describe and analyse the ways in which meaning is constructed through histories, power relations and places, and the structures of knowledge and power that construct and structure the social realms of everyday life and specialised knowledge. Discourses are ways of knowing, or regimes of truth, about the world, and they are made up of ideas, ideologies, narratives, texts,

institutions and individual and collective practices. Discourses help to create the institutions or realms of life that they describe. Michel Foucault is a key figure who theorised the relationship between knowledge, truth and power, arguing that knowledge itself is a potent form of power. For example, the 'discourse of development' (Escobar 1995: 39) created a set of relations between institutions, socio-economic processes, forms of knowledge and technologies which defined who could speak, with what authority and who had expert status to create and legitimate certain concepts, theories and practices. So for example, development discourse created a series of problems such as 'overpopulation', 'poverty' and 'lack of capital', which were constructed as inherent or natural problems of the 'Third World' that must be solved by specific interventions by development experts. Dominant discourses are all the more powerful because they are understood to be the natural state of the world, rather than historically specific constructions (Foucault 1980a, 1980b; Rabinow 1984).

[ii]Power (2003) provides more on the UK context of development geography, but the vast literature on development from Asia, Africa and Latin America are not well integrated into our theoretical discussions. Although Kay (1989) brings Latin American theories of development and underdevelopment to an English-speaking audience.

[iii]Although as late as 1996, we still saw textbooks on A Geography of the Third World (Dickenson et al.).

[iv]Throughout the 1960s, 1970s and 1980s, scholarly books and textbooks on development geography as a sub-field were few and far between. Instead, geogaphers produced introductory books on the geography of the 'third world' (see for example, Dickenson et al. 1996; Pacione 1988).

[v]Thanks to an anonymous reviewer for this ironic note.

[vi]These ideas emerged from a discussion at a National Science Foundation (NSF) strategic planning conference in Washington, DC in October 2003 and I owe a debt of gratitude to the participants, particularly Roger Downs, Bernie Bauer and Patricia Gober.

[vii]Material refers to the substantial conditions of life. The term is often associated with Marxist theory which argues that social change stems from the workings of economies, production and exchange rather than spiritual or intellectual ideas. The term has taken on a broader meaning in critical development geography, encompassing all substantial arenas of life, including those of production, consumption and social and environmental reproduction.

REMAKING DEVELOPMENT GEOGRAPHY

2.1 Intersections, inclusions and exclusions in development thought

The work of geography and development studies has always been intimately connected, through analyses of colonisation, modernisation, neo-liberalisation or more generally, the continual reworking of economic, political and cultural connections and spaces. I lay out here my framework for rereading development through our critical geographical approach. We are going to examine, in turn, the contexts of development knowledge, the geographies of development these theories have invoked and interrogated, and the subjects (people) deemed relevant to those formulations of development.

What, then, does it mean to talk about geographies of development? The term refers both to the ways development geographers analyse development processes, broadly taken, and to a geographical approach to reading and critiquing particular development theories. 'Geographies of development' have several important elements:

■ Geographers analyse the relationships between particular spatial or scalar representations of development and the kinds of processes, actors and institutions deemed relevant to that version of development. For example, Keynesian economic growth theories, which were foundational for development economics (see chapter 3), focus on national-scale processes and on formal state and economic actors, to the exclusion of household and community scales and actors engaged in social reproduction (Nagar et al. 2002).

■ Geographers examine the '...spatial and organic images and metaphors [that] have always been used to define what development is and does' (Crush

1995: 14). For example, within mainstream development discourse, places in the global South are imagined as backward, overpopulated, failing, fouled – as the mirror-opposite of constructions of the West.

■ Geographers attend to the ways in which development processes interact with places to produce different outcomes, producing, as Harvey (1996: 103) put it, a 'numbing effect' on abstract theorisations of development. We insist on accountability to place in our analyses of development processes, engaging in detailed case study research.

■ Finally, geographers situate development knowledges themselves. We examine how development knowledges are socially produced, and socially producing, of particular configurations of political, epistemological and institutional contexts and power relations. Development knowledges are also culturally specific. For example, much of the most influential development knowledge relies on Western, Enlightenment claims of universal, disembodied knowledge and private ownership of intellectual property. Despite the apparent universalism of Western development thought, it is in fact a culturally and historically specific product of the West. Other development knowledges are being produced actively in different cultural contexts, such as community-produced and shared knowledges emanating from diverse societies across the globe (Esteva and Prakash 1998; Rahnema and Bawtree 1997; Wright 2004).

The work of building a geographically informed critique of development theory and practice is not a distinct, overly intellectualised project, separate from the 'real work' of doing development. Rather, it is the hard and valuable work of making the self-evident problematical. This work of rethinking development can have a real impact by including silenced voices; by imagining alternatives that are negated by dominant development discourse; and by revealing what is at stake for us in the West in rethinking development. In my undergraduate development class, we examine the effects of mainstream discourses *here* in the West. We examine how a focus on 'overpopulation', 'hunger' and 'poverty' in the global South obscures the ways in which we benefit from dominant framings of development. These constructions of 'the problems' of development allow us in the West to elide responsibility for changing *our* practices and, more broadly, prevent us from having to critique or interrogate the very market capitalist system we are embedded in and continue to benefit from.

I use an exercise in class to show how difficult it is for us to engage in critique of ourselves. Students learn that critiquing Western ideas and practices often leads us to become defensive when our interpretation of the world is challenged. Often to their own surprise, it turns out that students have substantial investments in the order of things, their material lifestyles and the legitimacy of our social and economic system. Using a reading by Arturo Escobar (1995), which challenges the way poverty is constructed as *the problem* in mainstream development narratives and institutions, I ask students to discuss how analyses of development and resultant policies would be different if 'overconsumption' were defined as the major problem in the development industry instead of 'poverty'.

This exercise produces three major insights, and some surprisingly strong reactions from students. First, students became familiar with the idea that framing poverty as the problem and economic growth as the solution is *only one way* to understand global differences. Second, using Escobar (1995), together with a powerful testimonial called 'Becoming a development category' by Nanda Shrestha (1995), students investigate how development would look completely different if the problem were defined as 'overconsumption' and the solutions involved more equitable distribution and consumption of resources across the globe. When students see a completely different framing of (and, in turn, possible solutions for) the challenges of development, they begin to see that the focus on 'too many people' in the global South absolves them of the need to change or even to question their own lives. At the same time, I can point out that students themselves are unwittingly invested in a set of persistent discourses that point to the need for change *over there*, rather than *over here*. The very fact that some of my students become defensive provides a powerful illustration of the depth of our collective investments, and the degree to which these investments are masked and hidden in our lives, in public discourse and even in the academy (including, of course, geography). In other words, students come to see that our privilege is intimately linked to sustaining these enduring narratives about 'problems' and their solutions.

Geographers are deeply involved in demonstrating why rethinking, reassessing development is more powerful than tinkering with existing policies. Drawing on a broad range of critical social theory, geographers are deeply involved with reformulating what 'doing development' means, by analysing the making of development itself in ways that reveal the sorts of erasures, closures and exclusions that various bodies of development thought and practice have entailed historically. For example, Momsen and Kinnaird's (1993) volume *Different Places,*

Different Voices analyses the changing lives of women in the global South and demonstrates the importance of including voices and places frequently excluded from development debates. Townsend's (1995) book, *Women's Voices from the Rainforest*, on rainforest colonisation in Colombia, focuses on women pioneers, viewing women farmers as scientists who have been denied a voice in land use policy. This geographical (re)making of development (in concert with work in related fields), involves critical examination of the historical and geographical contexts through which development takes on particular meanings. It also involves analysis of the geographies of power through which development discourse and practice constructs and obscures its objects, subjects, places and interventions. In short, development geography is engaged in the work of analysing the geographies of power circulating through development and articulating progressive alternatives.

In the next section we discuss the contexts of development. Particular versions of development are produced through the interplay of geo-historically situated political and sociocultural power relations that shape our understandings of what development is, how it is thought to operate, and how it circulates through, and represents, places. We then examine the geographies of development produced by different bodies of theory: focusing on how their understandings of place and scale reveal key assumptions about development processes. In the final section of this chapter, I argue that analysing how subjects (people) in development are conceptualised reveals a great deal about who is included (and excluded) as legitimate actors or agents of development in each body of thought. In the following chapters I employ this framework to explore the ways in which development geographers are analysing mainstream development (chapter 3), Marxist-feminist understandings of development (chapter 4), and post-structural and post-development thought (chapter 5).

2.2 Contexts of 'developments'

> The form and content of geographical knowledge cannot be understood independently
> of the social basis for the production and use of that knowledge (Harvey 1996: 96)

As Cowen and Shenton (1996: 3) observe, '[D]evelopment seems to defy definition, although not for want of definitions on offer.' As I noted in the introduction, this has led to confusion within the discipline, about development as a form of purposive intervention; development as the unfolding of tendencies within economic and social systems; and/or development as the production of discourses and regimes of truth. Tony Bebbington (2002: 1) alludes to this confusion in his review of geographies of Latin American development:

> 'Development' has been used to refer to modernisation, economic growth, empowerment, the expansion of human capabilities and change of various forms and guises.... much has passed for development, and there have often been profound and perhaps irreconcilable differences between different types of development.

Confusion about the meaning of development emerges from our desire to define and fix a term that actually has myriad meanings, depending on the geo-historical, cultural and political context within which it is invoked. By context I mean the nexus of power relations comprised of discourses, material and intellectual histories, institutional practices and political milieux. These contexts are simultaneously spaces of articulation within which particular versions of development thought are produced, and sites through which these power relations and regimes of knowledge are consolidated and materialised. For us, contexts are sites of knowledge production that create and reproduce power. In this section, I focus on the forms of knowledge invoked by different bodies of development thought, and note that these are situated in particular institutional and geopolitical contexts (which are elaborated more fully in the following chapters). In other words, I map out a geography of development knowledge, looking at the places, thick with social relations, in which particular theories of development are produced. Geographers have differed in their engagements with development knowledge as either situated and contextual or universal (I discuss this range of positions in depth in subsequent chapters). This fundamental distinction has key implications for how development is conceptualised, assumptions about what development is, how it is thought to operate and the power with which development knowledges circulate in institutional and political contexts.

2.2.1 Enlightenment universalism

Universalism signals the position that ideas of development produced in Western social sciences hold for all times and places (Barnes 2000). The principles of modernist social sciences stem from the philosophies of Enlightenment thinkers of eighteenth-century Europe. In broad terms, Enlightenment thinkers argued that a single, stable 'Truth' about the world is knowable, and that we can produce accurate and objective (disembodied, unsituated) accounts of a world that can be ordered rationally. Rational and scientific thought, for these thinkers, has the potential to produce technical innovations and expert knowledge that can improve human life. As Harvey (1990: 29) notes:

> ...thinkers in the Enlightenment tradition, such as Adam Smith or Saint-Simon, could reasonably argue that once the shackles of feudal class relations had been thrown off, a benevolent capitalism...could bring the benefits of modernity to all.

Of course, throughout the sweep of history, these arguments have been challenged by philosophical debates, social upheaval, the horrors of science (such as the atom bomb) and the destruction of wars and genocide in modernist societies (for a discussion of this rich history of Enlightenment thought, see Harvey 1990; Livingstone and Withers 1999; Cowen and Shenton 1996). Nonetheless, some central principles of Enlightenment thought have endured: universal knowledge claims, a belief in linear progress and in the potential for technical and scientific solutions to the challenges of development (as defined within this same frame of thinking).

Scientific development knowledge is constructed as placeless, free of cultural specificity, as abstract and apolitical. It is technical, expert knowledge that can know all contexts and produce similar outcomes across places. Despite these claims, scientific development knowledge is a deeply culture-bound form of knowledge that is inseparable from its history, geopolitics and social relations of production. In other words, there is a distinct geography to Enlightenment thought in the sense that it was a product of a culturally and historically specific Europe. As Peet and Hartwick (1999: 125) point out, Enlightenment thought also produced a particular geography of hierarchy in which Europe was destined to guide the world.

> An Enlightenment map of the world saw global space divided between a center of reason, knowledge and wisdom in Western Europe and a periphery of ignorance, barbarity and only potential reason elsewhere.

This view of development knowledge was reflected in the arguments of modernisation theorists about the anticipated transformations of postcolonial societies (Harrod 1948; Lewis 1955; Rostow 1960; McClelland 1961), and this universalism remains a central assumption of arguments about neoliberal development emanating from institutions such as the World Bank. Heralding the decade of the 1990s, the World Bank pronounced:

> During the past forty years many developing countries have achieved progress at
> an impressive pace.... So if nothing else were certain, we would know that rapid
> and sustained development is no hopeless dream, but an achievable reality...
> (World Bank 1991: 1)

Despite a devastating record throughout the 1990s, including the Asian financial crisis and growing health and poverty crises in sub-Saharan Africa and Latin
America, the Bank's 1999/2000 *World Development Report* acknowledges that
development is multifaceted and complex, but the report retains a confident
'voice', bolstered by scientific evidence.

> The evidence of recent decades demonstrates that while *development is possible,*
> it is neither inevitable or easy. The successes have been frequent enough to justify
> a sense of confidence in the future. But while these *successes may be replicable* in
> other countries, the failure of many development efforts suggests that the task
> will be a daunting one... (World Bank 2000b:14, emphasis mine)

Mainstream development thought (discussed in more depth in chapter 3)
reflects and exemplifies universal knowledge claims, assuming universal relevance
and applicability for its theories, holding that value-free, objective scientific
practice produces development policies which will yield similar results, regardless of where they are implemented. Contemporary development geography
does not unproblematically mimic these truth claims; however, there remains
for many a sense that geography is producing foundational knowledge through
a systematic, rational and orderly process (discussed in Rose 1993; Dixon and
Jones 1998). For example, Peet and Hartwick (1999), in their book *Theories of
Development*, argue for the selective retention of certain beneficial aspects of
modernity within a critical modernist development. They suggest that development studies take up universal concepts of technological progress, productivity,
emancipation and democracy. They express a tense relationship with issues of
universalism and modernity, arguing for knowledge that transcends the local in
'...the critical modernist recovery not of sameness, but of similarity' (Peet with
Hartwick 1999: 205). Nonetheless, they argue for ethical and political principles
of development, which transcend the local to guide those in development to
respond through '...at least quasi-universal principles' (p. 205).

2.2.2 Development as situated knowledge

Feminist critiques of universal knowledge claims argue that they assert their superiority by actively subordinating, but fundamentally relying on, gendered, classed and

raced subjects and forms of knowledge produced in other cultures and places (Haraway 1988; Hartsock 1983; Harding 1986; Rose 1993). Claims to universal, technical, expert knowledge by some in the development field are a power move that constructs their analyses as disembodied, non-located and superior (see Escobar 1995 for an extended discussion; also Parpart 1995; Tapscott 1995). As Haraway (1988: 189) puts it, scientific knowledge performs a 'god-trick' wherein '...all perspective gives way to infinitely mobile vision...the god-trick of seeing everything from nowhere'. This 'god-trick' is a power move through which historically and politically specific analyses of development become universal truths.

Stuart Hall (1992) illustrates the way in which Enlightenment scientific accounts of progress and development in the West depended on the *prior construction* of the New World as savage, unrefined and backward. In relation to this 'other', Western civilisation and Western knowledge are constructed as superior.

> In Enlightenment discourse, the West was the model, the prototype and the measure of social progress. It was *western* progress, civilisation, rationality and development that were celebrated. And yet, all this depended on the discursive figures of the 'noble vs ignoble savage' and of 'rude and refined nations' which had been formulated in the discourse of 'the West and the Rest'. So the Rest was critical for the formation of western Enlightenment – and therefore for modern social science. (Hall 1992: 313–14)

Hall's quote also underscores that, despite claims of universality, Western scientific knowledge was itself culturally produced in very particular and unique histories, sites and relations between places – those of 'the West and the Rest'. Stories of Western civilisation and the progressive potential of modern science were/are actively constructed through histories of colonisation in Asia, Africa and Latin America, the development of extractive agricultural and mineral economies in the New World and trade in slaves and resources which institutionalised the economic and political power of Europe and North America. As Hartsock (1998: 207) argues:

> Inequality and domination were established in the name of universality and progress; ironically, power relations were institutionalised in and through a mode of thinking that denied any connections between knowledge and power or between the construction of subjectivity and power. The philosophical and historical creation of devalued Others was the necessary precondition, then, for the creation of the transcendental rational subject who could persuade himself that he existed outside time and space power relations.

Through historical and political analyses, feminist scholars are revealing the specificity of Western development knowledge, they are, in Visweswaran's terms (1994), engaging in 'homework' – the work of exoticising the West by locating powerful development knowledges. By this she means 'that a critical eye would necessarily be cast on a whole range of practices at "home" that authorised American intervention in the "Third World"' (p. 101).

Gillian Rose argues that '[T]he founding fathers of geography...sought a kind of knowledge that would apply universally.... They made no connection between the world as it was seen and the position of the viewer...' (Rose 1993: 7). Geography has its roots in this history of European exploration, discovery and mapping, and this has produced a series of 'epistemic exclusions' which have serious consequences for what counts as legitimate knowledge and who can produce such knowledge (Rose 1993; Gregory 2000).[i] Rose focuses primarily on exclusions of women, gender processes and the ways in which claims to universal, exhaustive knowledge in geography imply that 'others' cannot add significantly to this knowledge. She makes these arguments in order to understand the continuing marginalisation of feminist work in the discipline. Critical development geography draws on this feminist analysis to explore a range of epistemic exclusions in geographical analyses of development. In subsequent chapters I explore mainstream, Marxist-feminist and post-structural approaches to development geography and discuss the kinds of knowledge considered relevant to explaining development; the kinds of subjects who can construct development theory (discussed in section 1.4), and the scales and places through which development processes are refracted (discussed in section 1.3).

Critical development geography situates mainstream development (and indeed other streams of development thought), arguing that despite its universal knowledge claims, it is actually a situated and culturally specific (Western) discourse. Discourses are 'ways of knowing', or 'regimes of truth', about the world, and are made up of ideas, ideals, social conventions, narratives, texts, institutions, individual and collective practices. Discourses are both socially produced and socially producing – bound up in intimate power relations with the institutions and societies that they describe.[ii] Critical theorists examine how ideas about development are deployed by powerful actors as a regime of truth with substantial material and political effects.

For example, Said's classic book *Orientalism* (1979: 20) traces how intellectual authority over the 'Orient' was constructed in the West through the knowledge-space of the academy. Drawing on Foucault's work (Box 2.1) on power-truth-knowledge formations, Said argued that research and teaching in area studies, poetry, popular writings and in multiple aspects of Western culture constructed legitimacy for colonial administrations, through 'the relationship between texts and the way in which groups of texts, types of texts, even textual genres, acquire mass, density, and referential power among themselves and thereafter in the culture at large'. This 'Orient' was produced in and for Europe, serving as a foil that defines 'European civilisation' and that made processes of colonisation and imperialism in south-west Asia imaginable and possible by literally inventing the idea of the 'Orient'. Escobar's (1995) book *Encountering Development* extends this idea to post-Second World War Western development thought, arguing that a powerful discourse is constructed in *the relations between* academic arguments about the mechanisms of economic and cultural development, the institutions of the 'development industry' and development 'experts', which together form a knowledge-space which legitimates particular development 'truths' (see also Tim Mitchell's *Rule of Experts* 2002). This development discourse, reinforced by the political power of national development agencies and international institutions, determines who has the knowledge and authority to define both development problems and solutions.

Box 2.1 Foucault's impact on development studies

Foucault's thought has been influential in development theory for two reasons: first, his critique of Enlightenment thought – the basis for mainstream developmentalism – and second, for his analysis of power-truth-knowledge formations. Foucault rejects any form of totalising discourse, such as the claims of rational, scientific expertise and the possibility of universal 'Truth' in Enlightenment thought and, by extension, in Western developmentalism. He argued that there is no one absolute truth and that all versions of truth are political, struggled over by subjects in particular power-laden contexts. Foucault also analysed the fluid, multifaceted, multi-scaled, capillary nature of power that infuses language, social relations and the practices of social regulation (including bureaucracies). More specifically, he analysed discourse (rationalised expert knowledges), not merely as texts or structures of language, but as dominant knowledge systems comprised of meanings, institutional contexts, individual and collective practices that exercised authority and

---

power over subjects and other knowledge systems. Through discourse analysis, Foucault examined how subjects come to know and govern themselves in the mentality of dominating institutions (such as development agencies and programmes), and the ways in which dominant discourses come to be understood as Truth about the natural state of the world. Peet and Hartwick's (1999: 132) summary of Foucault's ideas reveals his impact on development thinking:

> Foucault believed all global theories, such as modernisation theory, Marxist mode of production theory, or world systems theory, to be reductionist (reducing complexity to a few tendencies), universalistic (making everyone and everything the same), coercive (implying force) and even totalitarian (implying total control). He attempted to 'detotalise' history and society as wholes governed by central essence, whether production in Marxism, World Spirit in Hegelian idealism, or progress in modernisation theory.

For Foucault, subjects exist in networks of power wherein they both experience oppressive power and exercise power themselves, such that domination is not singularly located in specific sites, institutions or social relations. His attention to the complexities of power opens the way for critical development theory to analyse the discursive power of the Development Establishment, but also to analyse the sorts of political openings that this reading of power suggests.

Building from these insights, critical geographers argue that all knowledge about development is culturally and historically specific, produced in what Turnbull (1997; see also Wright 2004) terms knowledge-spaces. Development knowledge does not exist in isolation, but rather is produced socially through discourses, power relations, institutions, material and intellectual histories and political dynamics in specific contexts. For example, the power of mainstream development is exercised in various influential ways. Institutions like the International Monetary Fund exercise direct control over billions in loans, currency rates, and government spending that have enormous direct consequences. Other institutions such as the World Bank, the Inter-American Development Bank, USAID and the Department for International Development (DFID) exert their influence more through their role as guarantors of the economic and political 'bankability' of a country, thus opening or slamming the door for large private-sector loans. But perhaps more importantly, these institutions of development shape everyday life in the global South through economic and political policies, regulations, legions of advisers dispensing 'expertise' and bureaucratic procedures. Development discourse, then, leads to Foucauldian self-governance, wherein global South states, communities and individuals come to understand themselves and their goals in terms of 'development' (see section 2.3 and chapter 3 for more on this). This dominant discourse is all the more powerful because it is understood as obvious knowledge about the 'natural' state of the world, rather than as a political construct that 'works' in certain interests (Foucault 1980a, 1980b; Gregory 2000; Barnes and Duncan 1992; Peet and Watts 2004).

For example, contemporary Development discourse sets the terms of debate, identifying development work as a series of technical and managerial problems that could be solved by the application of universal, objective, scientific knowledge and by 'experts' who are qualified to identify both the 'problems' of development as well as its 'solutions' (Escobar 1995; Ferguson 1990). A range of 'technical problems' have been identified since the mid-twentieth century – 'poverty', 'illiteracy' and 'overpopulation' (see Box 2.2). Once a problem like 'overpopulation' has been identified, it leads to particular policy interventions, while obscuring other processes that produce hunger and environmental damage – such as changing diets and commercialisation of agriculture for elites and export markets. In the process, the root causes of uneven development, ethnic conflict and persistent poverty were defined and 'solved' in scientific terms, rather than being understood as consequences of centuries of political and economic exploitation.

Box 2.2 Population as the 'problem'

Within Western popular culture, and also in the development 'industry' (funders and agencies engaged in a wide range of development projects), there is a remarkably tenacious narrative of 'overpopulation'. This common representation argues that countries of the global South are poor, hungry and environmentally fragile because they are 'overpopulated'. In other words, they are bursting at the borders and filled with people of unbridled fertility. This enduring Western representation is fueled on a number of fronts by anxieties over immigration to the USA and Europe from the global South, and by environmental rhetorics that associate 'overpopulation' with environmental degradation (Kaplan 1994; Connelly and Kennedy 1994). In US classrooms there is a particular geography to this representation. In teaching a large undergraduate development class, I question the students about which are the five most populous countries in the world. Students typically do name China and India as ranked one and two, but almost invariably Mexico is named as the third most populous country. Population data actually demonstrate that the United States is the third most populous country(!), followed by Indonesia and Brazil. In fact, Mexico does not even make the top 10 list. I then re-pose the question to students: why do Americans continue to believe that Mexico is the world's third most populous country when the data incontrovertibly refute it? Their response is rooted in generalised anxieties about Mexican immigration to the USA.

I use a classroom exercise to explore the tenacity of this idea that problems of hunger and poverty are a result of 'overpopulation', in the face of abundant evidence to the contrary. For my students, Timothy Mitchell's work, 'America's Egypt' provides a powerful critique of the commonly accepted 'overpopulation' argument circulating in international development institutions (Mitchell 1991a; see also Mitchell 1991b). Drawing on the empirical example of Egypt, Mitchell challenges the dominant, graphical and statistical representation of that country as a place with too many people and too little agricultural land. For development practitioners, these 'facts' are self-evident and continue to explain increasing hunger in the Egyptian countryside. What makes Mitchell's argument so powerful for students is that he refutes mainstream development arguments, by using the statistical measures and data employed by the development institutions themselves, and then by situating the image of a crowded, hungry Egypt in its larger historical and political context.

Mitchell contests the scientific representation from the World Bank that hunger in Egypt is primarily a mathematical problem of too many people on too little land, with too little technology to produce adequate food supplies. He employs World Bank data measuring numbers of people, food, growth rates, land densities and landownership to demonstrate that the dominant understandings of the problem can be, and indeed have been, refuted using the very statistical measures commonly employed by development institutions. Specifically, between 1965 and 1980, Mitchell showed that the population of Egypt grew at an annual rate of 2.2 per cent. Yet during the same period agricultural production grew at the even faster rate of 2.7 per cent per year, staying ahead of population growth (Mitchell 1991a: 20).

Nonetheless, even though data challenge this understanding of 'overpopulation' in Egypt and myriad other places (Jarosz 1996; Durning 1992; Greenhalgh 1996), mainstream explanations continue to influence both the policy field and popular understandings of Egypt in the West. Here again, as in the example of Mexico above, the claim of overpopulation has tenacity far beyond any evidence to support it. This raises the central question of why this particular interpretation is so trenchant and suggests that something else – something deeper – is at work.

By now, students should be asking the question: 'what else is going on'? If the facts do not fit the picture, why does the 'overpopulation' interpretation persist? The answer revolves around issues of power, which mainstream science, based on assumptions of objectivity and universalism, cannot measure effectively. Part of our response to the students' question is that a complex problem like hunger (or poverty, or inequality, or fertility) results from the intersection of geopolitical and economic power shaping material circumstances. After Mitchell demonstrates that, despite strong evidence, agricultural growth rates have kept up with, and even exceeded, population growth rates, he asks, '...why has the country had to import ever increasing amounts of food?' (Mitchell 1991a: 20). He demonstrates that a closer look at the geopolitical and economic history of Egypt in the world system offers up potential explanations that are considerably more persuasive than the equation of 'too many people/too little land'. This richer analysis considers international commercial food interests, food aid tied to political agendas, such as changing diets and opening markets for the West, and class and gender politics within Egypt itself.

To go further, yet another response to our student's question is that the very framing of 'overpopulation' as *the* problem is shaped through powerful discourses that continue to set the terms of the debate, consciously and unconsciously, in favour of Western interests. The focus on 'overpopulation' obscures our ability to 'see' other framings of the problem, such as 'overconsumption'. By focusing on the 'numbers problem', framed as a scientific argument, hunger and poverty are constructed as merely technical problems that can be solved with the rational application of technocratic solutions. In contrast, from a critical perspective, hunger must be understood in terms of differential access to resources in specific places and the ability of different groups to have an effective voice in defining both key issues and alternative ways of addressing them (Nagar et al. 2002; Escobar 1995; Shrestha 1995).

The third piece of our response to the question, 'what else is going on?' is that students must examine the effects of mainstream discourses *here* in the West. It is not only that these discourses have been limited, but that the persistence of certain discourses keeps the focus on 'them' (in this case, Egyptians) and obscures the ways in which 'we' are implicated and benefit from dominant framings of development. Part of the explanation for the persistence of mainstream discourses is their *effects*, in other words, the role these discourses play in reinscribing our place in the order of things. A fuller understanding of why discourses persist involves a reflexive analysis of our investments in them, whether we are aware of those investments or not. Keeping the focus on the global South through attention to 'overpopulation', 'hunger' and 'poverty', allows those in the West to elide responsibility for changing *our* practices (such as 'overconsumption') and, more broadly, prevents us from having to critique or interrogate the very market capitalist system we are both embedded in and continue to benefit from.

(Reprinted and modified with permission from Hickey and Lawson 2005.)

Box 2.2 illustrates how political, economic and cultural power relations come together in the construction and persistence of mainstream development representations of the technical problem of 'Development'.

Knowledge about development is also situated in another sense: our understandings are always partial, limited by our own social location (Haraway 1988; Marchand and Parpart 1995). In other words, all producers of development knowledge have 'a view from somewhere' (Haraway 1988). This means that multiple subject positions – of race, ethnicity, gender, sexuality, nationality – are crucial aspects of identity that significantly shape how people think about, experience and influence development (these ideas are elaborated in section 1.4 and chapter 5). Appreciating the situated character of development knowledge is not a simplistic exercise of personal revelation or 'navel-gazing', however. Rather it is a process of analysing how a particular individual or social group is situated in relation to power and influence. So, as Haraway quipped at a public lecture, this is not a process of simply listing one's personal characteristics, as in: I (Lawson) am a white, middle-class British woman and '...land-ho, I have discovered my situatedness'; rather, it is a serious process of questioning whether certain understandings and actions are more or less able to shape, challenge and transform development. So situatedness is about always thinking relationally and about working to uncover what relations of power are significant to the work at hand. Major lessons about the situatedness of development knowledge have come from postcolonial and feminist post-structural scholarship which argues that development processes look very different from the perspective of those subordinated and oppressed by colonial, imperial and Development relations (this point is elaborated in chapter 5).

Situating development knowledge is not an argument for an apolitical relativism, wherein social scientists cannot adjudicate among truth claims. Location is deeply political. Specifically, theorists of development are situated in power relations of gender, race, class, and contexts, with different claims on expertise and power; and these elements of theorists' subject positions influence both their understanding of development and their possibilities for shaping development debates and actions. As we discussed in chapter 1, Sarah Wright (2004) demonstrates the relative power of different knowledge-spaces and subjects in her analysis of struggles over intellectual property rights for rice seeds. The universalised knowledge-space of Western science and capitalist privatised property is wielded by corporations and the World Trade Organisation (WTO), and is being contested by Filipino farmers and NGO activists who have historically saved and shared diverse varieties of seeds to sustain their farming lives, and who understand rice as an expression of community, history, future and harmony. By understanding both these claims to rice seed, it becomes possible to see the connections between knowledge, power and privilege. In Wright's study, Western notions of knowledge as private property are legitimised through the formidable power wielded by corporations and Western states in global institutions. Institutions such as the WTO have legitimised and prioritised neoliberal economic and property regimes over indigenous claims to knowledge and forms of ownership.

To be sure, debates over development knowledge within geography cannot be characterised as a simple polarity of universal versus situated knowledge. Most development geography analyses development theory and practice as contextual to some extent, but for different scholars the meaning of context varies in significant ways. For some, situating development theory and practice entails an interrogation of the institutional and political-economic production of meanings and material differences, and the ways in which these construct Western authority and power over the global South (Watts 1993; Crush 1995; Shrestha 1995). For other geographers, contextualised development research is less concerned with the production of a regime of truth through development discourses and practices, but rather analyses historical, social and political processes as they come together in particular configurations in places to explain the spatially uneven character of development processes across the globe (Gaile and Ferguson 1997; Bebbington 2000; Hart 2002a). As Cooper and Packard (1997: 13) point out, '...the point is not to decide whether or not development is truly hegemonic, but to examine projects of building and fracturing hegemonies'. As students, I prompt you to think about the universal or situated nature of development knowledge claims as an analytical tool – a tool for thinking about the differential power exercised by various development institutions and policies, and about the limits to development ideas as they hit the ground in specific places and encounter social struggles.

2.2.3 Geopolitical contexts of development

These various knowledge claims about development arose in the context of political shifts and global upheavals – the geopolitical context of development. Geographers have examined how the rise of development knowledge has been intimately bound up with histories of exploration, early industrial capitalism and colonialism, and in the contemporary reworking of global political-economic power and the institutions through which this is enacted.

> [These] origins of development theory and practice as an academic and govern-
> mental enterprise – and development economics as its hegemonic expression –
> are inseparable from the process by which the 'colonial world' was reconfigured
> into a 'developing world' beginning in the 1930's but especially in the aftermath
> of the Second World War ... (Watts 2000: 167)

Theorists from across development studies have examined the geographies and histories producing concepts of development and inscribing them with particular meanings. Cowen and Shenton (1996) argue that the modern, positivist idea of development as 'trusteeship' emerged in the mid-nineteenth century as a set of political procedures, enacted by capitalists and state actors, seeking to ameliorate social disorder and disruption that accompanied early industrial capitalism within Europe. They argue that the concept of trusteeship bolstered statist (and later colonialist) aspirations to 'help people' or 'civilise people', and has justified substantial interventions in social and economic life. Michael Watts (1995) and Stuart Hall (1992) examine how the concept of development arose in scientific accounts of the West as modern and the simultaneous representation of the New World as chaotic, violent and virtually uninhabitable (Crush 1995: 10). For these theorists, concepts of development are rooted in historical processes of exploration, trade, religious conversion and governance, through which material and discursive difference was produced between the 'West and the Rest' (Hall 1992). Deploying arguments about civilising 'savages', Europeans justified their entry into the global South in terms of the necessity of bringing progress and Christianity to the colonies while actually securing access to trade and resources for Europe.

As Lucy Jarosz (1992) has argued in her analysis of the metaphor of Africa as the dark continent, 'darkness' is opposed to 'civilisation' and operates to justify exploration, conversion and trade. First, darkness signified Europeans' ignorance of the continent and the urgent need for scientific exploration. Darkness also served as a metaphor for 'evil, tribal' beliefs and the need for Christian conversion, wherein Christianity will bring light to the darkness (Jarosz 1992: 107). Third, 'darkness' requires

> ...enlightening Africa [which] could also mean 'open[ing] up her dark recesses to our commerce' (Lloyd, 1899: 13) and chasing away the darkness 'by the limelight of scientific discovery' (Kellersberger 1936: 39). Science, capitalism and Christianity – the hallmarks of colonising power – are encapsulated in the concept of the civilising mission... (Jarosz 1992: 107)

Despite important continuities with histories of European exploration and colonialism, the post-Second World War period also involves a series of reinventions of development in the context of the decline of the colonial world and the need to reinvent systems and practices of influence (Slater 1993; Corbridge 1997). In chapter 3 I discuss the relations between cold war discourses of freedom, democracy, anticommunism and the rise of modernisation discourses and the interventions of international development institutions to integrate societies of the global South into Western capitalist circuits.[iii]

> [T]he new beginnings in development thinking that many detect in the late 1940s are surely related to the beginnings of the cold war between East and West.

> Indeed, it is hardly possible to understand either the form or content of Western thinking about development in the post-war period without first recognising that a (new) discourse on North-South relations was always related to a parallel discourse on East-West relations. (Corbridge 1997: 731)

While 'communist threats' were foregrounded as the cold war rationale for Development, critics argue that modernisation secured markets, resources and trade relationships that bolstered economic growth and geopolitical influence in the West (Slater 1993). In chapters 4 and 5 I discuss efforts to reconfigure democratic thought and action in the context of global insurrections from the 1960s to the present. This period witnessed the rise of social movements which envisioned and organised for alternative developments.

In each of the following chapters I analyse the intellectual, institutional and political contexts through which the instability of development is transformed (in particular times and places) into something fixed and stable. This is important because particular definitions of development have served to justify policies that transform livelihoods, relocate communities, change the course of rivers, rework divisions of labour, and so on. For each approach to theorising development (mainstream, Marxian, post-structural), I analyse the epistemological grounding, institutional formations and political practices that have given rise to particular enframings of development discourse and practice. This analysis of the contexts of development does not lead us to paralysis or a helpless relativism, as some critics have alleged, but rather it reveals the ways in which power operates and is struggled over in various conceptions and enactments of development. Appreciating that development is situated knowledge, produced in particular contexts, can be enabling. If the term is contested and unstable, then there is room to renegotiate its meaning and to demonstrate the limits and slippages in particular renditions of the term. Furthermore, analysing the inclusions and exclusions authorised by particular versions of development destabilises the meaning of powerful actions carried on in the name of development. Our critical contextual reading of 'developments' in the following chapters reveals what is at stake in different versions of development theory, and whose interests are served by that version of development.

Understanding the contextual character of 'developments' demonstrates that development per se, as an outcome or an end point, does not exist, but rather, *development is a series of relations* between places, social groups, cultures and spheres of production and consumption. Development is both a politically powerful discourse and relentlessly material, entailing substantial transformations of society as a result of these power relations. Focusing on the contexts of development knowledge does not imply that it is merely discursive, but rather that 'development' is always simultaneously material and discursive, with transformative power in both realms.

2.3 Geographies of development

I argued above that ideas about development (regardless of their claims to universalism) are produced in particular contexts – comprised of power relations, discourses, material and intellectual histories, institutional practices and political milieus. Not only are development knowledges themselves context-specific, but development theories and development spaces are mutually co-produced. In this section I examine how particular development theories privilege some and exclude other representations of place/space and understandings of the scales at which development operates. I argue that a major contribution of development geography is to read approaches to development for these embedded (and often implicit) geographies. More specifically, geographers analyse the ways in which *place, space and scale* are conceptualised in development theories. Through these analyses, geographers reveal assumptions and power dynamics embedded in different development discourses and practices.

I begin by discussing the ways in which different approaches to development conceptualise place/space: as homogeneous, localised and bounded territories or places as fluid and constituted through diverse processes across scales. I then turn to the ways scale is employed by different approaches to development. For some, scale identifies a hierarchical ladder, including global, national, regional, and so on, through which development processes are thought to cascade down to local places and people. For others, scales are considered transient, constantly shifting and politically constructed through struggles among social groups over the discourses and processes of development.

2.3.1 Place, space and development

Geographers learn a great deal about development theories from how they represent the places and spaces of development. For example, the majority of mainstream development theory (chapter 3) does not explicitly theorise place, but implicitly juxtaposes localised and particular places to abstract and universalised spaces of modernisation which are unproblematically territorialised as nation states. Nonetheless, mainstream theories do construct places in two mutually reinforcing ways. First, place is understood in terms of discrete, all-encompassing categories such as 'failed place' or 'successful place', and second, the complexities of place are ignored in favour of a universal narrative of change.

All-encompassing categorisations of places circulate powerfully and influentially in the West, serving to homogenise entire regions or nations as passive and failed places, as in the following quote from *Time* magazine about Africa:

> At the end of the twentieth century, we are repeatedly reminded, Africa is a nightmarish world where chaos reigns. Nothing works, poverty and corruption rule. War, famine and pestilence pay repeated calls. The land, air and water are raped, fouled and polluted. Chronic instability gives way to lifelong dictatorship. Every nation's hand is out, begging aid... (McGeary and Michaels 1998: 35–6)

Just as one region is persistently represented as failed, another is constructed as uniformly modernising and successful. Even after the Asian financial crisis of the mid-1990s, the *World Development Report* (World Bank 2000: 17) persist in arguing that '[T]he success of East Asia provides some notable lessons in successful development strategies.... The East Asian countries implemented sound macroeconomic policies that helped control inflation and avoid recessions.' This version of place assumes that the roots of economic success are internal to a coherent, bounded region in which nations have inherent characteristics that lead to the implementation of successful development policies.

This conceptualisation ignores history lessons from the Asian financial crisis that revealed the deep dependence of the Thai, Indonesian and Malaysian economies on foreign investment and world demand for their exports (Johnson 1998). This idealisation of Asian spaces also ignores the US cold war strategy of growing the Japanese and South Korean economies as an economic and military hedge against the spread of communism in the region (Johnson 1998). Further, the fortunes of the South East Asian economies were not simply determined by domestic macroeconomic policies, but rather by political relationships external to these countries: between China, Japan and the USA. As Johnson (1998: 17) points out:

> ...actions by both China and Japan made Southeast Asian exports less competitive against those two countries. Thailand, which still tied its own currency to the now seriously overvalued dollar, was ruined as a result. Given the overcapacities that too much investment had generated and the competitive challenges from China and Japan, export growth in South Korea ... fell from 30 percent in early 1995 to zero by mid-1996. A balance of payments crisis was inevitable.

This critical reading of the geopolitical context for the Asian financial crisis highlights the fragility and vulnerability of economies pursuing 'market-friendly' policies, and contrasts starkly with idealised representations of Asian economies as in the *World Development Report* (World Bank 2000) quoted above. These representations of places fix and naturalise various characteristics of enormous and complex regions, and, in doing so, they have directly supported the widespread shift to export-led growth policies around the globe, while simultaneously eliding the gritty economic and political realities that bolstered these economies throughout post-war decades. Africa is constructed as poor and fouled, East Asia is constructed as successful, both measured in terms of the West – the silent benchmark in both descriptions.

These implicit comparisons reinforce the hegemony of Western ideas about ideal places and operate to justify a range of external interventions. These interventions are seen as essential to bringing development to places that are constructed as inherently lacking the necessary endowments. Lord Bauer of the London School of Economics, writing in the 1960s, builds precisely such an argument:

> [T]he advance of less developed countries (LDCs) depends on ample supplies of capital to provide for infrastructure, for the rapid growth of manufacturing industry, and for the modernisation of their economies and societies. The capital required cannot be generated by the LDC's themselves because of the inflexible and inexorable constraint of low incomes (the vicious circle of poverty and stagnation)...and by the lack of privately profitable investment opportunities in poor countries with their inherently limited local markets. General backwardness, economic unresponsiveness and lack of enterprise are well-nigh universal within the less developed world. (Bauer 1984: 27)

Here, economic development is hampered by backwardness, unresponsiveness and lack. Similar dynamics are still at work in framing places as in need of Development. A *New York Times* article, entitled 'Why Africa can thrive like Asia' (Kristof 1997), exemplifies this discourse of mainstream development. Kristof blames African poverty on high protections around domestic markets, saying: 'in Asia economic policies were ideal: the East Asian countries sooner or later adopted relatively open, market-oriented policies emphasising exports', while African countries '...often tolerated soaring inflation and overvalued their currencies' (Kristof 1997: 11). He argues that African poverty is also caused by the limits of Africans themselves, such as low savings rates, a lack of domestic investment in health and education infrastructure, the fragmentation of nations due to ethnic conflicts and high levels of corruption. Bauer's arguments from the 1960s have their contemporary echoes in the early twenty-first century, as complex histories of colonialism, geopolitics and contemporary shifts in global capital are ignored as nations are represented in ways that serve to justify specific Development arguments and interventions. Africa is currently the front-line target for neoliberal, 'market-friendly' policies that will purportedly allow Africa to 'thrive like Asia'.

By contrast, critical development thought conceptualises places and spaces as transnationally located and produced, meaning that places are constituted through multiple social relations and processes that reach outwards from specific places and inwards towards them. Massey (1994: 5) sees place '...as a particular articulation of [those] relations, a particular moment in networks of social relations and understandings...', which encompasses economic, political and cultural relations that intersect in places as geometries of power. In the same vein, feminist geographers emphasise the global openness of places and the differences within them rather than coherence and boundedness. Massey also recuperates concepts of space, working to '...uproot "space" from that constellation of concepts in which it has so unquestioningly – so often been embedded (stasis; closure; representation) and to settle it among another set of ideas (heterogeneity; relationality; coevalness... liveliness indeed) where it releases a more challenging political landscape' (Massey 2005: 13).

These reformulations of place and space unleash multiple trajectories of change and politics as coexisting across the globe, activated by the particular constellations of histories, political, economic and cultural processes that touch down in places in particular ways. As Pred and Watts (1992: 11) put it, '...how things develop depends on *where* they develop, on what has been historically sedimented there, on the social and spatial structures that are already in place there'. For example, Tad Mutersbaugh (2002) studied the ways in which inter-national standards for certifying organic coffee production played out differently for peasant farmers in several different communities in Oaxaca – looking at changes in earnings and also cultural and political shifts. The particular places in his study are linked to each other and to globalised flows (trade) and regula-tions (certification) through the international organic farming standards, which 'legislate' uniform local farming practices that, for some, did produce improved prices for their coffee. However, Mutersbaugh demonstrates that different communities had quite contradictory experiences of organic coffee production and that poorer communities, with weaker communal governance, had enormous difficulties tapping into the potential benefits of organic production. His work shows how places have complex relations to globalised forces and that experiences of development cannot be read off from broad representations of places that will predict local experiences unproblematically.

In other words, processes of development (such as economic growth or inequality) are produced/reworked spatially through the relations between places. Sheppard (2002) argues that we must attend to unequal power relations between places: what he terms 'positionality'. Positionality refers to direct connections between distant places and poses questions about the power relations expressed in those connections. His argument expands on network theory from Latour (1987) and Castells (1996), which posits networks as neglected forms of social organisation, including actors, resources, infrastructures, and flows into '...self-organising, collaborative, nonhierarchical and flexible....[n]etworks as social spaces that behave like complex systems, in which all participants potentially have significant influence over the collective outcome' (Sheppard 2002: 317). The term positionality extends network theory because it points to unequal power hierarchies for actors *within networks* that give rise to geographies of inequality.

Geographical analyses of the diverse positionings of social groups and places within global networks can reveal workings of power that help explain uneven development. This approach resonates with feminist analyses of positioned subjects discussed in section 2.4 (below). In both cases, analysis of positionality makes visible the power relations of difference, inequality and hierarchy that construct subjects and places. Spivak (1998: 335) terms this process 'transnational literacy', making visible the connections that subordinate certain subjects or places by virtue of their simultaneous positioning within a particular place and a network of places. For example, Spivak contrasts the positions of Bangladeshi women working in garment production in two very distinct places – London's East End and export-processing zones in Bangladesh – to reveal the ways in which ethnicity and 'development' are fixed in places to exploit women's labour. Thousands of Bangladeshi women are set up in unwitting competition with each other across these two locations. Women workers in London are constructed as informal workers, cheapened as an ethnic minority and by their competition with production from the global South, and women workers in Bangladesh are cheapened by their country's position as 'Fourth World', investing in development by attracting transnational capital that has fled places like the United Kingdom. The distinct constructions and valuations of these women, who are doing the same work, is only understandable in terms of the particular positions of these places in the context of globalised garment production – the deindustrialisation of the UK and the rise of export-processing zones as 'jobs for Development' in Bangladesh.

In these ways, critical development geographers are theorising place and space relationally, recovering a 'local that is constitutively global' (Katz 2001: 1214), and revealing how globalised processes operate through culturally constituted relations of gender, race and class, as well as localised forms of organising, resisting or accommodating broader forces. Particular places, and people positioned within complex geometries of power in those places, have contradictory relationships to neoliberal development policies. Continuing poverty in places within the global South cannot be understood simply as a problem of 'primitive cultures' that have not engaged sufficiently with global forces, but rather as a direct product of the ways in which globalised forces are worked out on the ground. For example, feminist research has demonstrated the complex and unpredictable relations between structural adjustment policies and poor women's activism:

> ...global indebtedness, structural adjustment policies, and the hegemony of neo-liberal development strategies have directly intensified women's triple roles in production, reproduction and community management.... Even as *women's poverty has deepened* under these globalised regimes, women have often collectivised their gendered work, such as food provision and struggles for community infrastructure ... (Nagar et al. 2002: 262; emphasis mine)

Geographers are also examining the World Social Forum (WSF) held in Porto Alegre, Brazil and Dumbai, India as another example of how social movements mobilise in place to rework globalised political and economic forces (Sparke et al. 2005). Since 2001, the WSF has gathered together otherwise geographically (and politically) dispersed activists, who organise around a range of issues (labour rights, environmental concerns, women's rights, farmers' rights), and are linked through their opposition to neoliberal, corporate-dominated globalisation. The place of the forum brings together groups with diverse critiques of neoliberal globalisation. This moment in place is powerful because it highlights the diversity of oppressions (cultural, racial, political, environmental, sexual, and so on) that constitute the monolithic category of 'neoliberal globalisation', and, at the same time, provides a space for working towards collaboration, solidarity,

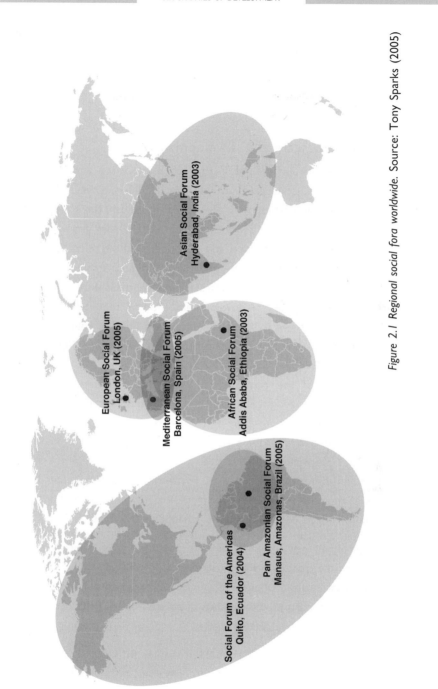

Figure 2.1 Regional social fora worldwide. Source: Tony Sparks (2005)

networking and collective action for changes across places and scales. This is one of many regional fora depicted in Figure 2.1 that have emerged in recent years. Coming together in one place each year is a central moment in strategies for building coordinated global justice movements (Corva 2004; Sparke et al. 2005).

2.3.2 Geographical scale and development

In much development thought, scale is also left untheorised and implicit, and yet, as with place/space, conceptualisations of scale differ in ways that matter across different bodies of development theory. At first blush, the scales at which development is conceptualised and practised seem quite similar, from the nation-state emphasis of both modernisation and dependency thought to the contemporary emphasis on the local scale by neoliberal and post-structural theorists. However, a closer examination of how scale is conceptualised reveals two key points. First, particular bodies of development thought tend to privilege one scale, while excluding others from consideration or political saliency. Second, different approaches to development conceptualise scales as either essential and fixed for all time or fluid and politically constructed.

Throughout much of the post-Second World War period, development studies and development geography privileged the national scale, while ignoring others such as community, household and body (Nagar et al. 2002). Dominant theorisations of development have assumed that nation states are fixed, sovereign entities that hold political power over a clearly defined territory and that contain bounded, homogeneous societies. Furthermore, the focus of development policies at the national scale is constructed as obvious, natural and essential – the scale at which development must happen, such that,

> [T]hese assumptions reinforce one another to produce a state-centered view of power in which the space occupied by states is seen as fixed, *as if for all time.* Thinking about the spatiality of power is thus put beyond history by assuming an essential state-territoriality to the workings of power (Agnew 1999: 1; emphasis mine)

Mainstream development theory (discussed in chapter 3) is characterised by this 'methodological nationalism' (Agnew 1999), resulting in an emphasis on the formation of national markets, democratic states and nationalism as a key form of collective identity (Schuurman 2000b). This nation-state focus has established the national scale as *the* legitimate site of development discourse and practice and, in so doing, effectively marginalised the explanatory role of global and local dynamics for understanding the paradoxes of development for much of the post-war period. Much development theory universalises a particular way of under-standing the organisation of political, economic and cultural life. Development '...starts with the spurious assumption of spaces already divided-up into parcels (the nation-states)' (Escobar 2001: 165). Even as globalisation discourse and practice is reworking the dominance of the nation-state scale, the Washington Consensus continues to frame economic crisis in Latin America as resulting from *domestic* failures of governance and macroeconomic management. In 1993, *The Economist* published its survey of Latin America, in which it reviewed the perfor-mance of structural adjustment policies. Success or failure is measured exclu-sively through a racist framing of the nation-state scale:

> ...the success or failure of this bout of reform depends on Latin Americans. Are they really determined this time to *become mature and responsible countries?* Or have they done no more than what they had to do in order to survive, under the tutelage of the IMF and World Bank, before reverting to type? Are they, in other words, still just *a bunch of mañana republics?* (Economist 1993: 8; empha-sis mine)

Furthermore, the World Bank, the IMF and the US State Department continue to locate neoliberal policy 'solutions' to economic crisis at the nation-state scale. For example, in the 1999/2000 *World Development Report*, considerable atten-tion is devoted to processes of globalisation and localisation that are trans-forming development landscapes. However, after a discussion of supranational trade and financial dynamics, global environmental issues and localised political movements and decentralisation, the World Bank still asserts the centrality of the nation state. The report stresses that national governments have a leading role in harnessing processes of globalisation and localisation in ways that are beneficial for national scale economic growth (World Bank 1999: 11).

In contrast to this hierarchical conceptualisation of scales as 'horizontal slices' of space, discussed above, some Marxist geographers have argued for the social production of scale and for the dialectical relations between space and human agency. Scales are, in this view, fluid, impermanent, interrelated and contested (Lefebvre 1990; Brenner 1998, 2001; Smith 1984, 1993; Peck 2002; Sheppard 2002). As Swyngedouw (1997: 141) argues, scales themselves are not ontolog-ically given, and so analysis should focus on the '...mechanisms of scale trans-formation and transgression through social conflict and struggle'. This pioneering work on the production of space and the politics of scale draws from Marxist theory's analysis of the social relations of production and the logistics of capital accumulation as central forces in the production and reworking of geographical scales. So, for example, the hegemony of the nation-state scale is seen as historically and geographically specific, resulting from a range of political and economic forces during the nineteenth and twentieth centuries.

In the late nineteenth century, dual processes of nation-building and nationalism in Europe and North America constructed economic and political life on a national scale. From post-Second World War until the 1970s, the hegemony of the national scale was reinforced by cold war politics, Fordist regimes of production and regulation, the disintegration of supranational colonial empires and the rise of postcolonial states as the dominant scale for regulating processes such as trade, human rights and development. In the last decades of the twentieth century, increasingly globalised networks of production and consumption, supranational modes of governance, such as regional organisations (such as the EU, NAFTA and CARICOM) and institutions (such as the IMF and WTO) and localised struggles over economic, political and cultural power (such as those of indigenous movements in South America) have revealed that the national scale is a social/political construction rather than a fixed and essential 'reality'. Rather than assigning certain processes to specific scales, as in mainstream theory's emphasis on the national scale, Marxian development geography poses questions about the ways in which *scales are produced* through multiple social processes at particular moments and sites:

> ...the association between a particular scale and a specific social process – say, the privileging of the national scale as the primary site of regulation, economic management, and political struggle under the era of Keynesian-welfarism or the current neoliberal preoccupation with privatised localism and global deregulation – is historically and geographically contingent. (Peck 2002: 337)

Conceptualising scale as the outcome and medium of multiple social processes and struggles opens up development studies in new ways. First, feminist geographers have argued that scales are produced not only through capitalist processes, but also through social relations of gender. Sallie Marston (2000) argues that scales are produced and reworked through deeply gendered processes of social reproduction and consumption. This insight has focused attention on scales excluded in mainstream development thought, such as community, household and the body. For example, feminist research on these frequently ignored scales reveals how gendered and racialised oppression creates feminised subjects who do the unpaid work of social reproduction (such as community kitchens and clinics) and undervalued work in the economy, which directly subsidises, and so helps to consolidate, both neoliberal states and globalised capitalism (Nagar et al. 2002; Marston 2000).

Second, critical development geography views scales as fundamentally inter-connected, meaning that social processes are not simply 'contained' at one scale or another. Women's activism in the face of structural adjustment demonstrates that the scope of national politics is not constructed exclusively through formal elections and national policies. Lind's (2000) research demonstrates that women community activists in Ecuador are organising politically in households and communities in ways that directly challenge the state for excluding women's claims as citizens and for its neglect of social welfare provision. Similarly, Perrault's (2003a, 2003b) research in Ecuador demonstrates the multi-scalar networks within which indigenous politics are embedded. Mondayacu is an indigenous community in the Amazon where residents are fighting for legal titles to their land in the face of an influx of mestizo colonists from the Andean highlands. In order to gain political and financial support for their fight for the land, community activists have actively built strong relationships with national indigenous federations and international non-governmental organisations in order to strengthen the position of their local fight through allying with strug-gles at national and international scales (see chapter 4 for a fuller discussion).

Third, thinking of scale as socially constructed raises questions about the substantive processes and moments through which economic or political scales are reconfigured, the process Smith (1993) terms 'scale-jumping'. Smith argues that scales are constantly being reworked, as the tensions between social groups are transformed over time and space. This insight has direct relevance for devel-opment studies. Whereas for decades, development institutions enhanced the capacities of national governments for the regulation of trade, production and society, the increasingly globalised power of corporations and supranational institutions is shifting the scales of governance in many places. Instead of assum-ing that governance always takes place at the national scale, critical develop-ment geographers are investigating the ways in which governance is being rescaled, as national elites in the global South (whose interests are increasingly aligned with global circuits of capital, rather than with their own poorer sectors) are embracing neoliberal (re)deregulation of their economies and societies. As a result, macroeconomic governance of many economies and societies is jumping scale as the IMF and the WTO become increasingly influential in poor nations, even as they enact the interests of corporate-led globalisation (see, for example, Lawson 2002). These shifts suggest that scales are not politically neutral; it is no accident that the global scale is currently so influential as transnational capitalist forces and governance shift upwards. As Peck (2002: 338; emphasis in original) points out:

> Although it is not *necessarily* the case that political actors occupying the highest ground are more powerful than those constrained to lower scales, it is often the case. Organisation at a higher spatial scale than the opposition typically confers advantages of mobility and evasion...multinational firms [who] engage in 'whipsaw' bargaining between plants is a case in point. The potential, frequently reiterated by management, for switching production and employment between plants, and often across national borders, erodes the capacity of labor unions to strike favorable deals at the local level...

Newstead (2002) explores the political reworking of scale in the Caribbean regional trading community CARICOM. This regional organisation has shifted the scale of macroeconomic governance upwards, and Newstead investigates efforts to rescale political activism by labour and women's groups. Specifically, she explores their efforts to appropriate discourses of 'regional community' that have been mobilised by transnational capital and political elites in support of their progressive political agendas. Here, scale-jumping is a means of acquiring political power by turning macroeconomic scalar restructuring back on itself to effect progressive social change. Perrault (2003a) notes that scale-jumping is not always upwards, from local up to regional, and so on. Drawing on Ecuadorian indigenous politics, he argues that scale may be jumped in many directions and focuses on the

> ...role played by local places as sites of political mobilisation and resistance to hegemonic globalisation... extra-local organisations may gain legitimacy precisely through their reification of place and their insertion of the local into national or transnational politics... the political claims and practices of many indigenous organisations, state institutions, and development agencies in Ecuador are *legitimated precisely through their relationship with...local indigenous communities...* (Perrault 2003a: 5; emphasis mine)

Critical development geography conceptualises scale as both an outcome and a product of struggles around gender, race/ethnicity, class, nationality, and so on.

From this perspective, scales in development thought are a socially constructed outcome of epistemological claims to know development, and material practices enacted as development, or in resistance to its hegemonic forms.

2.4 Subjects of development

> ...poor and hungry I certainly was. But underdeveloped? I never thought – nor did anybody else – that being poor meant being 'underdeveloped' and lacking human dignity... There was tension in the family. Educated children were viewed as future agents of *bikas* (development) and our parents were usually seen as *abikasis*.... in the eyes of the bikasis, whatever human capital, productive forces or knowledge our parents had accumulated over the years did not count for much. Many students felt ashamed to be seen in public with their parents. (Shresthsa 1995: 268)

Nanda Shresthsa provides a poignant account of growing up poor in rural Nepal. In his story, Nanda describes the way that contact with 'development' transformed his sense of self and the value he conferred on Nepali knowledges and practices, and even his relationships with his own family. Employing our critical geographical approach we think here about the ways *the subjects of development* (people in development) are conceptualised in different bodies of development theory. In attending to the roles and positions of people within approaches to development, we can reveal a great deal about how power is theorised, what axes of identity (if any) are significant to theorising the operation of development; and what or who are the agents of development in a particular approach (e.g. the state, the market, the worker, a multiply positioned subject). In addition, the ways in which the subjects of development are understood within a particular approach signals key differences in the research questions being asked, and in the strategies of interpretation employed.

The concept of 'subject' is not synonymous with the concept of 'individual', and this distinction is important to understand because of the centrality of both concepts in different approaches to development. 'Individual' captures the notion of unitary, autonomous actor whose actions are understood as 'free will', occurring in response to a direct and unmediated understanding of 'reality' (Scott 1992). By contrast, the subject is not free, but rather is positioned within webs of structural forces (discursive and material) that define and condition their agency. As Parreñas (2001: 24) explains,

...subjects cannot be removed from the external forces that constitute the meanings of their existence. At the same time, agency is not denied in this conception. Instead, agency is enabled and limited by the structures that constitute subjects.

Here, subjects understand life in the context of discourses and material conditions which, in particular ways, in specific places, shape the ways in which people interpret, and can engage with, 'reality'. Thus, development subjects are constituted, as Nanda Shrestha described in his evocative essay, through complex historical circumstances.

Attention to the subjects of development provides two key insights in our analysis of the making of development geography. First, the ways in which actors are conceptualised reveals different analyses of individual (object)/subject and structure/agency within various development theories. For example, we can examine whether a particular school of thought views people as individuals with free will, acting autonomously and exercising a notion of human agency that applies in all places and times. Neoclassical formulations of development assume that migrants 'vote with their feet' for development by moving to urban areas. Migrants are theorised as workers who are rational actors, responding uniformly to economic signals regardless of place or gender or class (Lewis 1955; Greenwood 1975; for a review, see Brown and Lawson 1985). Within these formulations, '[I]nequality is perceived only in terms of individual endowments; conflict takes the form of competition between individuals; and power implies decision-making power' (Kabeer 1994: 133). Within this individualist framework, the structural causes of mobility remain untheorised, such as the role of the state in compelling migration, or the commercialisation of agriculture disenfranchising peasant farmers and forcing migration in search of a livelihood in the urban cash economy (Lawson 1999; Radcliffe 1990).

By contrast, post-structural feminist approaches conceive of a subject that is constituted through structural forces, but nonetheless imbued with agency, and seeks to examine the limits and possibilities of that agency. People's experiences and actions in development are understood in terms of their subjectification by various axes of power, exercised through social relations of domination and subordination, such as those of class, gender, sexuality, race/ethnicity and nationality. In Rachel Silvey's (2000a, 2000b) work on low-income migrants in Indonesia, for example, she found that in the context of the 1997 economic crisis, women and men experience migration very differently. Silvey's work shows that since the 1997 crisis, when economic pressures on rural households intensified the need for EPZ workers to return home, women were subject to greater pressures than men. These pressures are directly related to the gendering of migrant subjects, wherein national gender ideologies have long supported higher wages and better jobs for men, thus constructing women as more available for return. In addition, given the need to draw workers home in the context of crisis, families have intensified their (gendered) scrutiny of the migration of young, single women in particular, and have pressed them to return home, employing gendered discourses about protecting their chastity and moral reputation. Silvey's work examines not only international and national power relations, defining 'good workers' and 'good women', but also ethnically specific ideas of femininity and masculinity, gender roles and meanings of morality among distinct ethnic groups within Indonesia. Her work exemplifies approaches wherein development subjects are theorised as constructed within, and acting through, multiple and intersecting relations of power.

Second, attention to the subjects of development thought also reveals how distinct intellectual streams conceptualise development subjects as inhabiting singular or fragmented identities. In other words, we can examine whether subjects are conceived as relatively homogeneous and uniform in ways that selectively silence certain aspects of their identities. Modernisation theories (discussed in chapter 3) conceptualise development subjects in terms of singular identities as objects of economic modernisation. For example, Rostow's stages of growth did not differentiate the processes of modernisation for people contained within his category 'the society'. In his description of the third stage of growth (Rostow 1960: 9), which he termed the drive to maturity, he argues that

> [T]he society makes such terms as it will with the requirements of modern, efficient production, balancing the new against older values and institutions, or revising the latter in such ways as to support rather than retard the growth process ... (emphasis mine)

This universal and singular rendition of 'the society' assumes that all people are equal members in this society and does not allow for the possibility that different people would have markedly different experiences and engagements with modernisation. His silence on women and gender, for example, assumed that within a particular nation state, all people's reactions to modernisation could be read off from their nation's location on the 'runway' as the country 'took off' towards the age of high mass consumption. Neoliberal development theory echoes these earlier assumptions about the nature and role of individuals in development. A World Bank study, *Voices of the Poor* (2000a), despite references to gender inequality, refers to the category of 'poor people' repeatedly, suggesting that their experiences are common within this category, and across many different places. Wolfensohn, then President of the World Bank Group, states at the beginning of the book that '...we needed to know about our clients as individuals...' with the assumption that given improved access to education, technology, credit and responsive institutions, all people in the category of 'poor people' would be able to improve their lives. Similar assumptions are rehearsed in a recent article in *Time* magazine, entitled 'Africa Rising', which argues that the secret to African modernisation lies in capitalist democracy (McGeary and Michaels 1998). The authors remark that '[w]hat really fuels Mozambique's climb...is the energy of individuals tackling problems from the bottom up' (p. 40). These quotes assume undifferentiated individuals who can all have the same experience of development, assuming they work hard and aspire to improve their lives.

By contrast, in post-structural feminist approaches, subjects are conceptualised as inhabiting multiple subject positions. This subject is positioned in, and constituted through, linguistic and cultural representations, as well as in relation to systematic processes of class, gender, racialisation, nationality and sexuality (Rose 1993: 138; Mohanty 1991). In these formulations, economic success is not exclusively an expression of individual attributes such as hard work, desire or ability. Rather, economic success is conditioned by a broader context of unequal power in which all are not simply equal individuals, but subjects who may experience discrimination and unequal access to opportunities. For example, the subjects of Parreñas' (2001) study, *The Servants of Globalization*, are Filipina domestic workers who are '...racialised women, low-wage workers, highly educated women from the Philippines, and members of the secondary tier of the transnational workforce in global restructuring' (p. 31). All these elements of their social location constitute them as constrained subjects and yet within the context of this positioning, Parreñas examines their exercise of agency in response to the dislocations they experience. Specifically, Filipina domestics in the USA are not able to control their destiny fully simply through hard work for several reasons. First, migrant Filipinas have vulnerable status in the USA as immigrants and non-citizens. They also experience upward and downward mobility in migration through their contradictory class positions in the USA and the Philippines. Middle-class Filipinas experience downward class mobility in their work as racialised, subordinated domestics in the USA, while upon their return home they take advantage of their higher social status (emerging from financial upward mobility) compared to that of poorer women in the Philippines, by hiring their own domestics (Parreñas 2001).

As these examples demonstrate, the (re)making of development geography, and development studies more broadly, has entailed a critical re-examination of the ways in which the subjects of development are conceptualised in diverse moments and places. Through careful attention to these constructions of the subjects of development, we can reveal the kinds of questions being asked and the forms of interpretation employed in development geography. In the following chapters I explore who is included (and excluded) as an agent of development and what aspects of identity are considered relevant to analysing geographies of development in recent decades.

Notes

[i] Chapter 1 of Rose (1993) on masculinism in social sciences and geography – note this is a complex and nuanced discussion of masculinism, as worked out in relation to diverse masculinities rather than one simplistic overarching masculinism.

[ii] The preceding discussion of discourse and this footnote are heavily indebted to work by Maureen Hickey (see Hickey and Lawson 2005). The examination of discourses and the rise of discourse theory in the humanities and the social sciences can be traced to the intense questioning by many scholars of Enlightenment theories of universal truth and meaning. Much of the interest in discourses can be attributed directly to the work of French philosopher Michel Foucault, who closely interrogated the relationships between knowledge, truth and power. Foucault argued that knowledge is itself a potent form of power. Power is constituted through knowledge and therefore knowledge is more than just a tool or technique to be utilised by the otherwise 'powerful'; instead, knowledge and power inevitably constitute one another. (For an introduction to Foucault's work, see Foucault 1980a, 1980b, 1984a; and the review essays, Gorden 1980 and Rabinow 1984. For Foucault's interview on the topic of geography and architecture, see Foucault 1980c, 1984b. For some articles on Foucault's influence on geography, see Gregory 1998; Hannah 1993; Philo 1992; Matless 1992).

[iii] This connection is perhaps most explicit in Rostow's *The Stages of Economic Growth: A Non-Communist Manifesto* (1960), which foretold the NITO ('there is no alternative') discourse of Thatcher and Reagan in the 1980s. David Slater reviews the geopolitical enframing of developmental thought (1993).

DEVELOPMENT AS INTERVENTION – FROM MODERNISATION TO NEO-LIBERALISATION

While not wanting to deny that the history of development over the past 50 years has been complex, we assert that the modernisation project continues to underlie any apparent change in the development project. That is to say, mainstream, dominant and powerful development ideology remains within the framework of neoclassical economics ... (Kothari and Minogue 2002: 7)

3.1 Contexts I: cold war global shifts and mainstream development

Mainstream development is not some dusty old body of thought, long since devalued in development circles. Quite the opposite is the case. The broad sweep of liberal economic theory *still defines* the agenda in powerful institutions of international development in the early twenty-first century, including the World Bank, World Trade Organisation, International Monetary Fund, Inter-American Development Bank, and so on. 'Market-friendly' development theory and policy dominates the mainstream agenda:

> It [successful development] can be summed up in the phrase 'letting the prices work'. That means low and stable inflation, an outward-looking approach to trade, an end to financial repression and a withdrawal from direct intervention in markets ... (Economist: 1989: 46)

> For developing countries, trade is the primary vehicle for realising the benefits of globalisation. Imports bring additional competition and variety to domestic

markets... trade exposes domestic firms to the best practices of foreign firms and to the demands of discerning customers, encouraging greater efficiency (World Bank 1999: 5)

In this chapter, we analyse debate and action within mainstream Development through the prism of a critical geographical approach. As you will see, what I term 'mainstream development thought' entails a range of theoretical and policy debates, but (as Kothari and Minogue note above) these debates are housed primarily within the theoretical and epistemological frameworks of neoclassical economics. We will first situate mainstream development thought in its geopolitical context, beginning with 'Contexts I'. In 'Contexts II' we turn to a discussion of the influential theoretical arguments that have shaped this body of thought and, most particularly, enduring debates over the relative importance of markets and states in effecting economic and social development. We then examine the ways in which geographers themselves engaged with mainstream thought, examining the spaces and scales of geographies of modernisation and 'market-friendly' approaches to development. In the final section of this chapter, forming 'rugged individuals', we examine how people are understood as subjects of mainstream development.

First, let us remind ourselves what we learn from situating development knowledge. Despite the universalism claimed by mainstream development knowledge, this body of thought is geographically and culturally specific to the West. By starting from the geo-historical, political and institutional context in which mainstream development knowledge became powerful, we can examine how this form of development knowledge was both socially produced, and socially producing. We can also analyse the sorts of economic and political tensions within the West, and in their relations to the rest of the globe, that development interventions attempted to resolve. For example, we will consider what sorts of pressures were influencing the global capitalist economy and Western economies (e.g. need for expanded markets, new means of access to colonial resources, need for new sites of investment, need for cheap labour either to in-migrate or to produce overseas). At the same time, situating mainstream development opens up consideration of the incompleteness, the unfinished nature of the project and the ways in which Development is continually being reworked in specific sites and places.

Situating mainstream development also means thinking through who benefits from the rise and consolidation of capitalist nation states. Efforts to promote mainstream development in the post-Second World War period were intimately linked to both an array of interests across the globe (elites, state actors, and so on) as well as to the continuation of Western strategic and economic interests. Situating mainstream development also reminds us that development is always about the relations between places, rather than being a purely national affair, taking place solely within the borders of global South countries. So, for example, during the cold war the legitimacy and influence of state power in the West was expanded through a development project that consolidated geopolitical spheres of influence. Finally, we read mainstream development to reveal the kinds of political and cultural rhetoric through which development was justified (e.g. the imperative to civilise; to free people from oppression; to solve hunger, poverty, overpopulation; to protect people from communism).

The project of mainstream development in the post-Second World War period is rooted in nineteenth-century histories of colonisation (which institutionalised European and US economic and political power). In chapter two I talked about how nation-building in Europe was linked with the military and economic colonisation of the global South (section 2.2). This European colonial presence was inscribed through arguments about the superiority of Western scientific ideas of 'progress' and 'civilisation'. The colonial era gave rise to social sciences that were based on '... an unconditional belief in the concept of progress and in the makeability of society, an essentialisation of First and Third World inhabitants, and the importance of the (nation) state as a frame of reference' (Schuurman 2000b: 4). Our discussion of the power of post-Second World War development is built on an appreciation of how these prior histories of conquest and economic exploitation under colonial rule constructed political-economic differences, and the vocabulary, for development interventions (Hall 1992; Gupta 1998; Sivaramakrishnan and Agrawal 2003).

Our focus here is on how these twinned discursive and material processes extended forward, but operated in new ways after the Second World War. Mainstream development thought took shape in the intellectual and geopolitical context of the cold war and the decline of the colonial world. As new countries emerged from the colonial world, Western thinkers and institutions deployed ideas about 'communist threats' to 'freedom' and 'democracy' in their efforts to integrate emerging economies and societies into Western capitalist circuits. A range of mainstream theoretical arguments and policy interventions have waxed and waned in influence, but as the quotations at the beginning of this chapter suggest, these debates are all derived from neoclassical economics.[i] During the 1950s and 1960s, the mainstream Development project consolidated through the emergence of particular theoretical arguments and powerful institutions. As the colonial world declined, mainstream Development discourse and practice became part and parcel of new mechanisms of influence and access to newly emerging states. Several authors have written about facets of these processes, including Tim Mitchell, *Colonising Egypt* (1991) and *Rule of Experts* (2002); K. Sivaramakrishnan and Arun Agrawal, *Regional Modernities* (2003); Arturo Escobar, *Encountering Development* (1995); Bjorn Hettne, *Development Theory and the Three Worlds* (1995); and James Ferguson, *The Anti-politics Machine* (1990). Each of these books addresses some of the forces producing powerful mainstream Development agendas and also argues for the power, and the limits, of this overarching project. While Development has been undeniably powerful, it is not a monolithic process of domination and homogenisation; rather, development in practice is open, ongoing and constantly reworked, as we discuss more fully in chapter 5 (Sivaramakrishnan and Agrawal 2003).

Our focus here is on how the power of mainstream development was consolidated in the West in the context of cold war struggles, the rise of influential development institutions and the political-economic agendas of newly emergent states around the globe. From 1945 to 1989, cold war politics were defined by an East-West fixation within which the development project focused on integrating newly independent states into capitalist, as opposed to communist, economic and political circuits.

> Anti-Fascist sentiment easily gave way to anti-Communist crusades after the war. The fear of communism became one of the most compelling arguments for development. (Escobar 1995: 34)

In this context, cold war discourses of bringing freedom, market economies and democracy to the global South took over from the language of the 'civilising mission' of the colonial era. Geopolitical influence in the West began gradually shifting away from Britain (and her declining Empire) and towards the USA. This shift was fueled by the dramatic post-war economic boom and the growing economic, military and political might of the USA during this period. As a result, we see successive US governments take on a major role in defining mainstream development as part of cold war ideological and material struggles over territory, markets and resources, and over the 'hearts and minds' of people in newly independent states (see Box 3.1 on Rostow). As Escobar (1995: 34) put it, '[I]t was commonly accepted in the early 1950s that if poor countries were not rescued from their poverty, they would succumb to communism'.

Box 3.1 Walt Whitman Rostow

The *New York Times obituary* for Walt Whitman Rostow in February 2003 reflects the intimate connections between mainstream development theory and geopolitics. Forty years ago, Rostow, an economic historian, made his mark on development theory with *The Stages of Economic Growth: A Non-communist Manifesto* (1960). His famous and much-critiqued book became emblematic of modernisation theory, wherein he argued that economic development was a linear and progressive process. In his formulation, countries move through a series of stages to reach the 'age of high mass consumption', after reaching 'take-off', which is stimulated by outside investments and the diffusion of modernist technologies and values. Rostow spent his career simultaneously as a professor in the academy and serving in a variety of capacities in the State Department and the Executive branch of the US government. Rostow was a professor of economic history at many distinguished universities, including Columbia, Oxford, Cambridge and MIT. Between 1961 and 1969 he held a series of government posts. As an adviser to President Kennedy in the early 1960s, he was a passionate architect and defender of the Vietnam War, and in the mid-1960s he joined Johnson's cabinet as his national security adviser. He personifies the connections between economic modernisation theory and the geopolitical struggles of the cold war that it expresses and represents. 'He argued that the United States should speed this process of modernization in places like Southeast Asia, and until it could be achieved, should make efforts to stop guerilla infiltration that threatened Communist takeover by all diplomatic or military means' (Purdum 2003: byline in the *New York Times*). Rostow was also among a core group that established the Center for International Studies (CENIS) at MIT in1951. A central preoccupation of its work was the relationship between economic growth and revolution. In 'A Proposal: Key to an Effective Foreign Policy'; they argued that when:

> …rapidly exposing previously apathetic peoples to the possibility of change… The danger is that increasing numbers of people will become convinced that their new aspirations can be realised only through violent change and the renunciation of democratic institutions… the dangers of instability inherent in the awakening of formerly static peoples would be present even in the

> absence of the Communist Apparatus. But the danger is, of course, greatly intensified by the focus which both Communist thought and Communist organisation give ... (Rostow quoted in Meier and Seers 1984: 243)

The Marshall Plan, a key element of cold war struggles, injected $19 billion into rebuilding Europe after the Second World War. The success of these massive infusions of capital directly supported mainstream development by bolstering arguments that modernisation could be engineered socially. Specifically, the success of the Marshall Plan was invoked in the design of institutions such as the World Bank. This bank was built precisely on the belief that large-scale investments in the global South could jump-start capitalist economic growth (see Box 3.2 below). As with the case of Europe, these large infusions of capital not only rebuilt infrastructure, but, more importantly, they created political obligations on the part of governments in the global South. Specifically, development aid and loans were tied to agreements to pursue economic policies that reflected mainstream development thinking.

For example, scholars have examined Western aid in the post-war period, linking flows of food, technology and loans to both cold war geopolitics and the growing economic crisis of deindustrialisation in the UK and the USA. After the Second World War, aid flows were typically tied to the purchase of goods and services from the donor country through USAID and, in Britain, through the Commonwealth Office (Power 2003: 31). For example, Public Law 480 was described as 'food aid' to Latin America in the 1960s and 1970s (George 1977; Goodman and Redclift 1991). However, a close reading of the 1954 law finds that it was designed as '...an act to increase the consumption of Unites States' agricultural products in foreign countries' (George 1977: 168). Through this law, the USA made 'concessionary sales', effectively dumping surplus wheat and rice into 'friendly' countries – selling food products below world market prices. This policy served to out-compete other country's food exports to those same markets and to shift diets and food preferences away from domestic staples, ensuring future demand for US food exports at commercial prices. Further, in the early years of Public Law 480, food was purchased in local currencies and deposited in local bank accounts, from which funds were spent in country without US congressional oversight. In many cases, these revenues were spent on military installations and internal police functions that responded to cold war imperatives in places such as Vietnam, Cambodia and Korea (Goodman and Redclift 1991; see George 1977 for an extended discussion). More broadly, aid to various countries, and the conditions attached, have ebbed and flowed in close relation to economic needs of the USA, the intensity of cold war politics and the strategic importance of specific places.

The United Nations Monetary and Financial Conference, held at Bretton Woods in 1944 is another specific expression of the politics defining this period. This conference was a struggle between the USA and the UK over nothing less than control of the post-war international economic order. The conference led to the creation of the International Monetary Fund (IMF), the World Bank (WB) and the General Agreement on Tariffs and Trade (GATT). These institutions, which came to define and dominate the mainstream development agenda, were created in the context of the rising economic and political influence of the USA and a struggle for access to Commonwealth markets previously controlled by the British. During the 1930s, the British maintained enormous power over currency and commodity markets within former colonies through the Imperial Preference System and the Sterling Areas mechanism. Imperial preference gave trade prefer-ences to Commonwealth imports into the UK and discriminated against imports from other countries, including the USA. Sterling Areas, fully established during the Second World War, meant that the UK held foreign exchange reserves of its Commonwealth members in London, in pounds sterling. This meant that in order for a Commonwealth country to trade with the USA, the transaction had to go through London, since dollars could only be converted into pounds by the British Central Bank. This meant that the British effectively controlled volumes of trade by limiting the amount of currency converted in any time period. In effect, these two mechanisms gave the British enormous control over world trade, limit-ing US access to growing markets in Africa, Asia and elsewhere.

This brings us back to Bretton Woods, a conference held in New Hampshire in July 1944. The United States pushed for greater multilateralism in world trade to fuel her post-war economic boom by gaining direct access to resources, investment opportunities and markets across the globe. While 44 nations partic-ipated in this conference, the USA and the UK dominated: Figure 3.1 depicts the cast of characters attending that meeting – an overwhelmingly white and male crowd. The USA provided support for many newly emergent states who were themselves vying for more independence from the UK. This conference was crucial in two ways. First, it signalled the end of the British Empire in terms of her economic control over many territories and states, and second, it created powerful multilateral institutions (along with national governments) that facili-tated the professionalisation of mainstream development. In other words, development came to be seen as a technical problem that could be fixed with appropriate policy interventions, thus obscuring its deeply political roots, which we are discussing here.

Box 3.2 The International Monetary Fund and the World Bank

The International Monetary Fund was created at Bretton Woods. Its members are countries (and a few territorial entities that are not states, such as Hong Kong as a special administrative region, People's Republic of China), who have voting rights within the fund, in proportion to the amount of money (subscription) they contribute. Voting rights and borrowing rights within the fund are defined by the relative size of a country's economy. This means that of the 184 members of the IMF, 5 countries (the USA, Japan, Germany, the UK and France) hold 39.2 per cent of the voting rights. The IMF has two main goals. The first is to facilitate the expansion and growth of international trade. The second is to stabilise the international financial system by preventing a foreign exchange crisis in one country from causing widespread economic recession (as in the Great Depression). To this end, the Fund lends money to countries to finance balance of payments deficits in order to prevent them from having to implement economic policies that would lead to stagnation and declining consumption. This model is based on the experiences of advanced economies during the Depression, wherein countries dealt with balance of payments deficits by cutting output, deflation, raising unemployment and cutting imports, which sparked a vicious downward cycle in their trading partners (called 'beggar thy neighbour' policies). The IMF founders argued that if short-term loans could be provided to tide over countries with a temporary trade deficit, then damage to the international financial and trade system could be avoided. This founding principle provides the rationale for the structural adjustment programmes implemented throughout the global South in response to debt crisis.

The World Bank was initially called the International Bank for Reconstruction and Development, reflecting the influence of the Marshall Plan experience in its founding rationale. The Bank makes larger and longer-term loans to countries than the IMF, in order to expand market economies and to 'modernise' societies. However, the World Bank is far

---

more than just a lending institution. It has a huge research and policy staff who have exerted substantial influence over the mainstream development agenda since the bank's founding. The emphasis of loans and programmes has shifted over the years, beginning with a focus on infrastructure projects (e.g. road, railways, dams and hydroelectric projects). The Bank's emphasis expanded to include education and agricultural investments seen as raising the productivity of the poor through 'green revolution' and 'basic needs' programmes. In the 1980s the focus shifted as the World Bank confronted macroeconomic and debt rescheduling issues, implementing structural adjustment policies (World Bank 1991). Later in the decade, the bank began paying more attention to poverty and environmental issues, as increasingly vocal civil society groups accused the Bank of not observing its own policies in some high-profile projects (World Bank 1999). All these policy interventions are framed in terms of mainstream liberal economic social science thinking about development processes. See the book *Unholy Trinity* (Peet et al. 2003) for an examination of how the World Bank, IMF and WTO have developed in distinct ways in recent decades.

Western states and international institutions did not unilaterally define the political context for international development. Indeed, mainstream Development's power and practices are constantly being interpreted, appropriated and reworked in specific times and places. For example, the participation of 20 emerging nations from the global South[ii] in the Bretton Woods Conference signals the growing independence and political influence of emergent states in development debates. Across the global South, nationalist movements powered the move to independence from former colonisers during the post-Second World War period (for detailed histories of colonial liberation, see Balogh and Imam 1988; Taylor 2002). Even as nationalist movements varied across places, many global South actors participated actively in economic development agendas. Two tendencies tied them to the mainstream development project, now promulgated by ostensibly politically neutral institutions rather than colonial governments. First, nationalist movements formed politically independent sovereign states, but in doing so, new leaders often espoused developmentalist ideals. Specifically, new governments prioritised policies and institutions that would increase economic growth and bring the nation into 'modernity'. As Gelvin (2002: 65) puts it in his study of independence

Figure 3.1 Bretton Woods Conference in 1944. Source: Bretton Woods Resort
Public Relations Office

movements in Egypt, Syria, Iraq and Iran: '...developmentalism was inextricably connected to the quest for national independence: full economic growth, it was believed, could be accomplished only by a complete political separation from colonial domination.' Second, newly emergent states in Asia and Africa consolidated their economic and political power through externally generated revenues. In many cases, these revenues came from international development assistance or loans and this served to continue various forms of engagement with mainstream development projects.

A range of alliances of global South states also wielded influence and voice in the shaping of Development from the early work of the Non-Aligned Movement and UNCTAD to the more recent formation of G-15 and G-20 Plus (among other coalitions). Economic development is a central aspect of the agendas of these coalitions as they have taken a place at the bargaining table to address international relations, access to development dollars and trade negotiations. Global South projects of nation-building and consolidation of power have often been closely tied with particular regional articulations of modernity, which have sufficiently engaged with mainstream development's analysis of economic growth and democracy to involve partnerships with Western actors and mainstream development institutions and resources (Sivaramakrishnan and Agrawal 2003; Gupta 1998). These processes of negotiation, engagement and development interventions have continued to both reaffirm and rework political and economic relations between state and capitalist interests around the globe.

Just as cold war geopolitical and economic interests framed the power of mainstream thinking, a series of dramatic shifts in the organisation of the global economy beginning in the 1970s, gradually reframed the dominant discourse of development from Keynesian to neoliberal policies (these theoretical and policy shifts are discussed in section 3.2). In other words, the political and economic contexts in which mainstream development was framed began to shift in some significant ways as a series of economic and political shocks rocked the USA and Europe (see Dicken 2003; Mitchell 2004; Sparke 2005 for a fuller discussion). These shocks were driven by:

- the powerful role played by OPEC in oil price shocks and shortages of the 1970s contributing to economic recession in economies of the global North;
- rapid expansion of transnational corporations in manufacturing, communications and banking, which decoupled their economic fortunes from those of nation states in the West;
- Thatcherism and Reaganism decoupling state practices, and nationalism leading to political demonisation of the welfare state and unionism;
- growing internationalisation of production and consumption and concomitant deindustrialisation of industrial heartlands;
- rise of the Asian Tigers (newly industrialising countries: Japan, Hong Kong, Singapore, Taiwan) that modelled export-led development and legitimated new development orthodoxy;
- institutionalisation of the free trade agenda in the World Trade Organisation;
- widening gaps of poverty and inequality between countries in global South, leading to loss of faith in discourses of universal progress.

These combined processes contributed to a reorientation of development thinking in international development institutions and by state actors across the globe. There was a shift away from an emphasis on protectionist developmentalist states and towards a free-market, export-oriented strategy that reduced trade barriers and state regulation of economy and society. In the next section, we trace the most influential theoretical arguments that worked in tandem with these politics to shape mainstream development thinking in the cold war and the subsequent period of neoliberal globalisation.

3.2 Contexts II: theoretical debates within mainstream development

Development is one of the oldest and most powerful of all Western ideas (Hettne 1995: 29)

Just as a series of geopolitical events set the stage for the rise of mainstream development, so a series of influential theoretical arguments framed out the project itself. While some of the leading architects of mainstream development were deeply embedded in cold war politics (see Box 3.1 on Rostow as an example), many individual theorists were not conscious conspirators in the creation of the 'Third World'. The structures of power that shape the mainstream (or indeed other) development agendas are often invisible even to those who inhabit them. Many of those who participated in building and refining the development project were motivated by the desire to contribute to social justice. In my own case, I was motivated by British colonial guilt and the desire to contribute to the improvement of lives in the global South. Although looking back now it is difficult to reinhabit that mindset, in the early 1980s I was a subject of the discourse of development, I was inside its logics, working for positive social and economic change and more enlightened policy. I suspect the same was true for many working in mainstream development geography more broadly (reviewed in the next section).

In other words, no one institution or set of actors had the power (even though some certainly had the intention) to *actually determine the course of events*. For this reason, we focus on the ways in which political and intellectual contexts *shape* processes, rather than determine them. Drawing on Ferguson (1990: 18), we think of mainstream development as a discourse in the sense that

> [t]he thoughts and actions of 'development' bureaucrats are powerfully shaped by the world of acceptable statements...within which they live; and what they do and do not do is a product not only of the interests of various nations, classes, or international agencies, but also, at the same time, of a working out of this complex structure of knowledge.

Inspired by a Foucauldian (see Foucault 1980a, 1980b) decentred concept of power, we examine mainstream development as a complex body of knowledge, constantly being produced and transformed by all the actors involved (academics, bureaucrats, politicians, activists, and so on). Even as we trace out the geopolitical and intellectual contexts of mainstream development, I am not arguing that mainstream development operates predictably, or at the bidding of any specific powerful subject. Rather, it is the coming together of geopolitical strategies, academic theories and actions in particular places in ways that *cannot be predicted in advance*. As you read the following account of influential theory underpinning mainstream development thinking, keep in mind that mainstream development is a fluid project that has constantly taken on board innumerable critiques (from the structuralist critique of Prebisch to the gender critiques of Women in Development (WID) theorists; see below). Despite the continuing hegemony of neoclassical development economics, mainstream development has nonetheless had to work hard to incorporate critiques within its theoretical frame. We discuss these limits of mainstream development's efforts to shift in response to gender and poverty critiques in the last section of this chapter.

Simply stated, students should not read mainstream development as a conspiracy to intervene in the global South. Rather, you should understand how political processes, particular institutional sites and certain theoretical arguments came together to shape the terms of development debate as well as its effects.

James Ferguson's (1990) book *The Anti-politics Machine* provides a nuanced and decentred analysis of mainstream development discourse and practice. Mainstream discourses of development exert their power in a range of diffuse ways, including through their representations of places in the global South. As we discussed in chapter 2, the discourse of 'failed places' establishes that problems of uneven development result from the inability of global South places themselves to adjust to 'modern nationhood'. Ferguson engages in a close reading of the World Bank Development Report from 1975, to demonstrate how Lesotho was constructed as a target for policy intervention. He details the ways in which Lesotho was represented as a primitive and uncivilised place; a place that lacked any productive connections to surrounding South Africa. He quotes the World Bank report which represents Lesotho as '…virtually untouched by modern economic development' and '…a traditional peasant society' facing '…rapid population growth resulting in extreme pressure on the land, deteriorating soil, and declining agricultural yields', such that the '…country was no longer able to produce enough food for its people' (World Bank 1975: 1). Ferguson argues that this representation has a job to do in development circles – setting up Lesotho as a target for development intervention. He counters this mainstream representation of this African place with historical scholarly research:

> Lesotho entered the twentieth century, not as a 'subsistence' economy, but as a producer of cash crops for the South African market; not as a 'traditional peasant society,' but as a reservoir exporting wage labourers in about the same quantities, in proportion to total population, as it does today. Lesotho was not 'untouched by modern economic development' but radically and completely transformed by it, and this not in 1966 or 1975 but in 1910 ... (Ferguson 1990: 27).

Ferguson's detailed study of rural development in Lesotho illustrates both how this place became a target for development intervention, and simultaneously how the closures of mainstream development discourse operate more generally.

The empirical social sciences, and especially development economics within US and UK universities, were key sites for academic research that further contributed to the power of mainstream development discourse. Their supposedly objective theoretical work prepared the ground for bureaucrats and 'development experts' to identify the 'appropriate' policy responses in Lesotho and many other countries. Their work was underwritten by neoclassical economic theory that assumed that the goal of Development was achievement of Western modernity and that this would be an evolutionary progression from 'traditional' to urban/industrial capitalist societies. Early theorists developed influential concepts of social and economic development (most famously those of David Ricardo, Adam Smith and Karl Marx), and these theories were all underlain with unconscious premises and unexamined assumptions about the superiority of the West as the pinnacle, the epitome of civilised society. For example, Adam Smith's argument contrasts American Indians, whom he describes as 'savages and barbarians', with the 'civilised nations' of Europe. While critical of capitalism, Marx's concept of an 'Asiatic mode of production' suggests the construction of an 'other' to dynamic and progressive European capitalist modes of production (Hall 1992: 315–17; for more discussion of Marxist theory see chapter 4).

Within the broad sweep of mainstream development studies, three major theoretical positions have duelled for prominence at different times since the Second World War. The first of these is the nineteenth-century classical economic liberalism of Adam Smith and David Ricardo, which emphasises open capitalist markets as the key to economic development and, in particular, the laws of comparative advantage that should govern international trade. Second are twentieth-century Keynesian arguments that assert an important role for the state in regulating growth and investing in societal development. And third are the structuralist economic arguments, beginning with Raúl Prebish in Latin America, but extended in other regions of the global South (Kay 1989).

Development economics in the post-Second World War period is a blend of these three arguments, with one position or another gaining strength at particular times. These theories all foreground economic growth and the rise of liberal, independent states and individuals, but they differ in their views about the role of states versus markets in regulating and enhancing economic development. Structuralist theorists also differ in their arguments about the relevance of Western assumptions and principles for countries of the global South, given their distinct positions within global economic circuits. These theoretical foundations for mainstream development have been thoroughly reviewed elsewhere and so I present a brief review of their major ideas (for extended discussions see Hettne 1995; Peet with Hartwick 1999; Kay 1989; Dickenson et al. 1996; Yotopoulos and Nugent 1979).

3.2.1 Classical liberalism

Adam Smith's classic tome 'The Wealth of Nations' (1776) argued that the 'invisible hand' of the market will lead profit-seeking individuals to extend their own gains in ways that are ultimately good for society as a whole. Smith's arguments – that societal development could best be achieved by the free operation of the market through the laws of supply and demand, are at the heart of liberal development theory. In the recent neo-liberal turn in mainstream development, these ideas have been employed as an argument against state involvement in economy and society. Further, neo-classical international trade theory draws from Smith's ideas about the efficiency achieved from economic specialisation and from national economies participating in an international division of labour. Trade theory argues that a country's economy would be most productive and efficient if it specialises in the production of goods for which it is particularly suited, and then engages in trade with other countries that have comparative advantage in other products (see Box 3.3). Ricardo was an early proponent of the unfettered operation of international markets arguing that 'all partners in trade benefited from an increase in total production in accordance with their comparative advantages' (Peet with Hartwick 1999: 29). In this view, the world economy produces and trades more goods at a constant level of inputs, if all nations specialise in producing the goods for which they have comparative advantage.

Box 3.3 An explanation of comparative advantage

Here I illustrate an argument for the concept of comparative advantage by Sam Nguyen (2004). This example is from the adamsmith.org weblog that discusses the merits of free trade policies.

He begins with a critique of the argument that some industries need protection from overseas competition because that is in the interests of the British economy. He goes on to illustrate the concept of comparative advantage, arguing that, in reality, protectionism may be good for particular groups of people, but it is never good for an economy as a whole. How does he build his case?

Nguyen argues that consumers buy goods from another country because they are better in quality or price than the goods available domestically. Sometimes it is because the good is only produced overseas. Being 'better in quality' should be taken in a broad sense, as some people regard British real ale as the best quality beer, while others regard Belgian beer as the best. Consumers have different tastes and imported beer from countries like Belgium enables different tastes to be catered for.

Nguyen continues that, odd though it might sound, trade would be beneficial even in the implausibly extreme case of Belgium being better than the UK at producing everything. This is because it is in Belgium's interest to specialise in those products that it can make most money on, and to use that money to buy in the other things they need. So the UK and Belgium – even in this example – would benefit from some specialisation and then trading their excess goods with each other. This is what is referred to as the Law of Comparative Advantage.

Nguyen concludes by following his logic to its own ends: trading allows more goods to be produced in total for the same amount of input, and therefore is more efficient. It is for this reason that proponents of free trade argue that protectionism and subsidies harm consumers and businesses alike. They prevent consumers from buying the goods they want at the prices they want, and they prevent businesses from taking advantage of their relative low costs and selling cheaply abroad.

Adapted from Nguyen (2004)

Following this logic, nations with large supplies of labour should have a comparative advantage in labour-intensive goods and should produce and export more of those.[iii]

Despite their provenance in the eighteenth and nineteenth centuries, these classical economic arguments have re-emerged as globally hegemonic in the late twentieth century in the form of neoliberalism. Neoliberalism refers to theoretical and political arguments which assert that economic and social well-being can be achieved only through reductions in the state's role in both the market and social transfer programmes, using tools such as deregulation, privatisation and marketisation (Peck 2001; George 1999). These policies are sustained by a belief in the virtues of individualism and personal responsibility, and the efficiency of market forces as captured in this quote from the Adam Smith Institute in Britain:

> The Adam Smith Institute is the UK's leading innovator of free-market policies. Named after the great Scottish economist and author of *The Wealth of Nations*, its guiding principles are free markets and a free society. It researches practical ways to inject choice and competition into public services, extend personal freedom, reduce taxes, prune back regulation, and cut government waste. (http://www.adamsmith.org/)

In the United States it was the Chicago School, led by Von Hayek and his student Milton Friedman, that institutionalised contemporary neoliberal thinking. Becoming known as the 'Chicago Boys', Von Hayek, Friedman and their followers were architects of neoliberal transformations in Europe, North America and, famously, Chile in the 1970s and 1980s (where Pinochet instituted neoliberal reforms after the violent overthrow and murder of the democratically elected socialist Salvador Allende). While our focus here is on the content of these theoretical arguments (see Box 3.4 for specific policies of neoliberalism), recall the previous section of this chapter and remember that neoliberal ideas became influential in the context of stagflation in Western economies in the 1970s and 1980s and with the rise of conservative governments of Thatcher and Reagan, who promised to solve economic crisis in the West by rolling back the state and 'freeing' market forces.

Box 3.4 The Washington Consensus

By the late 1980s, a broad consensus about the 'right policies' for neoliberal development had emerged between the IMF, the World Bank and the US Treasury Department (see Williamson 1990). This package of policies appeared in structural adjustment programmes throughout the global South and included the following policies (modified lightly from Peet with Hartwick 1999: 52 and Peck 2001: 448):

Fiscal discipline: capping government budget deficits

Public expenditure priorities: focused on supply-side investments rather than social redistribution

Tax reform: hold down rates and raise incentives for investment

Financial liberalisation: let the market determine interest rates and capital flows

Exchange rates: market forces should determine currency values, which should encourage rapid growth of exports

Trade liberalisation: tariffs and quota restrictions on imports should be removed

Foreign direct investment: barriers to the entry of foreign firms should be abolished

Privatisation: state enterprises should be returned to private ownership

Deregulation: restrictions to competition should be abolished, including social entitlement programmes

Property rights: legal systems should protect private property rights (including intellectual property)

Wage restraint: rollbacks in unionism, limits on minimum wages

Building from their initial consolidation as the Washington Consensus, neoliberal policies and politics have mutated throughout the last two decades, both in the advanced economies and in international development circles. During the 1980s and 1990s, mounting critiques from Latin American scholars and activists focused on the intense social costs of structural adjustment policies in the wake of the debt crisis (Green 2003; Petras and Veltmeyer 2001, 2003; Dezalay and Garth 2002). These powerful critiques prompted the World Bank to focus more on investments in social capital and incorporation of the agendas of social movements. Several worldwide initiatives have been launched to bring attention to the devastating environmental and social impacts of neoliberal policies such as the World Commission on Dams, the Extractive Industries Review and the Kyoto Protocol. Eventually, as social suffering became increasingly apparent during the 1990s, we also began to hear the 'Third Way' arguments of Blair in the UK and Clinton in the USA.

The Structural Adjustment Participatory Review Initiative (SAPRI) was launched in 1997 as a collabouration between the World Bank and social movements across the global South (countries involved were Bangladesh, Ecuador, El Salvador, Ghana, Hungary, Mali, Uganda, Zimbabwe, Mexico, the Philippines, Canada and Argentina). The project involved a detailed qualitative methodology, designed explicitly to focus on the perspectives of those impoverished by neoliberal policies. The initiative was to assess the social and economic impacts of Washington Consensus policies and to construct policy alternatives informed by a political-economic critique and a deep understanding of how these policies played out on the ground. Despite substantial evidence of social suffering from this effort, the World Bank has continued its structural adjustment policies and has refused to seriously engage with citizen groups. This quote from an April 2004 letter from the Structural Adjustment Participatory Review International Network (SAPRIN) steering committee to Wolfenson speaks volumes:

> Based on [SAPRIN] research, the Bank co-authored reports with SAPRIN that clearly demonstrate the failure of these [structural adjustment] policies. Unfortunately the Bank chose to ignore findings of this joint global investigation, as it has systematically dismissed other evidence of the failure of adjustment programs of the past quarter century to deliver promised results. ...In light of this, the *Bank's current rhetoric about the importance of civil society rings hollow* for the thousands of groups and individuals who contributed to the SAPRIN national exercises without remuneration but with the expectation that the Bank would make changes based on a better understanding of the impact of adjustment policies on their lives. ...Our organisations have put the World Bank to a test, *a test that it has badly failed.* (http://www.saprin.org/news_updates.htm; emphasis mine)

3.2.2 Keynesianism

Keynesianism, the second influential thread of economic theory, dominated the international development agenda from the 1950s until the 1970s. John Maynard

Keynes wrote *The General Theory of Employment, Interest and Money* (1936) in the wake of the Great Depression. Indeed, it was the crisis of the Depression that discredited liberal economic thinking and created space for the rise and influence of Keynesian ideas. His explanation for the Great Depression was that a lack of aggregate demand led to economic crisis. His solution involved government policies to stimulate demand and expand the economy in order to increase spending and consumption and so reduce unemployment (Brown, ch. 3 in Hall and Gieben 1992: 153). He argued, in marked contrast to the neoliberal standpoint, that the unfettered operation of free markets does not automatically improve human well-being. His ideas formed the basis for economic development policies that were designed to maintain full employment in Western capitalist economies through government spending on infrastructure, education and social services, along with monetary policy to control inflation.

These ideas, bolstered by the successes of European reconstruction after the Second World War, were foundational in development economics. Keynesianism promised the manageability of development and the need for managers such as development economists and policy 'experts'. At the same time, ideas about the 'makeability' of societies in the global South, in the image of Western economies, mandated a strong role for the state and this corresponded with the ambitions of emerging elites in many countries. As Hettne (1995: 38) puts it, 'the main message [in development theory] was that development necessitated plans, written by economists, and strong, active governments to implement them'.

A large number of development economists generated influential theories during the 1950s and 1960s that focused on maximising economic growth through industrialisation and urbanisation in the global South (reviewed in Peet with Hartwick 1999; Meier and Seers 1984). Here I mention only a few prominent thinkers as examples. For W. Arthur Lewis. the central questions in development revolved around how global South governments could modernise their traditional agricultural sectors and foment domestic industrialisation. He worked on the internal structural transformation of global South economies, examining flows of labour, goods and capital between domestic agricultural and industrial sectors. He argued for government investments in education, health services, water supplies and worker compensation as key elements of the economic modernisation process. Albert Hirschman argued that unbalanced industrial growth would stimulate efficient use of scarce entrepreneurial resources and maximise the growth effects of capital-intensive industrialisation. His ideas led to industrialisation strategies wherein investments, administrative energies and resources were spatially concentrated and focused on industries with many forwards and backwards linkages to the domestic economy, with the assumption that the benefits of economic development would trickle down to other places over time. Harrod (1948) and Domar (1946) argued that growth of national income was directly and positively related to the country's savings rate, leading to policies encouraging higher savings rates and developing banking and investment infrastructures. Their work also focused attention on the mobilisation of (domestic or international) capital as a major trigger for economic growth in the global South.

Taken together, these and other development economists built from Keynesian ideas to promulgate a range of policy interventions designed to increase economic growth and to effect the transition of global South economies into capitalist urban/industrial modernity. From 1960 to 1965, for example, the World Bank made 109 loans for power plants, roadways, railways and industries in Africa, Asia, Latin America and the Middle East (Table 3.1). By 1971–75, the Bank expanded this portfolio to 197 loans across these same regions, and substantially expanded loans for education and the commercialisation of agriculture, from 16 loans in 1960–65 to 93 in 1971–75.

Sociological modernisation theory emerged in close relation to Keynesian economic arguments about development in the global South. Pioneered by sociologists in the 1960s, modernisation theorists argued that certain cultural/social attitudes are a prerequisite for Western-style urban/industrial development. These cultural theories of development also adopted Enlightenment assumptions about societies passing through an evolutionary process from traditional to modern. Talcott Parsons' work on the evolution of social systems formed the foundation for this body of thought. Many authors built from his ideas about the limited 'adaptive capacity' of traditional societies and the importance of changes that prompt societies to specialise and transform their practical actions and value systems in response to problems. For example, Seymour Martin Lipset and Aldo Solari (1967) held that 'feudal' values and social structures in Latin America were holding back economic development. They argued that Latin American societies were imbued with elitism, that they scorned materialism, viewed work as a necessary evil and that society assigned status on the basis of family position rather than material achievements. In their view, these attitudes and values must change in order for 'nonindustrial traditional' Latin American people to become effective entrepreneurs who could then propel economic development forward. Lipset and Solari's solution was to

Table 3.1 Number of IBRD/World Bank Loans for 1960–1965 (A), 1966–1970 (B), and 1971–1975 (C) by type and region[iv]

	Africa			Asia			Europe			Latin America/ Caribbean			Middle East[a]		
	A	B	C	A	B	C	A	B	C	A	B	C	A	B	C
Agriculture	3	14	34	5	14	18	0	2	14	8	17	33	0	3	8
Education	0	5	7	1	3	8	0	1	7	0	11	11	0	0	4
Industry[b]	3	8	23	15	16	17	5	8	21	3	6	15	1	7	6
Power	10	9	11	12	14	9	10	7	11	17	29	18	0	0	6
Telecommunications	1	4	5	0	6	4	0	1	0	2	4	9	0	0	3
Transportation	6	25	25	16	20	21	6	7	11	22	19	29	4	2	7
Water supply/sewerage	0	2	7	2	3	5	2	0	5	0	4	11	0	0	2
Other[c]	0	2	10	0	0	7	0	0	1	0	0	9	0	0	4

Source: Anna McCall-Taylor, (2005)

Notes:

[a] The countries classified here as the 'Middle East' are: the Arab Republic of Egypt, Iran, Iraq, Israel, Jordan, Lebanon, Oman, and the Syrian Arab Republic. This is not a comprehensive list of Middle Eastern countries, but a subset of the countries receiving World Bank loans in this time period.

[b] The 'industry' category includes loans made for industrial development finance companies in each country.

[c] The 'other' category includes such things as family planning programmes, tourism development and loans for export expansion, urbanisation and technical assistance.

reform education so that it instilled high 'achievement motivation'. This concept, and the potential for instilling it in 'traditional' people, was derived from the work of psychologist David McClelland (1961). He argued that certain individuals had desire for achievement and so were suited to become entrepreneurs who would lead economic development forward.

Perhaps the most famous modernisation theorist was Walt Whitman Rostow (see Box 3.1), who pursued three key questions in his work: how could economic theory inform economic history? how did economic forces interact with social, political and cultural forces? and what is the relationship between economic growth and revolution? (Meier and Seers 1984: 229) In his famous book *The Stages of Economic Growth: a Non-communist Manifesto* (1960), Rostow postulated that countries would pass through a series of developmental stages on their (inevitable) path to modernity, eventually arriving at the stage of 'high mass-consumption'. This stage was the culmination of a process involving steady increases in savings, investment, economic growth and consumption, and a shift in people's attitudes and practices away from 'long-run fatalism' and towards entrepreneurial engagement with new economic opportunities.

3.2.3 Structuralism

Raúl Prebisch was the Argentinian pioneer of a structuralist perspective, the third major strand of mainstream thought. Prebisch argued that dominant Western arguments about economic growth were sorely limited in global South contexts. His major contribution to the economic development debate was to situate the experiences of Latin American countries in the context of an international division of labour. His work challenged the logic of international trade theory and arguments about comparative advantage as an appropriate strategy for long-term development. Observing the harsh effects of the Great Depression in Latin America, Prebisch (1959, 1962) argued that countries of the global periphery could not simply follow liberal trade policies formulated for advanced economies. Rather, he argued that peripheral economies were at a long-term structural disadvantage in relation to the advanced economies due to their disadvantageous terms of trade.

Prebisch argued that Latin America experienced 'primary export dependence', meaning that Latin American economies depended on primary exports as their principal source of national income. He argued that this was a very shaky basis for long-term economic growth and stability because of the disadvantageous terms of trade for primary exports. Specifically, he argued that prices for primary goods grew at a much slower rate than prices for manufactured goods, exported from advanced economies. Over time, then, Latin American economies would be forced to export ever-expanding volumes of primary goods to pay for their imports of manufactured goods. He also observed that demand for Latin American primary goods was not as elastic as for manufactured goods, meaning that if Latin American countries continue to pursue a comparative advantage approach to economic development, they would inevitably be faced with growing trade deficits, inflation and unsustainable international debts.

In addition to his arguments about primary export dependence, Prebisch also studied the role of the state in fostering high incomes for workers in advanced economies. He noted that immigration laws protected workers from cheap immigrant labour, that union bargains struck with the state and industry bolstered standards of living, and that the state played a redistributive role through social/welfare policies. These twinned economic and political analyses led him to conclude that Latin American development could best be achieved through state-led domestic industrialisation policies. He drew from Keynes' ideas about the need for the state to invest in and orchestrate economic development, but he added arguments about the need for trade protectionism in the global South. He argued that this was necessary because advanced economies held a technological and competitive advantage in the global economy due to their prior industrialisation. Prebisch advocated Import Substitution Industrialisation (ISI) strategies with a strong role for the state in building infrastructure, protectionist policies to allow infant industries to grow and intensification of domestic capital accumulation through tax incentives and preferences (see Furtado 1970 and Kay 1989 for detailed discussions of ISI). ISI policies were implemented across Latin America from the 1950s into the 1980s, until they were eliminated gradually by neoliberal policies of the Washington Consensus (see Box 3.4), which were foisted on the region by the International Monetary Fund in the context of the Latin American debt crisis (more on this in chapter 4).

Prebisch's structuralist arguments had an enormous impact both on the specific development policies pursued in Latin America and also through his intellectual leadership at the Economic Commission for Latin America (ECLA). In essence, his work foretold many subsequent analyses of Latin American dependency, variants of which drew on world systems theory, Marxian theories of imperialism and/or state–society relations, by authors such as Theotonio Dos Santos, Celso Furtado, Henrique Cardoso and Enzo Faletto and Andre Gunder

Frank (discussed in chapter 4; see also Kay 1989 for a detailed discussion of dependency analyses).

3.3 Geographies of mainstream development

By the sixties...there was a certain embarrassment about the whole history of empire, and a turning away from the idea that geography could or should have any global role, let alone shape geopolitical strategies (Harvey 2000: 2)

The project of mainstream development was inherently territorial, involving the formation and consolidation of nation states in the global South. And yet geographers were latecomers and minor players in the Keynesian/modernisation development project. Our absence is rooted in the history of relations between geography and Western, imperialist states such as the British, German and, later, the USA. Geographers served state projects of exploration, colonialism and imperialism of the nineteenth and early twentieth centuries (Peet 1979; Hudson 1977; see also Power 2003 on the history of tropical geography in the UK). For example, American geography was advanced by providing colonial administrations with regional expertise on specific places (such as the Philippines and Puerto Rico), providing 'experts' in mapping territory, identifying and exploiting natural resources and discovering commercial opportunities (Heyman 2004; Harvey 1996). However, as discussed above, the post-Second World War development project redefined Euro-American relations to the global South in objective, techno-scientific economic terms, deflecting attention from the territorial and political underpinnings that shaped that cold war geopolitical agenda. The discipline of economics was a central player in the redefinition of relationships between the West and the global South in terms of economic development and 'solving the problems' of the global South. In this transition, regional geographical knowledge was associated with colonising discourses, and it was only as theoretical geography was articulated in the 1960s that geography could reclaim any space within the development arena – once the discipline's new scientific identity served to 'cleanse' its own history of exploration and colonial and imperial expansionism.

Economists, regional scientists and planners were central players in the spatial analysis of disparities in income and growth in the global South (for a detailed discussion of all this work, see Gore 1984). Initially, they translated the mainstream theories discussed above into abstract spatial terms, assuming that an economic landscape at equilibrium would distribute factors of production evenly over an isotrophic spatial plane (a theoretical landscape with uniform characteristics, as in Ohlin 1933; Losch 1954; Isard 1956; Christaller 1966).ᵛ These theorists built models of locational interdependence, assuming rational responses by economic actors to prices and distances.

Gunnar Myrdal was one of the first to challenge this ideal of spatial equilibrium, arguing that the free play of market forces would inevitably produce regional inequalities through circular and cumulative causation that would disproportionately fuel the growth of dynamic regions. If not corrected through policy, Myrdal (1957) argued that growth in lagging regions would be retarded further as investments, migrants and economic activities were drawn into the dynamic centre of growth. John Friedmann (1966) focused on core-periphery dynamics in the global South, identifying growing core cities that led the process of industrial development; upward transitional areas that benefited from trickle-down growth; and regions in decline that needed to be targeted by regional development policies. For Friedmann, regional policy needed to achieve an interdependent system of cities that would transmit development across national territory. Overall, researchers assumed that spatially balanced development was desirable and that government policies could deliver on both spatial efficiency and equity goals.

Geographers entered the fray in the 1960s as the quantitative revolution gained strength in the discipline. In part because of their late entry, Browett (1980: 57) notes that '...the input of geographers to the formation of development theory has been minimal'. Geographers took up the idea that modernisation was transmitted across space through a matrix of cities and transport linkages. Their spatial approaches to modernisation conformed to the common assumptions of dominant mainstream theories reviewed above. For them, inequality and poverty were understood as a lack of development; inhabitants of the global South were seen as lacking, lagging and desirous of development; Western-style urban/industrial market economies were the unquestioned goal of modernisation; an evolutionary and progressive national transition needed to be set in motion; and the state was viewed as a benign actor, facilitating this transformation of societies (Gore 1984; Browett 1980). Peet (with Hartwick 1999: 84) aptly summarises this work:

> Modernisation was seen as a spatial diffusion process, originating in...port cities or colonial administrative centers, with patterns of change moving across the map, cascading down urban hierarchies, and funneling along transportation systems. This process could be measured by the spread of modern institutions like schools...and mapped as a *modernisation surface* ... (emphasis in original)

Geographers contributed to thinking about modernisation through their attention to the spatiality of development processes. They examined the uneven spatial spread of infrastructure and investment and sought to understand the patterns that emerged across national spaces. For example, Taafe, Morrill and Gould (1963) theorised how a dense network of roads emerges and facilitates the spatial diffusion of development. They constructed a generalised model of transportation development that analysed the diffusion of development to outlying areas, based on empirical work in Ghana and Nigeria. Their model examined the relationships between expansion of roads, population dynamics, the physical environment and processes of settlement and commercialisation. Ed Soja (1968) examined the spatial diffusion of modernisation in Kenya, looking at relationships between the spread of modernisation and the emergence of the modern Kenyan nation state. He mapped patterns of mobility, networks of social communication, links between cities and participation in national politics to reveal patterns of modernisation and their implications for national unity. Similarly, Barry Riddell (1970: 130) examined the human geography of modernisation in Sierra Leone, concluding that, 'Modernisation is a geographic phenomenon with obvious spatial expression; its pattern of spread is not a simple contagious process, but is strongly influenced and determined by the transport network and the urban-administrative hierarchy'. Figure 3.2 depicts spatial models of the diffusion of primary education across the national territory of Sierra Leone.

This geographical work aimed to inject space into the overly abstract and economistic theorisation of the categories and processes of economic development. For example, Norton Ginsberg's (1961) *Atlas of Economic Development* contributed to knowledge about global variations in economic development, and provided a richer and more nuanced representation of levels of economic development across the globe than the categories of 'rich' and 'poor' or 'developed' and 'undeveloped' that were circulating widely in development circles. Drawing on a range of variables, such as electricity generation, oil-refining capacity, international trade, transportation densities (of road, railways, vehicles), agricultural yields, and so on, Ginsberg attempted to dispel the idea of a homogeneous 'underdeveloped' world by mapping the varied socio-economic landscapes of countries across the globe. This atlas exemplifies geographic efforts to complicate the crude categories being employed in development circles. At the same time, this work by Ginsberg, Brian Berry and others seeks to join the technical debate about the nature of development processes. These geographers produce '...generalisations about the economic organisation of the world' (Ginsberg 1961: 11) by theorising development processes as a combination of

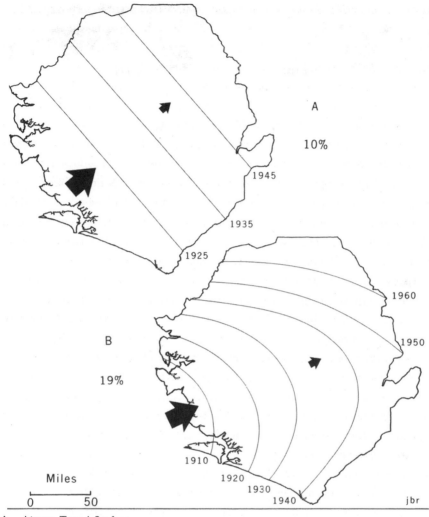

A – Linear Trend Surface
B – Quadratic Trend Surface

Figure 3.2 Diffusion of primary education. Source: Northwestern University Press, Riddell, J. Barry (1970) *The Spacial Dynamics of Modernization in Sierra Leone: Structure, Diffusion and Response* (p. 67, Figure 15)

context-specific resource endowments, the nature of social and economic settlement, transportation systems and as a result of the sorts of interactions taking place between peoples and places.

Geographers were motivated by a desire to analyse and understand the spatial complexity of economic development. Brian Berry (1961b) engaged in detailed empirical analysis to challenge some theoretical ideas about development.

95

Specifically, employing reams of data and multivariate analysis, he argued that tropical locations have little to do with levels of economic development in a direct challenge to environmental determinist arguments that still circulate today (recalling our discussion in chapter 1 of the book *Is Geography Destiny?*). Berry also challenged the argument that colonialism contributed to higher levels of poverty, and he extended these sorts of findings into policy recommendations about improving economic and social development.

Geographical work also entered policy debates on the 'optimal' spatial organisation of the urban hierarchy, assuming that transmissions of education, political and cultural change and economic diversification across these cities would deliver modernity. There was substantial debate about whether spatially concentrated development in large cities would maximise growth through agglomeration economies, eventually leading to trickle-down (Friedmann 1966; Richardson 1978, 1980). Researchers focused on mechanisms of developmental change, such as private and public investment flows, trade, migration, commuting and work dynamics, and the diffusions of innovations (modified from Gaile 1980: 24). Berry (1961a: 138–9, 1971) investigated a 'developmental model of city size distributions' to investigate whether a hierarchical urban system (as observed in many Western nations) would operate as a more effective transmission system for the diffusion of growth impulses than primate city systems found in some countries of the global South (and, not incidentally, also in France!). Berry's work argued that rank-size urban systems would promote integrated space-economies that would maximise efficient and equitable economic development.

On the latter goal, a great deal of energy and ink was expended on designing policies that would achieve spatially equitable development. Researchers and policy-makers promoted a host of urban development policies, ranging from growth poles (Richardson and Richardson 1975; Friedmann 1966) to intermediate size city strategies (Rondinelli and Ruddle 1978; Rondinelli 1983; Hackenberg 1980; Rivkin 1976; Hansen 1981). These policies were designed to redirect investments and migrants away from primate cities and to build linkages across the space-economy that would improve trade, commercialisation of agriculture and overall economic diversification. Michael Lipton (1977), by contrast, argued that urban bias systematically disadvantaged rural places. He highlighted the failure of urban/industrial growth policies to resolve rural poverty and advocated development policies delivering basic needs (such as land reform, health care, water supplies, sanitation and education) and increased agricultural outputs directly to rural places, instead of assuming that trickle-down would occur.

Rereading modernisation geography through our critical geographical approach, what do we learn about that project?[vi] In what ways was this work geographical? How did these theorists view the places of development? The places (cities, countries, regions) of mainstream development are understood in terms of a universal narrative of change. Despite the infinite social, cultural and geo-historical variations across Africa, Latin America, and Asia, particular places were viewed in terms of abstract spaces over which the processes of modernisation would play out, predictably, if not uniformly. These geographers acknowledged differences in the operation of diffusion and regional development, but they nonetheless produced generalised models and designed policies that were assumed to be broadly applicable everywhere. In other words, this work assumed that abstract spaces operate according to scientific logics and that one-size policies can indeed fit all places.

The 'spatial separatist' theme runs strongly through all this work: the assumption that space has independent effects that can be isolated and manipulated to reach policy goals (Sack 1974). Contemporary development geographers point to the limits of spatial separatism and argue instead for rich conceptualisation of place (as the confluence of geo-historical, political, social, cultural and economic forces and practices), empirical complexity and the spatiality of processes. For example, Charles Gore's (1984) book *Regions in Question* builds a detailed geographical critique of regional development theory and planning. He argues that spatial separatism is a fundamentally limiting feature of mainstream spatial development theory. Gore dubs this 'spatial fetishism', by which he means that a spatial structure (such as a city system, a core-periphery) is assumed to be the cause (rather than the expression) of a process. He notes that mainstream work is filled with mechanical metaphors about spread, backwash, trickle-down, pump-priming, and so on. These invocations of flowing water conjure up physical processes, implying that development is a natural, apolitical, engineering problem rather than a problem of social, political and cultural struggles. From our critical geographical standpoint, then, this work is limited in its assumptions that spaces act – that cities, hinterlands, transportation systems have causal powers/agency. Recent geographical work (reviewed in the following chapters) argues for a focus on the ways in which political and social forces come together in particular spatial formations (nations, cities, and so on) and that *actors in places* are actually shaping development.

97

Larry Brown also reassessed mainstream geographical approaches to development. Building from his prior work on innovation diffusion, during the 1980s he worked (with Lawson as trusty research assistant) on the intersections between development processes and migration in Latin America. Detailed empirical work in several Latin American countries led him to articulate a place-sensitive 'alternative view' of development. He moved away from universal theorisations of change and focused instead on place difference and specificity. His 1991 book *Place, Migration and Development in the Third World* examines the ways in which development and migration processes vary according to the 'local articulation of world economic and political conditions, donor-nation actions, and policies of Third World governments' (Brown 1991: 191). This research led him to propose empirically focused and place-sensitive research, involving

> ...a more idiographic perspective that takes account of places as entities in their own right and their unique experience of change. Particularly important is an ongoing dialogue with place reality... (Brown 1991: 192)

We can also employ our critical geographical approach to ask how these theorists and policy-makers think about geographical scale. Mainstream development privileged the nation state scale as the sole site of governance and development policy action. This scalar focus is a prism through which we can see the preoccupations and politics of mainstream development. As discussed above, mainstream development thought was firmly situated in its cold war and postcolonial political context. While many individual thinkers and policy-makers were critical of specific aspects of these development projects, the overarching focus of this work is to bring new nations of the global South into Western capitalist and geopolitical spheres of influence. Reflecting these politics, the modernisation project was explicitly about building liberal, secular, modernist, capitalist nation states in the global South.

As Soja's quote illustrates, mainstream development geographers unquestioningly analysed development processes within a national frame of reference:

> ...modernisation operates within the confines of a state to create a new behavioral system, mobilising the population into interdependent positions in empathy with a central government and sufficiently united to preserve stability and technological progress ... (Soja 1968: 1)

Geographers posed a range of questions about the spatial patterning of economic development across national territories. They investigated the spatial patterns of national urban systems, transportation networks and regional development. This work identified ideal spatial configurations that could hasten economic development and a corollary set of policy interventions that bolstered the power of state actors and justified relations with Western states and international development institutions. Developmentalist policies and dollars were attractive to many state actors in emerging nations, as they worked to consolidate their power through promises of economic growth and modernity as a means to build a sense of nationhood. As Gore (1984: 250) argues:

> One of the most important legacies of colonialism is that it created states with
> a 'national' territory, but no nation. Part of state policy in developmentalist states
> is thus directed towards *inventing* a nation. (emphasis in original)

This national scale focus continues to have a substantial impact on who has access to development dollars and influence. As we discussed in the introduction, for 50 years, the dominant institution of development principally dealt with state actors. One of the key contributions of Marxist, feminist and post-structural development geography (discussed in chapters 4 and 5) has been to disrupt this focus on the national scale and to reveal the limits of this scalar myopia. First, we will see how mainstream development identified the strategic field of intervention as the national territory, and in the process obscured other forces, operating across global and local scales, that might be responsible for spatially uneven development. Second, this nation state focus systematically excludes certain actors from development debates. Mainstream development's preoccupation with capitalist economic development served to marginalise those engaged in non-capitalist economic forms and those involved in non-economic spheres of household, community, service and care-work (Nagar et al. 2002). We turn to these critiques in the following chapters.

3.4 Subjects of mainstream development: forming 'rugged individuals'

Part and parcel of this mainstream focus on the national scale is a set of implicit assumptions about people in the global South. Mainstream arguments have consistently (albeit with different labels) argued that economic growth is the primary goal of development and that benefits would trickle down to countries who engage with the process. For example, Rostow's abstract invocation of 'the society' in his discussions of modernisation signalled that the characteristics of a country could stand in for the people within it. Development models and policies assumed that the people in Ecuador, Uganda or anywhere else were not differentiated either within or between countries, but rather were all assumed to be equal members in 'the society' with similar opportunities and experiences of the modernisation process.

Mainstream, growth-oriented modernisation work built on a Eurocentric model that normalised a discourse of whiteness, 'rational man' and national citizenship as a primary focus of political and economic identity. These theorists were silent about gender, indigenous identity, class differences and postcolonial subjectivity (we take up the limits of this thinking in the following chapters). To the extent that people were explicitly considered, sociological modernisation thought viewed people of the global South as malleable and in need of assistance in 'modernising'. These theorists drew from neoclassical economics to construct the ideal modern subject as an autonomous individual with free will, who chooses to engage in rational behaviour and to maximise his economic utility.

Geographers are disrupting these universal narratives through their grounded research in Asia, Africa and Latin America. John Brohman (1997: 297) nicely captures the limits of this neoliberal subject:

> ...neoclassical theory treats people as atomistic individuals who are bound together only through market forces. People are reduced to isolated creatures of the marketplace, devoid of history, cultural traditions, political opinions and social relationships beyond simple market exchanges.'

As early as the 1970s, a chorus of criticism emerged, challenging these assumptions and demonstrating the failures of mainstream development policies to incorporate poor people in general, and women in particular. Critics identified the exclusion of many from modernisation processes and called for policies that explicitly targeted redistribution with growth (Friedmann 1992). At conferences in Stockholm (1972 Conference on the Environment) and Cocoyoc, Mexico (1974 Conference on Patterns of Resource Use, Environment and Development Strategies) scholars and practitioners of development argued for a 'people-friendly' development and identified the crucial importance of both a 'basic needs ethic' and an environmentally sustainable approach to development. In 1974 the UN held its World Food Conference and called for an end to hunger, with a particular focus on the persistence of child malnutrition in the face of mainstream development interventions (Wisner 1989).

One outcome of these conferences was the basic needs approach (BNA) to development. Ben Wisner (1989) argued that the BNA emerged in two forms, the strong and the weak BNA, based on his grounded research in Kenya. The strong approach came from radical critics calling for alternative development, who argued for redistribution of land and assets, participatory democracy and strong voices for the poorest people. Weak BNA was promoted by mainstream development institutions and focused on developing 'human resources' through delivery of education, health and sanitation programmes to passive recipients. Wisner (1989: 38–9) argues that '[o]ne of the most striking features of the [World] Bank's version of the BNA is its specific rejection of any notion of distributive justice' and that '...basic needs have nothing to do with the redistribution of wealth'. Popular political participation is not the goal of the weak BNA; rather, people are encouraged to participate in development projects, such as building infrastructure, taking out credit, and so on. This approach to developing 'human resources' has its contemporary parallel in the social capital approaches of the new millennium (discussed below).

During this same period, feminist thinkers argued that mainstream thinking and policy focused on men – assuming they were primarily responsible for the business of development. Mainstream models, they argued, implicitly assumed that women would benefit as members of families, adopting a Western model of the nuclear household, headed by a male breadwinner and supported by a dependent housewife (Kabeer 1994). Ester Boserup's (1970) pioneering work inaugurated the Women in Development (WID) approach, which demonstrated that development projects were excluding and marginalising women, depriving them of livelihoods and status (see summaries of WID in Kabeer 1994; Marchand and Parpart 1995; Schroeder 1997). Her pioneering work pointed to evidence that women did not have equal access to the (presumed) benefits of modernisation, due to the gender biases of colonial administrators, postcolonial policy-makers and officials who assumed that men were the primary agents of production while women were wives and homemakers. Her work inspired a meeting, sponsored by the United Nations in Mexico City in 1975, that proclaimed an International Decade for Women (1976–85) to focus attention on projects that would bring women into the development fold. The Nairobi conference marking the end of that decade found that women remained among the poorest in the global South and that mainstream policies had failed to address women's struggle for power and access to resources (Wisner 1989).

WID scholars represent important alternative voices within mainstream development, putting women firmly on the agenda. However, even these critiques remained firmly situated within mainstream thinking, assuming development to be synonymous with Western modernity. The goal for WID was to recover women from the passive, dependent status assumed in Western economic thought, and to demonstrate that women too could be classical liberal individuals, engaging in rational behaviour, being involved directly in economic activities and as keen to maximise their economic utility (Boserup 1970; Tinker 1976). However, WID constructed a homogeneous 'Third World woman', associated with a series of problems, such as illiteracy, high mortality, high fertility and poverty, that were holding her back. These were construed as technical problems (rather than gendered political ones) that could be solved by the right development policies. As a result, the figure of the 'poor Third World woman' became a symbol of the promise of development and the ideal subject of development. She is constructed as one who, if given the opportunity, can realise development's full potential. This woman is also constructed as an altruistic agent of development who will invest in her family and community. This idealised woman is a recurring trope and rationale for mainstream neoliberal development. Ultimately, WID mounted an internal critique of development, focusing on the exclusion of women from educational and economic opportunities, rather than an external critique of the fundamental assumptions and goals of this development project.

The social costs of both modernisation and neoliberal development policies have been a repeating refrain, brought into clearer focus in large part by the actions of people marginalised by five decades of mainstream development. Indeed, the World Bank's 2000/2001 report states that '2.8 billion people – almost half the world's population – live on less than $2 a day', and that 'the average income in the richest 20 countries is 37 times the average in the poorest 20 - a gap that has doubled in the past 40 years' (World Bank 2000). Within the mainstream development community there is a deep awareness of what the Brookings Institute describes as billions living in dire poverty alongside a billion in widening splendour in an unsustainable scenario.

The combination of this awful track record and these critiques about the exclusion of the poor, and women in particular, has led to a flood of programmes across the global South, targeting women and, as the World Bank puts it, 'mainstreaming gender and poverty'. The World Bank has begun to focus on 'social capital' in the global South (Fukuyama 2001; Rankin 2002; Hart 2001; Radcliffe 2004). Social capital refers to the glue that holds societies

together, 'local forms of association that express trust and norms of reciprocity...' and networks that enhance efficiency by facilitating cooperation (Rankin
2002: 1; Radcliffe 2004). Mainstream policies for enhancing social capital focus
on building networks and associations that are intended to fuel development by
building social cohesion and cooperation, providing a pool of shared knowledge
and building accountability (as, for example, with village banking programmes,
where the availability of loans depends on repayments by other community
members). Sources of social capital are thought to include families, community
groups and identity-based groups.

Mainstream social capital approaches implicitly assume that people targeted
by these policies have equal access to the market and they are viewed as legitimate participants in development *only* to the extent that they engage with the
market. So, for example, people and communities are compelled to take on the
organisation and continued funding of projects such as community banks that
lend small start-up funds for small businesses. Communities apply for loans to
build their own neighbourhood services, roads, electricity supply, sewers, and
so on, rather than municipal or county government building basic infrastructure
(for more detailed examples see the USAID Women in Development Program,
the World Bank Gender and Development section, and the Poverty Reduction
Strategy of the International Monetary Fund).

While these programmes do respond to immediate needs, these self-help
approaches also depoliticise development. They divert attention from questions
of conflict and power and deep inequalities in access to resources within
societies (Harriss 2001). Equally importantly, social capital programmes divert
attention from deeply political questions about the role of the state in the provision of social goods, putting the onus back on to poor communities themselves
(Radcliffe 2004).

Critical geographers question the construction of a universal, market-oriented
subject in these social capital projects and instead situate actors in their cultural
and geo-historical contexts. Despite prevailing assumptions that these alliances
are voluntary, cooperative and mutually beneficial, contextual research identifies the limits of these arguments. Katharine Rankin's (2002) work on microfinance projects in Nepal examines the potential for social capital policies to
advance poor women's economic well-being, solidarity and political voice. Her
work suggests that while these policies have the *potential* to empower women
and to transform entrenched gender relations, this is not necessarily so. In the
Nepali case, microfinance policies have perpetuated cultural ideologies that

reproduce social inequalities. Her ethnographic work reveals that not all forms of associational life are necessarily progressive and that some actively reproduce structures of domination and oppression. For example, the Nepali *Guthi* associations are often invoked as a culturally specific example of community solidarity and collective microfinance distribution. Rankin finds that these caste-based associations are hierarchical and exclusive of lower castes. In addition, membership is mandatory within the society and the costs of building that social capital are extremely high in terms of time, work and money. *Guthi* obligations become a matter of household honour, with the majority of the work of preparing feasts, participating in worship and festivals being borne by women. Furthermore, women bear the burden of representing household morality, purity and honour. In other words, these social capital obligations reinstate gender relations and hierarchies through cultural and religious codes, rather than being an emancipatory space for Nepali women (see also Radcliffe 2004). We take up questions of subjectivity and difference raised by this example more fully in the following chapters.

On one hand, debates over social capital have held open some space for a social development agenda within powerful institutions during our era of neoliberal globalisation. In addition, social capital ideas have created room for non-governmental organisations to have more voice and role in the decentralisation of resources and programmes around the globe. However, the well-funded programmes run through international development institutions have legitimised certain forms of social connection and association (community organisations, small-scale banking programmes, barefoot doctors, and so on), while ignoring other forms of association that have articulated political protest and alternatives which critique neoliberal development orthodoxy (recall our discussion of SAPRIN earlier in this chapter). Geographers today are deeply engaged with questions of social and environmental justice that are elided by these mainstream engagements with social capital. While early geographical work challenged mainstream debates, by revealing spatial inequality and inserting space and nuance into overly economistic debates, categories and understandings of development, current geographical work pushes much harder (as in Rankin's work above). As we shall see in the following chapters, contemporary development geography has moved away from internal critiques towards a more thoroughgoing questioning of the underlying assumptions of mainstream development thought.

Notes

[i] Sociological, political and psychological modernisation theories were also influential in mainstream debates, but they too drew their foundations from economic debates about development as economic growth.

[ii] These nations included 19 Latin American countries, 3 from Africa (Egypt, Ethiopia and Liberia) and 4 Asian countries (India, Iran, Iraq and the Philippines). None of the colonised countries of Africa, Asia or the Caribbean had any part in this conference.

[iii] However, a cursory examination of labour costs quickly reveals that institutional and political factors have a greater impact on labour costs than the amount of labour in an economy. The mix of unionism, state welfare supports and non-waged benefit costs adjust the real costs of labour far more than the mere numbers of workers in an economy.

[iv] This table was compiled by Anna McCall-Taylor and I am grateful for her excellent work. The projects listed here include loans made by the International Bank for Reconstruction and Development and the World Bank during the fiscal years ending when indicated. Other development-related work of the World Bank Group (such as the granting of International Development Association Credits and the activities of the International Finance Corporation) is excluded. It is assumed that the International Bank for Reconstruction and Development and the World Bank are the same organisation for these purposes, and that IBDR Annual Reports from 1960/1961–1965/1966 and World Bank Annual Reports from 1966/1967–1974/1975 can be treated as belonging to the same series of publications. In some cases, the total number of loans listed in tables included in IBDR/WB annual reports differs slightly from the number reported within the accompanying text. In other cases, reports giving overviews of past years featured data different from the past years' reports of data. The data here are drawn directly from the tables listing loan country, purpose and dollar amount that can be found in every IBDR/WB report for the period covered. This table was compiled using the following sources:

World Bank. *International Bank for Reconstruction and Development Sixteenth Annual Report 1960–1961.* Washington, DC: World Bank. Data from 'List of Loans' on page 10.

World Bank. *International Bank for Reconstruction and Development 1961–1962 Seventeenth Annual Report.* Washington, DC: World Bank. Data from 'List of Loans 1961/1962 – Expressed in U.S. Dollars' on page 10.

World Bank. *International Bank for Reconstruction and Development 1962–1963 Eighteenth Annual Report.* Washington, DC: World Bank. Data from 'List of Loans 1962/1963 – Expressed in US Dollars' on page 11.

World Bank and International Development Association. *International Bank for Reconstruction and Development/International Development Association Annual Report 1963–1964.* Washington, DC: World Bank. Data from 'Bank Loans and IDA Credits 1963/1964 By Purpose' on page 9.

World Bank and International Development Association. *International Bank for*

Reconstruction and Development/International Development Association Annual Report 1964–1965. Washington, DC: World Bank. Data from 'Bank Loans and Credits 1964/1965 by Purpose' on page 9.

World Bank and International Development Association. *International Bank for Reconstruction and Development/International Development Association 1965–1966 Annual Report.* Washington, DC: World Bank. Data from 'Bank Loans and IDA Credits 1965–1966 by Purpose' on page 9.

International Bank for Reconstruction and Development and International Development Association. *World Bank and IDA Annual Report 1966/1967.* Washington, DC: World Bank. Data from 'Bank Loans and IDA Credits 1966/1967 by Purpose' on pages 8–9.

International Bank for Reconstruction and Development and International Development Association. *World Bank/International Development Association Annual Report 1968.* Washington, DC: World Bank. Data from 'Bank Loans and IDA Credits 1967/68 by Purpose' on pages 8–9.

International Bank for Reconstruction and Development and International Development Association. *World Bank/International Development Association Annual Report 1969.* Washington, DC: World Bank. Data from 'Bank Loans and IDA Credits 1968/1969 By Purpose' on pages 10–11.

International Bank for Reconstruction and Development and International Development Association. *World Bank/International Development Association Annual Report 1970.* Washington, DC: World Bank. Data from 'Bank Loans and IDA Credits 1969/1970 By Purpose' on pages 10–11.

International Bank for Reconstruction and Development and International Development Association. *World Bank/International Development Association Annual Report 1971.* Washington, DC: World Bank. Data from 'Bank Loans and IDA Credits 1970/1971 By Purpose' on pages 10–11.

International Bank for Reconstruction and Development and International Development Association. *World Bank/International Development Association Annual Report 1972.* Washington, DC: World Bank. Data from 'Approved Bank Loans and IDA Credits 1971/1972 by Purpose' on pages 12–13.

The Executive Directors of the International Bank for Reconstruction and Development and the International Development Association. *World Bank/IDA Annual Report 1973.* Washington, DC: World Bank. Data from 'Approved Bank Loans and IDA Credits 1972/73 by Purpose' on pages 10–11.

The Executive Directors of the International Bank for Reconstruction and Development and the International Development Association. *World Bank Annual Report 1974.* Washington, DC: World Bank. Data from 'Bank Loans and IDA Credits Approved in 1973/74, by Purpose' on pages 10–11.

The Executive Directors of the International Bank for Reconstruction and Development and the International Development Association. *World Bank Annual Report 1975.* Washington, DC: World Bank. Data from 'Bank Loans and IDA Credits Approved in 1974/1975, by Purpose' on pages 10–11.

^v The concept of economic equilibrium was formulated by Pareto and states that '...in any economy, with a given set of factors of production and commodities to be exchanged, there is a unique pattern of output and prices which will always be attained through individuals striving to achieve the "best" position for themselves' (Gore, 1984: 26).

^{vi} I focus here on early mainstream work, informed by Keynesian and modernisation thinking. There is growing attention in geography paid to neoliberal development, but the majority of this work begins from a Marxian perspective and is discussed in chapter 4.

chapter 4

DEVELOPMENT AS IMMANENT PROCESS: MARXIST AND FEMINIST POLITICAL ECONOMY

> Development studies is explicitly normative, as teachers and researchers who are
> attracted to the field tend to see current reality as sickening... They want to change
> the world, not only analyse it (Hettne 1995: 12)

> Political economists have always been clear about the purpose of their analyses: to
> understand the world in order to change it (Perrons 1999: 92)

Marxist and feminist geographers offer very different readings of development
processes to those provided by mainstream thinkers. Michael Watts, a key figure
in radical development geography, delineates two questions as central to his
work: how do the dynamic and restless processes of capitalism articulate social,
political and economic relations in specific times and places? and how do people
experience these processes and what are the costs, consequences and resistances to them? (paraphrased from Watts 2001b). More broadly, Marxist and
feminist geographers are centrally concerned with questions of social and
environmental justice. Marxian development geographers employ historical-
materialist analysis to analyse the contradictions of capitalism, class struggle,
uneven development and imperialism in the global South ('little d' development).
Their work examines patterns of accumulation, class formation and politics in
rural and urban areas, the role of the state, struggles over resources and the
articulation of peasant production with agrarian capitalism across Africa, Latin
America and South Asia. Marxist geographers also pioneered the field of polit-
ical-ecology (see Rod Neumann's 2005 book in this series). Feminist political-
economy researchers examine the ways in which these multifaceted processes

are gendered and insert a serious consideration of social reproduction in its relations with capitalist production processes (Carney 1992; Lawson 1995).

The rest of this book considers the various strands of critical thought that have shaped development geography and geographical contributions to development studies. I separate this discussion into chapters 4 and 5, even though there are continuities in the ways that geographers have taken up Marxian political-economy and Marxist-feminist theory (discussed in this chapter), and post-structural theory (discussed in chapter 5), which builds understanding by taking difference seriously. Here we focus on geographers who have analysed little 'd' development: the unfolding of capitalist social, economic and political processes in particular places and moments. As you will see in this brief review, Marxist work in geography has a 30-year tradition of debate and theoretical elaboration, continuing now in its engagement with the 'posts' discussed in chapter 5.

We begin by situating critical development geography in the context of global shifts and intellectual streams. As you will see, 'critical development geography' refers to scholarship, inspired by social movements emerging worldwide in the 1960s and 1970s, which engages with a Marxist critique of capitalism to examine the growing inequality, exploitation, racism and sexism embedded in Development. This critical development geography struggles for the relevance of geography as a discipline through its political commitment not only to writing the world as geographers, but also to changing injustice around the globe.

I begin by looking at the decades Michael Watt's (2001) describes as '1968 and all that' – the political, economic and cultural upheaval of the last decades of the twentieth century that set the broad context for radical thought in US geography. The 1960s and 1970s witnessed the disintegration of colonial empires, the civil rights and antiwar movements, and deepening crises of poverty, inequality and environmental degradation across the globe. The turn to Marxist theory in geography emerged from this tumultuous societal context that led these theorists to critique mainstream development geography. The following section sets up our discussion for both chapters 4 and 5. Read this to think about how radical development geographers were shaped by and engage with political struggles through their work.

4.1 Contexts I: the 1960s and beyond

I want to transport you back in time, across recent decades, to think about the political upheaval, economic change and cultural shifts that formed the context in which radical development geography was produced and practised. Recall from chapter 2 that we situate the development for each body of thought. In chapter 3 we discussed how development took on particular meanings and political heft for mainstream thinkers in the context of the cold war. For radical geographers, an alternative reading of these post-war decades gave rise to a very different set of understandings about development. Theorists who were part of the struggles I describe here began to rethink the project of development, with a commitment to understand the world in order to change it.

During the 1960s, social movements organised in protest against imperialism, racism, sexism, consumerism and the larger social order.[ii] As you read on, imagine yourself living through the 1960s – a pivotal moment in modern social history. What were some of the defining events in this period? How might modernist development thinking and practice be challenged, and ultimately changed, by these events?

4.1.1 Political upheaval

Every social context poses questions for those who inhabit it, construct it, and are in turn constructed by it (Hartsock 1998: 1)

The 1960s heralded a momentous period of paradox and upheaval. This was a time of dramatic successes for modernism – exemplified by the moon landing in 1969 (whose grainy images I saw as a nine-year-old) that represented a world of technological and scientific achievement in which literally anything seemed possible. This was the period of US post-war boom; of countries across South East Asia and Africa gaining national liberation from formal colonialism; and of the cold war rebuilding of war-torn European cities. Development was represented as a realisable project that claimed to bring the benefits of modernity to every place and person around the globe – orchestrated through the United Nations and the World Bank. Despite this belief in the possibility of constructing social order through the rational application of absolute truths, post-Second World War modernism was nonetheless firmly situated in its cold war context. Against a background of rising US hegemony, American cultural icons were appropriated by political and corporate elites as symbols of individual expression and as the apparently politically neutral successes of capitalism. High art and culture of the modernist period (such as abstract expressionism) served as symbols of freedom of expression, in contrast to communist censorship. So, as Harvey (1990: 37) argues:

> What was distinctively American had to be celebrated as the essence of Western culture. And so it was with abstract expressionism, along with liberalism, Coca-

Cola and Chevrolets, and suburban houses filled with consumer durables...'values that were subsequently assimilated, utilised and co-opted by politicians, with the result that artistic rebellion was transformed into aggressive liberal ideology...' (embedded quote from Guilbaut 1983: 200, quoted in Harvey)

It was precisely at this zenith of US power and wealth, and the seemingly unstoppable influence of consumer capitalism, that the contradictions and paradoxes of Western modernism came clearly into view. Persistent poverty, inequality, environmental injustice and multiple forms of discrimination fomented the rise of countercultural, anti-imperialist and anti-institutional social movements.

And so this was also a time of dramatic social and political uprisings that led many development scholars and activists to believe in a major historical discontinuity that reworked modernist teleology and philosophy (Best and Kellner 1997). In '1968 and all that...' Michael Watts (2001a) provides a vivid account of the 1960s as generative and pivotal in refiguring democratic thought and action around the globe. An enormous number of social movements surfaced in what Watts terms a 'global insurrection', in settings as diverse as Paris, Mexico City, San Francisco, Lima, Manila, Seoul, Delhi, Cape Town and literally hundreds of other places, involving broad segments of civil society. These movements were 'doing politics' differently – such as the student rebellions of Mexico; the millions of students and striking French workers in the streets; the stone-throwing intifada of Palestine; protests against the Vietnam war and civil rights struggles which coalesced in diverse forms and performances on the streets in the USA (Watts 2001a). People began building transnational movements, organising in protest against repressive social discrimination. These efforts continue in the global justice movement, protesting neoliberal policies of free trade and the power of the World Trade Organisation; in the World Social Forum that meets as a counterweight to the World Economic Forum in Davos, Switzerland; and indigenous movements that coalesced around the twin forces of democratisation and neo-liberalisation in Latin America in the 1990s.

It is important to appreciate that this insurrection was global, emerging from both political organising and intellectual foment across the global South as well as in the West. Activists and scholars witnessed the empirical failures of modernisation while working in South Asia, Africa and Latin America, where new and radical ideas were circulating. Myriad influences shaped these times, including the Cuban Revolution, Latin American dependency thinking, national liberation movements which gained momentum throughout the twentieth century and struggles for the liquidation of the colonial system in Asia and Africa (see Balogh and Imam 1988 for an accessible summary of the political history of national liberation movements). These projects of mass mobilisation presaged the social movements that oppose the nationalism, cronyism, elitism and patriarchy of postcolonial states and the failures of Western developmentalism. Scholars and activists also came together across the global South, creating new centres for research and intellectual exchange that interrogate development alternatives and alternatives to development (see Box 4.1).

Box 4.1: Centre for the Study of Developing Societies, Delhi

A group of scholars founded the Centre for the Study of Developing Societies in 1963 to create a space for research on social and political processes in South Asia, Afro-Asia and Latin America. Some of the key early pioneers were Ranji Kothari, Ashis Nandy, Bashiruddin Ahmed and Ramashray Roy. Members of the Centre examine critically the dynamics of democratic politics across a range of postcolonial nations and interrogate the exclusions produced in competitive, electoral politics as well as questions of dissent and cultural survival. The Centre is also a space for cross-cultural and interdisciplinary research on civil society, grassroots movements and human rights struggles. The Centre faculty also researches postcolonial nation states and the ways in which struggles over culture, ethnicity and religion are producing tensions and exclusions in the transition to modern, mass societies. Much of the work of the Centre focuses on those who are poor and politically marginalised, critiquing mainstream notions of 'Development' and 'progress' as dominant and oppressive knowledge systems. Scholarship from the Centre is premised on the idea that dominant development discourse has muted (or indeed subverted) alternative visions of sustainable and ethical societies, and that analysis and collaboration with grass-roots communities and alternative world views is needed to construct a 'vision of the possible'. (See http://www.csdsdelhi.org for a fuller description of the Centre.)

More recently, in Latin America, organisations such as the FMLN (Frente Farabundo Martí para la Liberación Nacional – Farabundo Martí National Liberation Front) in El Salvador, the MST (Movimento dos Trabalhadores Rurais

Sem Terra – Brazil's Landless Workers' Movement) in Brazil and CONAIE (Confederación de Nacionalidades Indígenas del Ecuador – Confederation of Indigenous Nationalities of Ecuador) in Ecuador emerged – encompassing trade unions, indigenous organisations, guerilla groups, ecological movements and women's movements, protesting bureaucratic authoritarian military dictatorships, the neoliberal turn to free trade and the withdrawal of the state from social provisions and protections.

These diverse movements mobilised a new politics of antistatism, self-governance and freedom to organise around radically different identities and principles (rather than national identifications), and at diverse scales, from transnational to local. These politics empowered different institutional arrangements as well as a massive increase in social movements and non-governmental organisations around the globe, including new community organisations and civic institutions – such as indigenous movements, women's groups and environmental struggles. These institutional and political shifts have fundamentally challenged mainstream development, such that '...the critique of growth determinism has now become an orthodoxy itself' (Watts 2001a: 181). And of course, these intellectual and political challenges go further than just the development establishment, questioning the social and environmental impacts of globalised capitalism, attacking corporate liberalism and focusing on global justice. The 1960s stressed a politics of collective identity formation in ways that have since been challenged by activists and theorists who organise politically around diverse identities and in diverse contexts. 'Post' theorists and actors work with an ongoing tension between collectivity and difference as they struggle to understand the forces of social change and seek ways to build alliances to strengthen their movements.

In Western advanced economies, the social movements of the 1960s protested against crass consumerism, sexism, racism and a professionalised liberal democratic politics. Activists organised around civil rights and a New Left radicalism in Europe and the USA. Women activists who found themselves in a subordinate role within male-dominated radical movements (making coffee, typing and xeroxing) organised second-wave feminism. For example, Dorothy Height's account of the civil rights march on Washington in 1963 recalled the absence of women from any speaking role on that historic day (Clemetson 2003). Dorothy was the only female member of the Council for United Civil Rights Leadership that organised the march. She was also the only woman sitting on the platform, and she recounts how, the very next day, the National Council of Negro women met and '...we discussed our goals and the need going forward to point out that women needed to speak as women, to voice the double discrimination of racism and sexism that we felt' (Clemetson 2003: 12). In the early 1960s, Rachel Carson's famous book *Silent Spring* built a feminist argument against agricultural chemicals and in favour of a holistic philosophy of ecology that connected nature–society relations. *Silent Spring* and Borlaug's very public rebuttal contributed to the mobilisation of an environmental agenda that inaugurated Earth Day in 1970 (Box 4.2).

Box 4.2 The clash of environmentalism and developmentalism

Rachel Carson was a writer and a biologist. Her fourth book, *Silent Spring*, made the best-seller lists in 1962. The book is an argument against pesticide use, a warning about the dangers of DDT and an elaboration of the holistic philosophy of ecology. Later that same year, state legislatures around the United States discussed and debated some 40 newly introduced bills to regulate pesticide use. Federal regulation to address water and air pollution, as well as pesticide use, was also influenced by the publication and ensuing debates the book engendered. The book is now viewed as a precursor to the environmental movement of the 1970s, as well as the continuing interest in ecology and rising awareness of the linkages between nature and society around the world.

Dr Norman Borlaug received the 1970 Nobel Peace Prize for his work in developing hybrid wheat strains. He is known as the father of Green Revolution technology – agricultural technology that consists of irrigation infrastructure, hybrid seeds and the application of synthetic fertilisers and pesticides as a concrete manifestation of modernisation theory to underdevelopment and hunger in Asia, Africa and Latin America. Green Revolution technology was designed to increase yields of wheat, rice and corn. In a speech he delivered in 1971 at a United Nations conference, Borlaug had this to say about *Silent Spring*:

> The current vicious, hysterical propaganda campaign against the use of agricultural chemicals, being promoted today by fear-provoking, irresponsible environmentalists, had its genesis in the best-selling, half-science-half-fiction novel 'Silent Spring'.... This poignant, powerful book...sowed the

> seeds for the propaganda whirlwind and the press, radio, and television circuses that are being sponsored in the name of conservation today (which are to the detriment of world society) by the various organisations making up the environmentalist movement.
>
> Borlaug's remarks presaged the ongoing debate within development as to the relationship between science, society and environment as it concerned development.
>
> Lucy Jarosz, University of Washington

In communist societies, social movements stood against bureaucratic party politics and political closure and corruption in the Prague Spring of 1968, and were involved in efforts to build socialism with a human face in Czechoslovakia. In the wake of the 1989 fall of the Berlin Wall and the dissolution of the Soviet Bloc, a crisis on the left ensued, fueled by a crisis of human rights violations in socialist countries – Tiananmen Square in China in 1989 and Castro's crackdown on dissidents in Cuba in 2003.

4.1.2 Economic change[iii]

In the midst of the political and social upheavals of this period, an equally important challenge to mainstream Development emerged from the empirical record itself. Recalling the grand claims for scientific development from chapter 2, that '...sustained development is no hopeless dream, but an achievable reality' (World Bank 1991: 1), the record is actually one of enormous paradoxes. To be sure, this record includes successes, such as improved life expectancy, lower infant mortality rates and increased access to education around the globe. Tschirgi (1999: 1) summarises these global gains:

> ...infant mortality rates have dropped to less than 60 per 1000 live births (a reduction of 60 per cent); adult literacy has been cut in half; primary-school enrollment has come to include more than three quarters of the school age population with notable increases for girls; life expectancy has increased to age 40 for 75 per cent of the world's population.

However, when you consider the immense resources – billions of dollars, millions of person hours, over more than five decades, the failures of development loom large. Many critics argue that mainstream Development is a failed project when measured in terms of the increasing numbers across the globe living without adequate food, clean water, a sustainable livelihood or adequate shelter, in both the North and South. Consider the findings of the *UN Development Report* (1999: 1) that 800 million people across the globe are malnourished. The Economic Commission for Latin America and the Caribbean (ECLAC) reported that in 1994 39 per cent of households in Latin America were below their country's poverty line (using most recent reported data at the time). In Africa, the World Bank reported that 39 per cent of people were living on less that US $1 per day in 1993 (the most recent comparable data at the time).[iv] On income inequality, the World Bank PovertyNet website reports diverse trends:

> ...Malaysia saw declines in inequality...during the 1980s, but this trend was reversed in the 1990s. Korea and Indonesia experienced rapid growth during the 1980s with little change in inequality, while China and Russia experienced large increases in inequality over the same period (www.worldbank.org/poverty/data/trends/inequal.htm)

Both poverty and inequality are fueled by economic restructuring and massive expansions in 'flexible' (unregulated, unprotected) work. For example, my research in Quito, Ecuador found that over 70 per cent of working people interviewed labour without job security, any kind of employment contract or benefits (Lawson 2002). More broadly, Gausch (1999) found that 54 per cent of the Ecuadorian labour force worked informally by 1999. These trends are widespread across the globe and have exacerbated inequalities, as Potter (1999: 8) points out:

> [S]ince 1960, the start of the first UN Development Decade, disparities of global wealth distribution have doubled, so that by the mid 1990s, the wealthiest quintile of the world's population controlled 83 percent of global income, compared to less that 2 percent for the lowest quintile.

Growing inequalities over the decades of development emerge when looking at non-income measures as well. For example, a child in sub-Saharan Africa can expect to attend school for 3 years, whereas a child in Europe can reasonably expect to spend 17 years in formal education (for more information see http://www.oxfam.org/en/programs/campaigns/education). Looking at health issues, the Jubilee Campaign website reports that in Canada women's life expectancy is 82 years, infant mortality is 6/1000 live births and less that 1 per cent of people aged 15–49 live with AIDS. By contrast, in Zambia, women's life expectancy is 39 years, infant mortality is 112/1000 live births and 19 per cent of people aged 15–49 live with AIDS, as reported in the year 2000. Within the global South patterns are also extremely diverse, with people in sub-Saharan Africa having a life expectancy of 47 years, compared with 70 years in Latin America (United Nations Development Program 2003: 265).

The contradictions of the urban/industrial development model emerge even within oil-rich nations such as Nigeria. In the two decades since 1985, the country has invested substantial oil revenues into infrastructure development (power grid, water systems, telecommunications), into expansions of oil and gas export capacity, and into education services, yet poverty has risen substantially, such that 70 million people (66 per cent of the population) are now classified as poor. In Ogoniland, where 60 per cent of Nigerian oil was pumped in the 1980s, the politically weak region saw only 5 per cent of its legal allocation of oil revenues. As Watts (2003: 65) details:

> Few Ogoni households have electricity, there is one doctor per 100,000 people, child mortality rates are the highest in the nation, unemployment is 85 per cent, 80 per cent of the population is illiterate and over half of Ogoni youth have left the region in search of work.

The paradoxes and contradictions of mainstream Development have also emerged in agriculture. The widespread adoption of Green Revolution technologies in the 1970s substantially increased yields of rice and wheat, when coupled with intensive fertiliser use. Indeed, tens of millions of extra tons of grain per year were produced. In India and Asia, however, fertiliser use rose many times more rapidly than increases in crop yields, because over time the soil requires more and more of these inputs since chemical fertilisers do not replenish the land. Furthermore, since expensive inputs are necessary to remain competitive in farming, '...then wealthier farmers will inexorably win out over the poor, who are unlikely to find adequate employment to compensate for the loss of farming livelihoods' (Rosset, Collins and Lappe 2000), meaning that this much hailed 'revolution' has displaced many poorer farmers from the land.

Mainstream development orthodoxy also advocated the shift of formerly protected economies (from Indonesia to Bangladesh to Guatemala) to an emphasis on export-oriented assembly/manufacturing. This global expansion of capitalist industrial relations involved the deindustrialisation of Western economies and the concomitant destabilisation of Western state–capital–labour relations in ways that contributed to the social and political unrest described above (for discussions of these shifts, see Peter Dicken's (2003) *Global Shift* and David Harvey's (1990) *The Condition of Postmodernity*). Harvey (2003) argues that the 1970s witnessed the shift from production to finance capitalism in the USA as Nixon took the dollar off the gold standard, arguing that this was pivotal to a set of changes in economic and political relations globally. This is coupled with the rise of export-processing throughout the global South that has transformed communities and prompted massive migrations of workers to export-processing zones such as the US–Mexican border. Here again, the record is contradictory since these shifts have provided large numbers of (primarily) young women with new industrial jobs, reworking households and gender relations as women become breadwinners and household heads. At the same time, the rise of this female industrial workforce has been accompanied by high rates of male unemployment, male departures from households or startling increases in alcoholism and domestic violence (Fernandez-Kelly and Nash 1983; Cravey 1997; Chant 1992). Other economic shocks and shifts arose from the punishing Latin American debt crisis and imposition of structural adjustment policies and neo-liberalisation, discussed later in this chapter.

Taken together, these economic changes form a second key element of the disenchantment with mainstream Development that forms the backdrop and momentum for radical theory and politics over the last five decades.

4.1.3 Cultural shifts

One man had much money,
One man had not enough to eat,
One man lived just like a king,
The other man begged on the street.
Long ago, far away;
These things don't happen
No more, nowadays.

One man died of a knife so sharp,
One man died from the bullet of a gun,
One man died of a broken heart
To see the lynchin' of his son.
Long ago, far away;
Things like that don't happen
No more, nowadays.

Gladiators killed themselves,
It was during the Roman times.
People cheered with bloodshot grins

As eye and minds went blind.
Long ago, far away;
Things like that don't happen
No more, nowadays.
('Long Ago, Far Away' *by Bob Dylan*)

The upheavals challenging corporate capitalism, diverse forms of oppression, consumerism and bureaucratic governance were not limited to the political and economic spheres, but permeated every aspect of life. Within the arts and architecture substantial shifts set the stage for new understandings of society. Cultural forms emerged that rejected the elitism of 'high culture' (that is, the notion that art holds a stable, essential meaning produced by the artist) and the claims of grand narratives that retell modernist stories of redemption and success (Best and Kellner 1997). These popular cultural forms are playful, pluralist, democratic and eclectic. These cultural expressions included forms of performative protest, such as feminist activists tossing their bras and girdles into the 'freedom trash bucket' at the Miss America protests in 1968, to symbolise their opposition to unrealistic and commodified ideals of beauty in American society (Whelehan 1995). They also included the folk/rock movement, symbolised by the Woodstock concert that connected the realms of popular culture and politics as captured in Dylan's song, above. There were many expressions of the link between politics and cultural expression, as Michael Watts (2001a: 160) illustrates so colourfully:

> [N]eed I remind anyone that the late 1960s produced Jerry Rubin, Alan Ginsberg and company attempting to levitate the Pentagon; the Yippies causing havoc on Wall Street by throwing money on to the floor of the exchange; the Strasbourg Situationists denouncing boredom; the Dutch Provos unleashing pandemonium in Amsterdam by releasing thousands of chickens in rush-hour traffic; the Diggers declaring love a commodity; and not least Ed Sanders and the Fugs setting off on their own march to Prague to masturbate on Soviet tanks?

More recently the turtles, trade unionists and anarchists marching together in Seattle in 1999 symbolised these forms of expression in protest of exclusionary, state-focused institutions such as the WTO ministerials and IMF board meetings.

Of course, these efforts are all imperfect themselves. For example, the UN Beijing Women's Conference in 1995, while on one hand was another important step forward, also operated to silence some groups of women. The UN conference was only open to official delegates of member states of the UN, and a parallel non-governmental organisation conference was arranged to lobby official delegates. Controversy erupted when the parallel NGO conference was moved from a building close to the official conference to a location more than two hours away. In addition, NGOs had to apply for accreditation to enter China and attend their conference, and this allowed the Chinese government substantial control over which NGOs would have access to the conferences. Despite these hurdles, participation by NGOs and the success of their lobbying efforts in Beijing signalled the growing influence of alternative voices in development debates.

These street and cultural performances called attention to alternative analyses of global justice and to the voices of silenced subjects. Much of the post-structural research we will discuss in chapter 5 was deeply informed by these movements and the assertion of the importance of cultural processes of meaning-making in the larger context of political-economic shifts. Returning to my question, how could development theory and action possibly look the same after all this upheaval? the answer is that it does not. The 1960s heralded the gestation of other politics and visions, some not fully cohered or expressed until later or under different epistemologies (see chapter 5). Some of these visions engage with modernist development and others might not be called development at all, but perhaps human-friendly or freedom-friendly projects. Despite seeming to be all over the 'map' – geographically, politically and in terms of substantive focus – these varied movements nonetheless cohere into a series of political and intellectual challenges to Development, the political and social status quo, the norms of the nation state and neoliberal democratic principles and practices.

The 1960s and 1970s stressed a politics of collective identity formation and a set of intellectual and political challenges that go further than just the Development establishment, to question the social and environmental impacts of globalised capitalism, attacking corporate liberalism and focusing on global justice. These grounded politics are one of the forces contributing to the rise of critical development geography. A second major set of influences comes from intellectual work around the globe that formed a theoretical basis for critique.

4.2 Contexts II: intellectual strands of Marxist-feminist development geography

4.2.1 Marxist development studies

Geographers came to the study of Marx as they grappled with these swirling issues of power and politics. Richard Peet's celebration of 30 years of radical geography notes that in the late 1960s and early 1970s, '...radical geography tried to transform the scope of a conventional discipline criticised as irrelevant to the great issues of the time – civil rights, the Vietnam War, and environmental pollution...' (Peet 2000: 951). Harvey (2000: 2) reflected on his turn to Marxist theory by saying that he '...arriv[ed] in Baltimore a year [1969] after much of the city had burnt down in the wake of the assassination of Martin Luther King. In the States, the anti-war movement and the civil rights movements were really fired up... I realised I had to rethink a lot of things I had taken for granted in the sixties'. David Slater tells of travelling and working in Peru and Tanzania in the late 1960s and early 1970s, where his world view was influenced by the negative effects of imperial power, exploitation and oppression, as well as by the vibrant and challenging literature being produced by Latin American and African scholars working with dependency and Marxist ideas (Slater 2005, personal communication).

So, how does Marxist theory reshape development geography? The oft-told and familiar story locates the rise of Marxist geography in urban/economic research in the West, as scholars grappled with questions of declining inner cities and deindustrialisation. Indeed, scholars such as David Harvey, Doreen Massey and Neil Smith built influential arguments about capitalist crisis, urban and regional decline and the gentrification of urban and regional spaces (Harvey 1973; Smith 1984; Massey and Meegan 1982; Castells 1983). However, there is another important and overlooked story of how Marxism came into geography – through critical work on uneven development, imperialism and the 'periphery'. Early issues of *Antipode* (the radical journal of geography founded at Clark University in the 1970s) published a series of landmark papers arguing for a radical geography of imperialism and underdevelopment in the global South (see, for example, Slater 1973, 1977; Folke 1973; Santos 1974; McGee 1974; Susman 1974; Blaut 1973, 1975). Other influential geographers began from questions about the persistence of the peasantry under agrarian capitalism and about the politics of peasant–state relations in Africa, Latin America and Asia (Blaikie 1981; Watts 1983; Hecht and Cockburn 1989; Hart 1986; Porter 1987; Wisner 1989).

Marx's writings, and those he inspired across the social sciences, are vast in scope and have been summarised, reviewed and debated in many pages of print. It is beyond the scope of this volume to deal directly with Marxist theory, but see Box 4.3 for some guidance on key concepts relevant to development geography and a reference list of Marx's writings.

Box 4.3 Marxist theory

Karl Marx, writing about European capitalism in the nineteenth century, produced a general theory of capitalist society. Marx revolutionised thinking about the nature of production, arguing that over the course of history there have been distinct modes of production, distinguished by the social relations through which members of society relate to the means of production and to each other (e.g. feudalism slavery, subsistence production, capitalism). Through historical processes of struggle and dispossession the capitalist system emerged as a historically specific mode of production. His work critiqued the neoclassical economics of Smith and Keynes (discussed in chapter 3) for its superficial analysis of capitalism – focused on market mechanisms and the exchange of objects. By contrast, Marx argued that the most fundamental relationship in capitalism was between people and labour, captured in his *labour theory of value*. For Marx, production is irreducibly social, defined by processes of exploitation and power (Watts 1988). He argues that labour has 'use-value' which is set to work by capitalists to produce more value in a working day than is returned to the worker in wages. The existence of this difference between the 'use-value' of labour and its 'exchange-value' – that which is returned to the worker as wages – is the foundation for arguments about exploitation, class struggle, commodity fetishism, alienation, the tendency for profits to decline, crisis theory and transformative class politics (for excellent summary discussions of Marxist theory see Harvey 1982; Corbridge 1986; Bottomore 1991; Peet (with Hartwick) 1999).

Marx's work lays a foundation for understanding uneven development across the global South. However, Marx did not theorise space or uneven development per se, but rather the capitalist mode of production. In the last chapter of *Capital* Volume I, Marx discusses primitive accumulation and the 'problem' of the colonies. He uses examples from the colonies of North America and Australia to identify the central challenge for the expansion of the capitalist mode of production – that of 'freeing' labour from direct access to the means of production. He argues that as long as workers remain in possession of their own means of production and so accumulate capital for themselves, capitalism cannot develop and social progress towards the collapse of capitalism will be deferred. In a sense, this discussion opens the door for understanding the geographical expansion of capitalism across the globe, but Marx does not go through it. Authors such as Lenin and Luxemburg extend these ideas to develop theories of imperialism that form the basis for much of the early radical development geography (see Box 4.5).

The (nearly) Complete Works of Karl Marx (in order of original publication)

(1970) *Marx's Critique of Hegel's Philosophy of Right.* Ed. J. O'Mally, Cambridge: Cambridge University Press.

(1992) *Early Writings.* New York: Penguin Books.

With Frederich Engels (1998) *German Ideology: Including Theses on Feuerbach and Introduction to The Critique of Political Economy.* Amherst, NY: Prometheus Books.

(1997) *Wage-Labour and Capital Value, Price and Profit.* New York: International Publishers.

With Frederich Engels (1998) *The Communist Manifesto.* Introduction by Eric Hobsbawm, New York: Verso.

(1990) *The Eighteenth Brumaire of Louis Bonaparte.* New York: International Publishers.

(1993) *Grundrisse: Foundations of the Critique of Political Economy.* New York: Penguin Books.

(1993) *Capital: A Critique of Political Economy,* Vol. 1. New York: Penguin Books.

(1993) *Capital: A Critique of Political Economy,* Vol. 2. New York: Penguin Books.

(1993) *Capital: A Critique of Political Economy,* Vol. 3. New York: Penguin Books.

(1999) *Capital: Theories of Surplus Value,* Vol. 4. New York: Prometheus Books.

(1982) *A Contribution to the Critique of Political Economy.* Ed. M. Dobb, New York: International Publishers.

(1996) *Marx: Later Political Writings.* Ed. T. Carver, Cambridge: Cambridge University Press.

For a biography of Marx see Wheen (2000).

Marxist thought has a rich history of over 30 years of scholarship in geography and I cannot do justice to the full sweep of this work. I focus on two broad questions that preoccupied Marxist development geography. First, what causes capitalism to expand and spread geographically, and to create international uneven development? As we shall see, these authors turned to Marxian theories of imperialism and dependency theory in Africa and Latin America. Second, what are the characteristics of capitalism in the global South (often referred to as the periphery) and what social forces of repression and/or progressive change will it unleash? This led geographers to engage with ideas about the articulation of modes of production and the peasant studies literature on the agrarian question. Here I trace some of the foundational work that opened up development geography to debates around imperialism, primitive accumulation, articulation of modes of production, peasant studies and agrarian change. I also talk about how feminists extended political-economy arguments in crucial ways. Having set the stage with a discussion of early strands of Marxist-feminist development geography, the following sections employ our critical geographical approach to think about the geographies of Marxist-feminist development and the ways in which the subjects of development were theorised in this work.

Radical geographers did not speak with one voice, except in their fulsome critique of the mainstream development geography we reviewed in chapter 3. They critiqued mainstream theory for its ahistorical application of Western concepts of modernity and for '...scientific dogmatism which is more concerned with the verification of hypotheses than with the source and nature of those hypotheses' (Santos 1974: 5). Santos, Armstrong and McGee, Connell and Logan all argued against separate, dualistic capitalist and non-capitalist sectors within the global South. Connell (1973) appeals for micro-geographic studies of rural villages to understand spatial and social interconnections and in response to the '...pompous irrelevance of most macro theories of development' (Lipton 1970: 15, quoted in Connell 1973). Logan (1972) also advocates detailed empirical studies that take account of the variation within global South countries to challenge Western ideas about spatial dualism. Santos (1974) decries arrogance in Western geography and calls for more attention to be paid to Latin American geographers.

Intellectual influences from Latin America and Africa did indeed shape radical development geography. Geographers were inspired by dependency scholars, including Frank, Furtado, Cardoso and Faletto, as well as the influential work of Fanon, Rodney and Mugubane (see Box 4.4; Brookfield 1973; Logan 1972; Slater

1973, 1977; Blaut 1973, 1975; Watts 1983). Brookfield's (1973) work argued for attention to processes (rather than spatial patterns) of inequality and to the structural aspects of development, and also attacked the value-free stance of mainstream research, arguing instead that this work is imbued with Eurocentric assumptions and interests, calling attention to '...the rising bitterness of some writers in the Third World, together with those Westerners who have come to share their views' (Brookfield 1973: 9).

Box 4.4 Dependency thought

Latin American dependistas, writing from the 1940s to the 1970s, critiqued both mainstream and classical Marxian theories of capitalist development. Dependency thought is rich and diverse, and yet, in the early years, Anglo scholars mostly relied on Gunder Frank, who wrote in English. Dependency's fundamental contribution to development debates is to turn mainstream logic on its head, by arguing that under-development resulted directly from contact with the West. These scholars are united in their insistence that development must be theorised from their postcolonial global South context (for an excellent review of this broad literature see *Latin American Theories of Development and Underdevelopment* by Cristóbal Kay 1989).

Gunder Frank (1969), often viewed as a world systems theorist, argued that 'underdevelopment' is not a traditional state, but rather is developed directly through contact with Western capitalism. He conceptualised a world system of metropoles and satellites, in which the metropoles (which may be countries, regions or cities) are exploitive, draining resources from their peripheries. His ideas produced a storm of critique from Marxist dependistas because he argued that Latin America had been capitalist since the sixteenth century, when European merchant capital invested in and traded with the region's economies. This was controversial because it defined Latin American economies as capitalist solely because they are producing for world markets and, in the process, ignores the social relations of production and state–society relations within Latin American countries. Wallerstein's (1974) *The Modern World System* provides an extended, but related neo-Marxist argument.

Marxist dependency thinking emerged at the Center for Socioeconomic Studies at the University of Chile under the leadership of Theotonio Dos Santos (other key authors include Marini 1969; Bambirra 1972; Quijano 1971). Marxist dependistas examine the particular forms of capitalism that have arisen within Latin America, arguing that underdevelopment results from the penetration of the region's economies by foreign capital, technology and finance. While they were influenced by classical theories of imperialism (Box 4.5), Marxist dependistas were critical of the idea that progressive political consciousness and a transition to socialism would result from Western capitalist penetration. They examined the roots of dependency in specific social relations between foreign and domestic elites and state actors that produced technological and financial dependence and allowed for the superexploitation of labour. They argued that these processes occurred to compensate Latin American capitalists for falling profit rates, as value is exported to the core through unequal exchange (identified by Prebisch in chapter 3).

Reformist dependistas Furtado (1970), Cardoso and Faletto (1979) and Evans (1979) shifted the analysis from the economy to a consideration of state–society relations as they worked out differently in various Latin American countries in the period after the Second World War. They argued that no abstract form of dependency exists and developed a historical-geographical analysis of dependency. These authors focused on how Latin American governments across the region incorporated and excluded various social sectors as Import Substitution Industrialisation, advocated by Prebisch, began to fail. They examined the relations between foreign, domestic, industrial and agrarian capitals and argued for the possibility of a reformist Latin American state through which nations could be agents of their own development if they addressed the unequal and repressive social and political relations that had emerged.

Beginning from Marx's insight that the economy is irreducibly social, Marxist geographers attacked mainstream development for its assumption of spatial separatism – the idea that spatial forms are ontologically separate from social structures and processes (Smith 1986). Geographers such as David Slater opposed claims that mainstream development would bring progress and modernity to all, arguing instead that 'Development' was concerned with resolving capitalist crises in, and for, the West. Similarly, Griffin (1969) critiques dualism and stages of growth theories of development. His detailed empirical study of nine Latin American countries argues for historical analyses of the ways in which indigenous societies were destroyed by mercantile capital and colonial administration. He draws on Frank to argue that underdevelopment is a product of history, examining dispossession of indigenous populations by colonial administrations and postcolonial states. Folke (1973) argues for analysis of imperialism, calling for more attention to the work of Lenin and Frank. These geographers were inspired by scholars from Latin America, Asia and Africa, who were writing about histories of colonial and imperial exploitation and violence, and who explained inequality and underdevelopment in terms of economic and political domination and dependency (Brookfield 1973; Slater 1973, 1977; Santos 1974; Blaut 1973, 1975).

4.2.2 Imperialism and the geographical spread of capitalism

Marxist geographers provided an alternative reading of development as underdevelopment, rooted in histories of colonial territorial expansion and imperial expropriation and transformation of peripheral economies (reviewed thoroughly in Slater 1973, 1977). David Slater (1973, 1977), working at the University of Dar es Salaam in Tanzania in the early 1970s, critiques mainstream development geography for three inadequacies: its confusion of regional growth with regional development; its neglect of class concepts and their contradictions; and its failure to consider any analysis of imperialism (paraphrased Slater 1973: 21). Slater draws on scholars such as Desai (1966), working on Indian society under colonialism, Laclau (1971), on peasant economies in Latin America, and Arrighi's (1970) work on African peasantry to argue that mainstream development geography has ignored the rich histories of underdeveloped societies and their relationships to Western capitals.

In short, Slater argues that colonial histories of dispossession and extraction are continued with 'Development' − sustaining the theme from Brookfield above. Slater draws on theoretical arguments about imperialism (see Box 4.5) to set a radical agenda for development geography. Specifically, he argues that uneven development in the global South must be understood (in specific places and historical moments) in terms of the relations between external and domestic capitals, by the particular ways in which distinct modes of production are co-produced, and by the relations between peripheral states and international capitals. In these respects, both Slater and Brookfield argue that capitalist penetration of the global South is exploitive and extractive, and that our work

Figure 4.1 Argentinean graffiti from 2004. Source: Bill Beyers (2005)

should examine the forms of capitalism that emerge, the forms of class relations that develop, and whether these contain the potential for a progressive transition to socialism or to peripheral stagnation. Many of these authors draw on Lenin and Luxemburg's Marxist analyses of imperialism (Box 4.5) to argue that mainstream development is but '...Old Colonialism writ large' (Brookfield 1973: 8). These radical analyses of the exploitive nature of capitalism are alive and well in Latin America as depicted in this Argentinian graffiti from 2004 (Figure 4.1).

Box 4.5 Marxian theories of imperialism

Theories of imperialism extended Marxist theory, providing explanations for the spatial spread and impacts of capitalism in the global South. Marx and Engels wrote a series of articles and letters, reporting on developments in Ireland and India, that revealed their ideas on colonialism and modernisation – but they did not develop a theoretical argument. As Blaut (1975: 2) points out, 'Marxist thought begins but does not end with

---

Marx', noting that Marx himself did not fully elaborate a theoretical analysis of colonialism and imperialism. It was later theorists, such as Lenin (1965) and Luxemburg and Bukharin (1972), who argued the fundamental importance of the non-European world to capitalism – thus providing the foundations for a radical geography of development and underdevelopment. Specifically, these authors argue that the export of capitalism to the global South resolves crises in Western capitalism, and therefore the benefits of imperialism accrue to the West. They also argue that capitalist social relations are profoundly disruptive of non-capitalist societies and forms of livelihood in the global South, highlighting the violence and dispossessions that inevitably follow from the penetration of capitalism from the West.

Lenin argued that imperialism is the highest (presumably inevitable) stage of capitalism, wherein the concentration of production in Western capitalist economies leads to the formation of monopolies and to the merging of finance and industrial capitals. These monopolies require new sites of investment to resolve capital over-accumulation in the West, and they struggle for control over areas of the world as new sites of investment and accumulation (reviewed in Slater 1977; Corbridge 1986). Lenin viewed the 'backward nations' and geographical inequalities in development as functional for metropolitan capitals. Luxemburg emphasised contradictions within Western capitalism as the low wages of workers led to a realisation crisis (inability to sell all the commodities produced within Western capitalist societies) and a need for new markets in the global South. Luxemburg argued that capitalism faced barriers to its spread into the global South that had to be overcome. These included: the continuation of non-capitalist means of production and a shortage of wage-labour, which is overcome through violent means; competition with local commodity economies and, finally, international competition among Western capitals for the remaining conditions of accumulation and the industrialisation of the global South. Luxemburg stressed the close relations between postcolonial states and international capital, and the importance of the expansion of transportation infrastructure for the appropriation of non-capitalist forms of production (reviewed in Slater 1977; Corbridge 1986).

There were lively debates among the pioneers of Marxist development geography. Jim Blaut (1973, 1975) also argued that Marxian theories of imperialism provide critical tools for understanding geographies of development in the global South. He drew from authors such as Fanon (1965), Furtado (1970) and Cardoso and Faletto (1979) to argue that in the global South capitalism assumes a different, dependent form to Western capitalism. While many Marxists assumed that socialism would follow from mature capitalism in the core, Blaut argued that proletarianisation and oppression had been exported to the global South in the guise of Anglo-American superiority and civilisation since 1492. He further argued that the shift from feudalism to capitalism in Europe was itself possible because of the appropriation of surplus value by merchants from Asia and Africa. Blaut's argument echoes Gunder Frank's focus on merchant capital and exchange relationships, viewing medieval extraction of surplus from the global South as a prior condition for the full emergence of capitalism, and subsequently colonialism, from Europe to the globe. In other words, rather than seeing imperialism as emerging from European capitalism, he sees surplus value extraction from the global South as making core capitalism possible. Slater argues that Blaut misreads Marxian theory, confusing the production of surplus under merchant capital with the capitalist mode of production. This conflation leads Blaut to broadly attribute proletarian status to the geographic space of the global South, rather than to people experiencing specific class relations within capitalism.

However, Blaut's work (along with much dependency writing) is very influential because he decentres Eurocentric arguments within Marxism: that capitalist development emanates initially from Europe and then radiates out across the globe. He focuses on violence, extraction and exploitation since early exploration and trade relations between Europe and the global South. Blaut's work identifies these histories of linkage and foretells more recent arguments about the ways in which development discourse echoes and continues colonial narratives of civilisation, progress and development (for more on the latter, see chapter 5; Mathewson and Wisner 2005).

4.2.3 Peripheral capitalist societies and peasant studies

Taking the geographical spread of capitalism as a starting point, peasant studies in the 1980s posed questions about the nature of peripheral capitalism. This was a resolutely interdisciplinary affair through which Marxist development geography became increasingly concerned with the political-economy of agrarian transformation and the relations between peasantries and capitalist development within the global South. Geographers began to produce grounded studies in Africa and Asia as they sought to understand social and political differentiation in the context of ecological change (Watts 1983; Blaikie 1981; Hecht 1986; Porter 1987; Carney 1988; Wisner 1989; Jarosz 1990; Watts and Bassett 1986). These geographers were concerned to inject theoretical analysis into studies of agrarian change in response to an early disciplinary emphasis on detailed historical descriptions of peasant landscapes that characterised the Sauerian tradition at Berkeley. Michael Watts, a pioneer of this work, tells of being inspired by Marxists such as Chris Hill and E. P. Thompson, who wrote a people's history of how British people experienced being a peasant or a landless worker and of struggles over the privatisation and defense of common lands (paraphrased from Watts 2001b). Just as early work on imperialism was inspired by scholars from the global South, here too influential texts, such as Franz Fanon's *The Wretched of the Earth* (1965) and Walter Rodney's *How Europe Underdeveloped Africa* (1972), inspired a move beyond Anglo-Marxist theory towards a less Eurocentric reading of these complex processes.

This Marxian peasant studies research also gave rise to the field of political ecology which firmly situates analyses of hazards such as famines, soil erosion, tsunami, and so on, in a Marxian analysis of social relations of production and consumption (Watts 1983; Blaikie 1981; Blaikie and Brookfield 1986; Wisner 1989). See Rod Neumann's (2005) *Making Political Ecology* volume, which addresses the rise of this field in detail. Let me just note here that radical geographers unpack the 'natural' in natural hazards and examine how the political-economy of agrarian change is intimately related to ecological changes and to the production of hazards such as famine (see case studies in Peet and Watts' (2004) *Liberation Ecologies*; Bassett 1988). For example, Watt's *Silent Violence* (1983) was a broad examination of the political-economy of underdevelopment which examined food crisis and the changing character of food systems in northern Nigeria. Watts analyses the articulation of capitalist and peasant modes of production across northern Nigeria in order to understand how peasant societies' ability to withstand drought and famine shifted over time. He reveals how peasants lose their adaptive capacities, as pre-capitalist cultural and productive practices are eroded by the penetration of first colonial and then globalised forms of capitalism. Watts simultaneously chronicles the relationships between household marginalisation and ecological instability as land managers are forced to exploit their own environment due to unequal access to land, labour and capital.

Exemplified by Watts' work above, geographers also pose questions about the persistence and transformation of the peasantry in the face of diverse

131

national capitalisms (Watts and Bassett 1986; Bassett 1988; Wisner 1989). A crucial element of this work questions the articulation of capitalist and peasant modes of production, drawing on theorists such as Ernesto Laclau (1979) and Eric Wolf (1969). For example, Lucy Jarosz (1991, 1993) looks at how a land reform initiative, designed to address class inequalities among the peasantry, actually exacerbated those very inequalities in Madagascar. Her research demonstrates how land reform aimed at incorporating peasant producers into capitalist agriculture actually increased share-cropping rather than eradicating it.

A few geographers also raise questions about the dynamics, contradictions and struggles over control of agrarian resources between peasantries and the state. This work raises questions about the role of the state in creating and stabilising specific regimes of accumulation (Bassett 1988; Watts 1983; Samatar 1989, 1999; Samatar and Samatar 2002; Crush 1987). Linking with themes discussed by dependistas (Box 4.4), some geographers examine how state actors ally with various factions of domestic and international capital in ways that shift and shape interventions and trajectories of capitalist development (Cardoso and Faletto 1979; Samatar 1989; Hecht and Cockburn 1989). Arguably, this remains an underdeveloped area within Marxian development studies in geography (see Glassman and Samatar 1997 for an extended discussion) that has now been prematurely overshadowed by concerns with Foucauldian governmentality, in the wake of debates about the changing role of the state in the context of globalisation (see a discussion in Lawson 2002).

4.2.4 Feminist political-economies of development

Feminist work in development studies was inspired by the same political foment as the Marxist work reviewed above; however, the feminist critiques push further in important ways. The early WID pioneers, discussed in chapter 3, had already established the neglect of women in mainstream development and so created space for this more radical feminist critique.[v] Despite the groundbreaking importance of WID, it did not critique the unequal power relations of gender or race/ethnicity, nor the systematic marginalisation of women by globalised capitalism. Early Marxist development work was also silent on issues of gender, assuming that the primary identity for analysing economic and political change was through one's class position and that men's class adequately reflected that of other household members, most notably women. Marxist work was nonetheless very important for critical feminist work, most particularly in the Marxist analysis of the systematic relationships between the spread of capitalism and the marginalisation of women. Ironically, the Marxist analysis of women's oppression resonates somewhat with the WID position! To the extent that Marxist theorists considered the position of women, they understood their oppression in women's relegation to social reproduction and the household, and assumed that women would be empowered through participation in work, building solidarity with other capitalist workers (Kabeer 1994; chapter 3).

As feminist researchers looked closely at women's experiences across the globe, this Marxist assumption of women's empowerment through work was roundly challenged. A range of empirical studies found that women have dramatically differing access to paid work in different places and that women's entry into wage work is profoundly gendered (Sokoloff 1980; Hartmann 1981; Bandarage 1984). Feminist research reveals how discourses of gender difference construct divergent valuations, remunerations and opportunities in paid work for women and men (Raju 1982; Ong 1987; Beneria and Roldan 1987; Moser 1987; Wolf 1992). These sorts of findings: that women are systematically disadvantaged even within paid work, called for an explanation of women's subordination to men rather than only to capitalism. Here researchers examined the ways in which the expansion of patriarchal capitalist systems across the global South disrupted prior gender divisions of labour and led to the differential valuation of reproductive and non-capitalist work. Inspired by Marxian concepts of social relations of production, feminists introduced the concept of social relations of gender, which focuses on men's role in the continuing subordination of women at all scales and in all realms of life (Whitehead 1979; Young et al. 1981; Kabeer 1994). These researchers see capital accumulation and gender as closely related, but not in predetermined ways, and so they take context seriously. This work is an advance over prior abstract arguments about women's subordination by capitalism, arguing that social relations of gender take on specific forms in specific times and places.

Kabeer (1994: 54) nicely frames the challenge for feminist development studies:

> ...to steer a path somewhere between the liberal individualism of WID scholarship and the structural determinism of certain Marxist accounts, so that analysis could move beyond demonstrating the adverse/marginalising impact of development/capitalism on women to a deeper understanding of the ways in which unequal relations between women and men may have contributed to the extent and forms of exclusion that women faced in the development process

This work does not focus (necessarily) on the behaviour of individual men, but rather pushes beyond the formal economy to examine how families, communities, informal and unpaid work, and the institutions of nation states and development are shot through with gender relations and gendered discourses that construct different access to life chances, resources, programmes and so on.

Feminist geographers are ideally positioned to develop this context-specific research. Janet Townsend, Janet Momsen, Sylvia Chant, Lynn Brydon and Saraswati Ragu were early contributors to feminist development work, providing broad surveys of the position and experiences of women across the global South (Momsen and Townsend 1987; Brydon and Chant 1989; Raju 1982). Joni Seager's (1997, 2003, 2005) feminist atlases contribute to understanding the geographies of gender difference around the globe, posing a research agenda on environmental change and gender differences. Feminist work such as the International Geographical Union Working Commission on Gender and Geography brings together researchers from around the globe, as in the *Different Places, Different Voices* (1993) volume (Momsen and Kinnaird). This collection foregrounded regional differences in development concerns across Africa, Asia and Latin America. In early Africanist research there was more focus on gender and environment, agrarian change and basis needs. In Asia, feminist researchers were concerned with demographic changes, such as fertility and migration. In Latin America, more research focuses on feminism and revolutionary struggles for justice for groups differentiated by class and ethnicity. While certainly not all the authors mentioned above would claim Marxist influences in their work, they clearly laid crucial groundwork for those of us who came later to explore how capitalist and gender processes worked together to shape development.

Geographers blended Marxist and feminist analysis in their context-specific analyses of the social relations of gender in development. Their work took seriously the cultural construction of gender difference in its relation to substantial reworkings of power relations in work, social reproduction and politics. For example, early geographical work analysed ideologies of women's domesticity, gender divisions of labour and the gendering of paid, unpaid and informal work (Hays-Mitchell 1993; Raghuram 1993; Townsend 1995; Faulkner and Lawson 1990; Radcliffe 1986; see also England and Lawson 2005 for an overview). Feminist scholars also examined social reproduction, gendered household relations and complex contestations of power in households and communities around divisions of labour and access to resources (Lawson and Klak 1990; Carney 1992; Townsend 1993;

Sage 1993; Lawson 1992, 1995). Geographers examined the varied responses of peasant households to the encroachments of agrarian capitalism, looking at gender, environment and sustainability (Hart 1986; Watts 1989; Jarosz 1991; Rocheleau 1991; Ardayfio-Schandorf 1993). All these processes are profoundly political, of course, and researchers are building a feminist political geography of the global South (Radcliffe and Westwood; 1993; Peake and Trotz 1999; Nelson; 2003; Van Eyck 2002; see Kofman 2005 for an overview).

To be clear, I am referring here to feminist political-economy research, which does not break with its Marxist roots within geography, but rather builds from Marxist work on imperialism and peasant studies. A major contribution of this feminist work is to explicitly consider households, communities and women as centrally important sites and subjects for development studies. Feminist research on global economic restructuring, gender relations and development policy (especially structural adjustment programmes) owes a huge debt to Marxism (Massey 1984, 1994; Lawson 1992, 1995; Cravey 1997, 1998; Mullings 1999; Wright 1997, 2004; Nagar et al. 2002). Much work on gender and mobility also begins from Marxian roots to think about mobility in relation to work, households and the nation (Radcliffe 1990; Chant 1992; Tyner 1994; Lawson 1998; Silvey and Lawson 1999; Silvey 2000a, 2000b). These researchers foreground the systematic marginalisation of women through the geographic spread and intensification of capitalist accumulation in the global South, and, at the same time, they take seriously the ways gender inflects every aspect of those processes. Chapter 5 discusses research which largely has its roots in these feminist and Marxist literatures, but which goes further in raising questions of difference, postcoloniality and gendered discourse.

4.3 Geographies of Marxist-feminist development

4.3.1 Political economies of space and place

Despite the substantial insights into little 'd' development that emerged from early Marxist-feminist political-economy work across the social sciences, the 1980s witnessed an impasse within Marxist development studies (Corbridge 1986, 1990; Schuurman 1993; Perrons 1999). Classical Marxism (of Marx, Lenin, Luxemburg) was seen as determinist: reading off similar economic and political outcomes from capital accumulation across the globe. Marxist theory was also criticised as economistic: reducing a complex mix of economic circuits and flows to a dominant and determining capitalist mode of production, focused on the logic of capital accumulation and on workers and capitalist classes. Feminist researchers in particular argued that the Marxist emphasis on exchange detracts from thinking about the fullness of human life, including its spirituality, connection with nature, dynamics of social reproduction and care-work. As we shall see in chapter 5, the early Marxist-feminist work also downplayed (ignored) other crucial aspects of identity and politics, such as race/ethnicity and postcoloniality, invoking global class and gender solidarities that did not exist. Impasse critics argue that Marxist development theory constructs an imagined space of a coherent 'third world' at odds with the fragmentation of the last decades of the twentieth century – including the uneven emergence of newly industrialising countries (the NICs), the rising power of OPEC countries, the breakdown of the Bretton Woods financial system and the growing internationalisation of capital, the persistence of peasant production across much of Africa, and so on (Corbridge 1990). Critics also argue that early Marxist development work placed too much focus on the shift to urban/industrial economies as part and parcel of progressive change, neglecting the persistence of peasantries, agrarian economies and the complex articulations of diverse modes of production in many places around the globe.

Geographic contributions to development studies push beyond the limitations of this impasse to construct 'post-Marxism', not ex-Marxism (Slater 2005, personal communication). Geographers articulate how capitalist processes restlessly reconfigure space, place and scale, and so take Marxist analysis beyond determinism and economism. Much radical development geography retains its roots in Marxist thinking, with a continuing commitment to causality and analysis of the relations of production, while paying serious attention to the diverse ways in which these combine with other forms of power (relations of gender, religion, ethnicity, nationalism, and so on) to constitute specific social and political formations. Marxist-feminist development geographers have refused to build any predictable or universal narrative of change and focus their work on understanding the diversities and commonalities in D/development processes to inform progressive political possibilities. This work in geography theorises concrete instances in order to understand the ways in which struggles over resources and labour are inseparably bound up with struggles over meanings, identities and the exercise of power (Hart 2001: 27). Pred and Watts' book *Reworking Modernity* (1992: 11) foregrounds the multiple ways in which locally situated actors rework the forces of modernity. Their argument captures our geographical sensitivity to place and space:

...there are both national and local capitalisms... [T]he global reach of capitalism has transplanted capitalist relations onto foreign soils whose different social
structures produce different class configurations and different institutional forms
of capital and labor

Early Marxist geographers gave great weight to local culture, tradition and
history, paying attention to the articulation of processes in places in irreducibly
local ways (Watts 2001). For example, Susman's (1974) work on Cuba linked
urban primacy and inequality to American domination and virtual colonisation
through control of land and the sugar industry. His work assesses post-revolu-
tionary Cuba, arguing that Castro's policies of land reform, nationalisation of
key industries and social redistribution have been successful in reducing inequality. Terry McGee's (1974) work on hawkers in Hong Kong draws on Marxian
thinking to underscore the crucial importance of neocolonial relations in shaping
uneven development in the global South. McGee's detailed empirical work
critiques modernisation assumptions of a smooth transition to modernity in the
global South and argues for a more ecological and historical approach to understanding traditions (such as street hawking). He also draws on Santos' (1974)
work to argue that hawkers play an integral part in the economic growth of
Hong Kong as the lower circuit that subsidises the expansion of the upper
circuit, or modern retailing sector.

Geographers have been at the forefront of moving beyond the impasse, while
retaining the analytical power of Marxist development theory. Geographical
contributions take place and space seriously by acknowledging the indetermi-
nacy, the openness of D/development processes and the politics they set in
motion. Stuart Corbridge argues that development can only be understood in
terms of the diverse conditions of existence of national and international
regimes of accumulation, regulation and alliances among and between diverse
nation states and social classes (see also Corbridge 1990). Michael Watts'
detailed historical and empirical body of work on Nigeria examines the ways in
which global forces articulate with local forces through multi-scalar and
grounded analysis. He looks at how petro-capitalism has unleashed a particular
version of modernity, producing new social classes and state–society relations.
Watts examines how these shifts were experienced by landless workers in the
North; how they produced a certain sense of ethnic identity; why local political movements in northern Nigeria had such power; and how oil exploitation
has led to a series of exclusions and to political resistance by those excluded.

Through this body of work, Watts employs Marxian theory to analyse local, grounded situations and simultaneously asks how these empirics inflect theory itself (Watts 1983, 1989, 2001b, 2003).

In addition to geographers' detailed empirical engagements with Marxist-feminist development theory, David Harvey stands out for his theoretical extensions of Marxian thinking through which he theorises the differential production of place, space and political activism under capitalism. While Harvey has not worked explicitly in development studies, his theoretical insights have substantial relevance for our argument here. Harvey's work stresses the restless spatiality of capitalist processes and pushes beyond the essentialism of stagnationist and underdevelopment theses of early dependency and imperialist arguments. He draws on Marx's theory of crisis to argue that capitalism must have its fixes, but that we cannot predict in advance what fixes will be implemented, nor what forms they will take (this idea of a fix is evocative: fix as in stabilise, fix as in heal or solve, fix as in a junky needing a fix – to prevent feeling worse, in order to feel better[vi]). Harvey's foundational work in 1973 and 1982 argued that one palliative for the political crises engendered by exploitation of workers is the devaluation of capitalist production in one place, coupled with the spatial relocation of capitalist investments and the remaking of labour relations in places more advantageous to capital. His *Limits to Capital* (1982) is a key text that delineates an overdetermined, spatially restless capitalism, coupled with the spatiality of crisis formation and its resolution. Harvey's work has been invaluable for understanding the contradictions of capital accumulation and international movements of capitalist modes of production and money flows (Corbridge 1990).

Harvey's more recent work examines contemporary global capitalism and *The New Imperialism* (2003): the connections between capitalist crises in the USA and the remaking of places around the globe through the penetration of investments, international debt and military intervention. This has enormous relevance for radical development geography, as Harvey extends early arguments about imperialism (Box 4.5) to argue that crises in Western capitalism (and particularly the USA) are sufficiently deep, and the conditions for accumulation sufficiently altered, that new strategies are required to maintain capital accumulation, including new rounds of 'accumulation by dispossession'. This term refers to the opening up of profitable investments (in the USA and around the globe) through privatisation of common rights and resources, such as water, education, health care and housing; displacement of peasant populations; privatisation of national industries and utilities; expansion of intellectual property rights to include medicinal plants and food crops; corporate fraud and dispossession of retirement assets; asset destruction through inflation; rolling back of regulatory frameworks for workers' rights; and elimination of benefits such as pension plans and social security (see also Box 3.4).

As Sparke et al. (2005: 376) argue, Harvey's formulation of primitive accumulation can potentially serve as a 'hinge concept' that opens the door to thinking about the multiple extra-economic power relations in specific places through which domination is being exercised in the early twenty-first century. This is important because it helps us to understand why diverse social movements have come together to create a politics of opposition to neoliberal policies. This is because these policies (redefining indigenous claims to communal property rights, eliminating state supports for care-work, which serves to reinscribe oppressive gender roles, and so on) bring together diverse groups around a common goal of anti-neoliberalism. In sharp contrast to mainstream arguments about maximising growth through free trade for the good of all societies, Harvey reads the turn to neoliberalism through the interrelations between places, the unfolding of neoliberal capitalist relations and the multiple axes of domination and politics that are emerging in response.

The shift to neoliberal orthodoxy in development policy emerges, Harvey argues, from the push to resolve crises of stagflation and deindustrialisation in US and UK capitalism in the 1970s. As we discussed in chapter 3, a series of economic shocks rocked Western countries, leading to a political shift towards neo-liberalisation, including privatisation and free trade to open up new territories and new spheres (such as services, utilities, and the like) for investments by Western capitals. Harvey's theoretical analysis complements a variety of research by development geographers on the '...*different variants* of neoliberalism, the *hybrid nature* of contemporary policies and programmes, or [to] the *multiple and contradictory aspects* of neoliberal spaces, techniques and subjects' (Larner 2003: 509, emphasis in original). Development geographers have responded to Larner's appeal for research on the context-specific variations in neoliberal processes, producing a range of empirically rich research across the global South (see for example Ould-May 1996 on Mauritania; Kelly 1999 on the Philippines; Gwynne and Kay 2000, 2004; Klak 1998; Konadu-Agyemang 2000; Chase 2002a; Harris 2000; Perrault and Martin 2005, all on Latin America). Geographers are also bringing together Marxist-feminist and post-structural arguments about the forms of governance and governmentality at work in these new economic and political forms (see for example Bridge and Jonas 2002;

Nagar et al. 2002; Sparke and Lawson 2003; Sparke 2005). In addition to clearly situating the shift to neoliberal policies in the relations between Western and Latin American capitalisms, these researchers are raising crucial questions about social and environmental justice under these regimes of accumulation (more in section 4.3.2 on scale, below).

Box 4.6 Latin American debt crisis

As we discussed in chapter 3, the implementation of neoliberal reforms in Chile in the 1970s and 1980s inaugurated neoliberal legitimacy, and this was followed swiftly by structural adjustment programmes throughout Latin America, implemented in the wake of the debt crisis of the 1980s.

A Marxist reading situates the roots of the debt crisis in capitalist crises in the West (Figure 4.2 depicts this view). Profit declines in the core prompted a growing internationalisation of production and banking just as a vast influx of petrodollars came into the international banking system. The concomitant search for new investments landed bankers in Latin America, where the costs and inefficiencies of Import Substitution Industrialisation led to a high demand for capital imports (Stallings and Kauffman 1989; Harvey 2003; Perrault and Martin 2005).

Latin American countries took on large loans at low interest rates in the early 1970s, but as economic crisis hit the Western economies, interest rates skyrocketed by the early 1980s, such that the interest payments on loans rapidly became unmanageable. In the wake of Mexico's 1982 announcement that they could not sustain debt service payments, several Latin American countries followed suit and requested emergency loans from the IMF to stay afloat. As a condition of receiving those loans, the IMF required structural adjustment programmes (summarised in Box 3.4) in order to qualify for continuing bank loans. From a Marxist perspective, these policies created the conditions for accumulation by dispossession, and were intimately related to resolving economic crises for globalising capital and for Western and other cash-rich economies, such as the OPEC investor nations. Indeed, the managing director of the IMF, Michel Camdessus, made clear that the success of structural adjustment programmes was based on their ability to strengthen the economic recovery of the advanced economies:

> I referred last year to the impressive performance of the thirty five successfully adjusting countries: their performance has been maintained, with an annual growth in per capita incomes averaging 4.5 per cent over the past five years. U.S. exports to China, the Middle East and Latin America grew in 1991 and 1992 at ten times the increase in U.S. exports to Western Europe. Ten times! And Japanese exports to the same markets grew ten times faster than Japanese exports to the U.S... The successful developing countries not only show the way forward for other developing countries. They have also shown to the industrial countries that there is no action more effective in...strengthening their own recovery...than the full integration of the developing and transforming countries into the global economic system... (Camdessus 1993)

Marxist analyses of debt crisis present a significant rereading of development. In contrast to mainstream World Bank and IMF arguments, wherein these SAPs were required to fix national problems of economic mismanagement *within the global South*, Marxist scholars interpret debt crisis in terms of the intimate relations between capitalist economies across the globe. The *National Catholic Reporter* goes further and asks for whom is this a debt crisis, pointing out that indebted countries are exporting capital and enriching the West and global institutions.

> The overall global debt of all developing countries, according to U.N. statistics, was $567 billion in 1980 and $1.4 trillion in 1992. In that same twelve year period, total foreign debt payments from third world countries amounted to $1.6 trillion. This means that, having already paid back three times over the $567 billion they had borrowed, far from being less in debt, in 1992 they owed two hundred and fifty per cent more than they owed in 1980... (Ambrogi 1999)

Doreen Massey's work also pioneered radical Marxist-feminist development geographies of place and space, which moved beyond the impasse and contributed substantially to development geography. Her book *Spatial Divisions of Labour* (1984) sets forth influential arguments about both spatialised and gendered divisions of labour under capitalist accumulation. She focuses on uneven regional development within Britain and makes links to the offshoring (often to the global South) of production in the restless search for profitability. Her insights about

Figure 4.2 It's not that Third World countries are getting poorer, it's that we're getting richer.
Source: Carlos Bernales, North American Commission on Latin America *Report on the Americas* XXXIII(1): 23, July/August 1999

the power differentials that accompany these spatial divisions of labour laid the groundwork for critical analyses of global economic restructuring and the relocation of production to the global South in subordinate relation to Western spaces of control and domination.

> ...if these divisions of labour which are stretched out over space...consist, as we
> have said they do, of mutually defining elements, then the functional (and social)
> characteristics of some areas define the functional (and social) characteristics of
> other areas. If one region has all the control functions...then other regions must
> have all the functions that are controlled, the subordinated functions. This has
> clear political and policy implications. (Massey 1994: 89)

Massey's contributions are important both in mapping out these spatial processes and relations in contemporary capitalist restructuring, and in her attention to place specificity and the constant remaking of space. Massey takes place and space seriously and argues that spatial and gender divisions of labour, and struggles over class power, are tendencies that take on particular forms in specific places and times (Massey 2004, 2005). For Massey, exemplified in her book *For Space* (2005), spaces are in constant motion, being restlessly remade by shifting relations between places and through multiple trajectories of power and heterogeneity. As Matt Sparke (2006a: 4) so aptly summarises her project, 'Massey's account...enables us to reimagine place as a venue in which space-relating and space-making processes come together in conjunctural events'. This insight is important because it opens up places and spaces to politics so that the kinds of places being made in struggles over D/development are in contestation rather than being produced from on high. Her work is deeply informed by Marxism and feminism, and her geographical theorising moves us away from determinism and economism, through serious attention to the cultural construction of gender, race/ethnicity and class difference in their complex relations to the economic processes at the heart of Marxist theory.

Inspired by this theoretical work, many Marxist-feminist development geographers take a relational and critical analysis of place seriously. They draw from the theoretical abstractions of Marxist-feminist thought to examine how these processes, contestations, accommodations and politics constitute places across the globe today. For example, Cindi Katz (2001, 2004) analyses the interconnectedness of places undergoing D/development in two ways. She begins from thick, historical descriptions of processes of production and social reproduction in particular places, and then identifies connections between apparently disparate processes in distant places. Katz explores how an agricultural modernisation project, civil war, IMF-imposed structural adjustment and international investments in commercial food production combine in Howa, a village in Sudan. She traces dramatic shifts in land use and access to communal wood and grazing resources and the resultant food insecurity, male outmigration, dramatic reductions in health and education investment, the changing lives of children and deskilling of community members. Katz then maps out the parallels in social disinvestments and economic restructuring between Howa and Harlem in New York. Looking at job flight from New York to cheaper labour pools elsewhere, she identifies similar rollbacks in social services for working-class people in Harlem. Katz argues for structural comparisons of Howa and Harlem to call attention to the topographies of capitalism in order to be able to imagine a spatial politics of connections. This resonates with Sheppard's (2002) arguments for positionality and Spivak's (1998) call for 'transnational literacy' (discussed in chapter 2), which posit the analysis of spatial interrelationships as a technique for revealing the sorts of power differentials produced through systematic connections between places that actively produce uneven development.

Gillian Hart's (2002) book *Disabling Globalization* also builds relational analyses of D/development. She argues against what she terms 'impact studies' of global-isation or development, which assume that their effects are unidirectional, radiating outwards from a dominant core and having predictable effects 'on local places'. Hart argues, by contrast, that globalisation is produced *in the relations between* processes operating across multiple and intersecting scales, and through 'history, place, practice and power in multiple, interconnected arenas' (Jarosz 2003: 506). Drawing on detailed research in South African townships, she challenges the notion that development 'models from elsewhere' (Hart 2002: 5) – in this case, neoliberal industrialisation models from East Asia – can be uniformly and unproblematically applied in very diverse places with predictably positive outcomes. She argues that

> ...critical human geography has a major role to play in developing politically enabling and non-reductionist understandings of political-economy, culture and power in an increasingly interdependent world... (Hart 2003: 813)

Hart first charts dramatic differences in the conditions for, and performance of, industrial development in East Asia and South Africa, and then goes on to demon-strate profound differences in the trajectories of industrial development within two South African townships. Through in-depth field research, Hart traces histories of Taiwanese industrial investments and demonstrates how land dispossession in South Africa predicated very different forms of industrial development and labour politics to those which had occurred in East Asia, where redistributive land reforms were pivotal in creating the social conditions for rapid rural industrialisation. Hart also examines 'multiple trajectories of socio-spatial change' (Hart 2002: 13) within post-apartheid South Africa, examining the diverse political identities and alliances that form in relation to the local state and industrial development in each township. Her comparative histories of the two townships examine how political identities and alliances are formed through racial, gendered and ethnic differences in partic-ular places that produce dramatic differences in connections to national and local liberation struggles, to the labour movement and to struggles to secure the condi-tions for social reproduction. Her work deconstructs the very possibility of a universally applicable neoliberal development trajectory, recovering the ways in which different histories of dispossession, political identity formation, access to the state, and ethnic and gender struggles articulate with forces of capital accumula-tion and postcolonial state-building in particular places.

A host of processes come together in the production of the places/spaces of development. Geographers' attention to the political-economic production of places has been critical to moving development studies beyond the impasse in Marxist thinking. In so doing, radical development geography moves our discussion away from a mainstream preoccupation with the inherent limits of global South places that must be fixed by external intervention, and towards an analysis of the ways in which political and economic relations with other places contribute to precisely the 'problems' that mainstream Development identifies.

Marxist scholars in geography are analysing commonalities across places as well as diversity and specificity (Perrons 1999). Their work integrates theoretical analyses of capitalist processes with the gendered production of difference, processes of identity formation and of state–society relations to understand the myriad forms that D/development assumes. I have not provided an exhaustive review of geographical work taking up a critical engagement with place/space. In previous chapters we have considered many examples of critical empirical analyses of D/development, such as Rachel Silvey's (2003) 'The Spaces of Protest' on different gendered labour activism in two export-processing zones in Indonesia; Rick Schroeder's work on agrarian change and gender in the Gambia (chapter 1); Melissa Wright's analysis of gender, maquiladora work and the devaluation of women in Ciudad Juárez (chapter 1); Sarah Wright's analysis of struggles over representations of rice and farmers' livelihoods in the Philippines (chapter 1); and Tad Mutersbaugh's research on the differential effects of international organic crop certification across villages in Oaxaca (chapter 2). These same themes continue and are further extended in the 'post' research we discuss in chapter 5.

4.3.2 The social production of scales

As we discussed in chapter 2, Marxist-feminist geographers have also been at the forefront of theorising the social and political construction of geographical scales. This theoretical work pushes beyond earlier dependency arguments that rested on unexamined regional divisions into core and periphery. Dependency formulations of the scales of development and underdevelopment are crude and undifferentiated, and do not allow for the possibility that specific patterns of investment and circulation take on very different forms at various spatial scales. Smith (1986) argues for a nuanced reading of the ways in which uneven development plays out across geographical scales, noting that

>...the discovery that geographical space is 'the product of socio-economic processes' should lead not to the dismissal of space but to a recognition of its

importance. Space is not a 'dead factor', but comes alive neither as a separate thing, field or container but as an integral creation of the material relations of society... (Smith 1986: 94)

Smith goes on to argue that scalar differences in the operation of capitalist processes should be a central concern of development studies. From this vantage point, the rise of the East Asian Newly Industrialising Countries (NICs) of the 1980s cannot be read off as a triumph of industrialisation over the development of underdevelopment because many parts of the global South slipped further behind as the NICs were forging ahead. Rather than claiming a coherent 'periphery' as a container for the uniform operation of capitalist relations, Smith theorises uneven development as integral to the working out of the contradictions of capital. The failures of dependency theory lie in its inability to theorise the differentiated production of spaces and scales at particular moments of capital accumulation.

Marxist-feminist development geographers are building a more rigorous theorisation of space and scale, as produced through capitalist social relations. As Ron Johnston (2000: 726) puts it:

> ...the construction of geographical scale is a process of profound political importance. 'Scaling places' – the establishment of geographical differences according to a metric of scales – etches a certain order of empowerment and containment into the geographical landscape.

Marxist geographers analyse the social construction of scales as the '... geographical resolution of the contradictory processes of a capitalist economic system' (Marston 2000: 232). More specifically, they examine the ways in which geographical scales are produced and transformed by capitalist processes of accumulation, regulation and de(re)valorisation of capital and labour (Brenner 1999; Smith 1984, 1993). Further, Marxist and feminist geographers have examined the scalar dynamics at work in creating particular identities to consolidate political legitimacy for a nation state or a social movement. As we discussed in chapter 2, Neil Smith argues that social groups can act strategically to create their own politics of scale, and we see this as they work to resist D/development processes (more below). Marston (2000) has further insisted on theoretical attention to the household and body as crucial scales for understanding the ways in which gender systems and patriarchy operate in relation to economic, political, consumption and social reproduction processes. How, then, does this Marxist-feminist work on the social and political construction of scale advance critical development studies?

Attention to the dynamic production of scales shifts our analytical lens to new questions and new scales of analysis, leading geographers to rethink development in a range of ways. First, globalisation – a term implying a radical rescaling of almost everything (from Watts 1993) – threatens to overshadow development studies (Schuurman 2000a).[vii] Marxist-feminist geographers have refocused discussion away from the fuzzy and overdetermined globalisation debate and towards analysis of the ideological political-economy and policy shifts of neo-liberalisation (Peck 2001; Peck and Tickell 2002; Larner 2003). In doing so, our analytical focus shifts away from a supposedly unidirectional 'globalisation' and towards a complex set of rescalings of capitalist uneven development (or little 'd' development). As we discussed in the previous section, geographical work links neo-liberalisation to particular shifts in regimes of accumulation from Keynesian protectionism towards liberalised and de(re)regulated economies, which facilitate global flows of capital, trade and resources (Harvey 2003; see also chapter 3, Box 3.4). This critical Marxist-feminist work contributes to development studies by way of its critique of celebratory renditions of growth through market efficiency in mainstream development. By contrast, this critical work reveals how deep changes in development orthodoxy and policy are systematically linked to the resolution of capitalist crises in Western economies.

Second, and building from these insights, Marxist-feminist geographers are interrogating the changing scalar geographies of governance and state power over economic, social and environmental life accompanying processes of neoliberal development (Brenner 1999; Peck 2001; Peck and Tickell 2002; Bridge and Jonas 2002; Perrault 2006; Sparke 2005). In Latin America, the rush to privatise seemingly everything has transformed historically social goods such as water, communal lands, health care and forests, into economic commodities, and these processes are fomenting new politics of scale. For example, Perrault's (2006) work on the privatisation of water rights in Bolivia traces a series of political rescalings. The Bolivian government centralised control over water rights in national-level superintendencies, taking them away from local-scale municipalities and campesino groups. Under neoliberal reforms and the search for new sources of national revenue, the superintendencies have the power to negotiate the export of water into world markets (in this case to Chile). In this process, governance over a key social and environmental good is rescaled to facilitate new rounds of capital accumulation at the national scale in Bolivia and Chile. This rescaling process prompted massive mobilisations by peasant

farmers, who themselves jumped political scales from local groups to the formation of a national-level peasant network, organised to reassert their rights to
control water. Perrault (2006: 279) points out that farmers resist state central-
isation of water rights by

> ...engaging in a complex politics of scale, reasserting the importance of local
> autonomy and authority through their emphasis on *usos y costumbres*, while
> forming translocal networks with campesino and indigenous organisations, leftist
> political parties, and national and international NGOs.

The social construction of scale raises crucial questions for development studies
by calling attention to these transformations of governance and the formation
of new political identities and organisations that accommodate and/or challenge
neoliberal reforms (see also Swyngedouw 1997; Bebbington 2001; Nagar et al.
2002; Sparke and Lawson 2003; Bridge and Jonas 2002; Lawson 2002).

The rescaling governance is also jumping to the international scale (Glassman
1999; Lawson 2002). Lawson traces the shift of economic governance away from
the Ecuadorian state and towards supranational institutions (World Bank,
International Monetary Fund) and treaties (NAFTA, GATT (now WTO,) Andean
Community; see Figure 1.8). The Ecuadorian economy fell into crisis in the
1980s and 1990s, labouring under a steadily increasing international debt and
massive capital flight. In the context of this crisis, state elites worked ever more
closely with international financial institutions and private, globalised capital to
keep the economy afloat. These institutions frame economic crisis as resulting
from *domestic* failures of macroeconomic management and so justify their role
as the new arbiters of economic policy within vulnerable and debt-ridden
countries like Ecuador. Elite actors in states like Ecuador have implemented a
suite of policy reforms that align their economies with the needs of globalised
financial and productive capitals, dismantling protectionism, slashing state spending on social provision and curtailing unionism. These actions internationalise
the Ecuadorian state, reflecting the class backgrounds and interests of those in
power that are closer to global elites than to the mass of working Ecuadorians.
As macroeconomic governance has jumped to the global scale, Ecuadorians have
massed in multiple protests, recognising their diminished control over their own
economic, social and environmental futures (see Lawson 2002 for more detail).
By examining these shifts in policy regimes, processes of governance and development ideology through the social construction of scale, we see the ways in
which power over the Ecuadorian economy has shifted away from the territo-

rially defined state (the scale at which national politics are enacted) and towards the unbundled spaces of international financial institutions and private capitals (see also Newstead 2002, 2005), discussed in chapter 2). Glassman (1999: 673) examines similar processes of internationalisation of the state in Thailand, explaining it as '...a process in which the state apparatus becomes increasingly oriented towards facilitating capital accumulation for the most internationalised investors, regardless of their nationality'.

Third, geographers are researching ways in which these new scalar geographies of capitalism, state power and D/development are contested by social movements who organise across a range of scales, from transnational networks to local community groups. Research by geographers reveals the ways in which women's movements, labour unions, indigenous organisations, farmer's groups, and so on, are reframing scales of identity formation, action and cooperation (see selected chapters in Klak 1998; Chase 2002a; Swyngedouw 1997; Wright 2004; Perrault 2003b, 2006). For example, Tom Perrualt's (2003) work in Ecuador examines the ability of indigenous groups to push their claims on the state by jumping scale and allying with other groups at national and transnational scales. In the case of the Mondacayu community Perrault studies, the community has forged alliances with national indigenous federations, international NGOs, financial institutions and the state. More specifically, the community organised to secure formal legal title to community lands that were threatened by an influx of colonists from the highlands. In order to legitimate their ownership, Perrault traces how the Mondacayu shifted from historic practices of hunting, fishing and small-scale horticulture to make their presence in the landscape more visible by clearing forest lands for cattle pasture, which fitted with Ecuador's rural development programme and land reform agency criteria. This act of producing a visible space of production allowed the Mondacayu to build political alliances that defended their control over community lands. As this example illustrates, scale-jumping has contradictory effects. On one hand, the Mondacayu defended their ancestral land claims, while at the same time they became integrated into globally subsidised commodity chains and circuits of capital accumulation which lead to deforestation.

Our earlier discussion of Sarah Wright's (2004) work on Filipino farmers' efforts to resist the privatisation of rice seed illustrates how social movements contest the scale-jump embodied in contemporary intellectual property rights, policies and laws (see chapters 1 and 2). Wright traces the ways in which corporate, scientific and policy actors took one culturally specific knowledge about rice seed (rice in Western property law and scientific vernacular as private property) and jumped scale to this as the globally legitimate (and legally protected) view of rice. This scale-jump creates new spaces for capital accumulation on the part of corporations and governments, as these patents on rice seed become valuable assets that secure markets, profits and new investment opportunities. Wright traces how farmer social movements have jumped scale by creating alternative spaces of knowledge and property rights, as well as working to change existing national and global laws and regulations about the privatisation of rice seed. MASIPAG, the social movement with which she worked, articulates a concept of Farmers' Rights which

> ...encompass[es] a broad array of rights and responsibilities including rights pertaining to land, to seeds and genetic resources, production, biodiversity, politics and decision-making, culture and knowledge, information and research... this definition is based on the idea that farmers have a responsibility to feed their families, community and society... [this] creates a moral economy in which the right to subsistence needs, in particular the right to collect seed, trumps the right of investors to control the dissemination of products... (Wright 2004: 20)

This Filipino social movement is contesting and actively working to disassemble the claim to power embedded in the global scale-jump of intellectual property rights laws. Wright identifies their political strategy as constructing different conceptions of scale and space, specifically 'woven space', in response to this hegemonic global regime of property rights over rice. This woven space is made up of both opposition and alternatives, springing from specific local knowledge, struggles and strategies.

> It is this space that the farmers of MASIPAG work to construct as they create spaces free of individualised intellectual property; spaces based on communal ownership, sustainable agriculture and farmer empowerment. In creating these spaces, defying norms and technoscientific knowledge spaces on offer from elites, they draw upon, nourish and create anew the networked spaces of multiscalar resistance... (Wright 2004: 22)

Recreations of space and scale by subaltern groups can be overtly political, as in the above examples, or can enable economic and social practices that sustain livelihoods (Bebbington 2003). For example, Nevins (2001) and Newstead, Reid and Sparke (2003) examine the ways in which Mexican migrants construct a transnational scale encompassing both sides of the US-Mexican border.

Figure 4.3 Filipino farmers' and organisers' rally. Source: Sarah Wright (2003)

Notwithstanding the militarised border zone, many migrants engage in repeated recrossings and produce cultural imaginaries, representing this transnational space to their communities, as one of economic possibility.

Fourth, scholars are rethinking development by pointing to the rescaling of social reproduction from the state to households and to individual women under structural adjustment programmes (SAPs) (Moser 1987; Dalla Costa and Dalla Costa 1993; Elson 1990; Emeagwali 1995; Nagar et al. 2002; Lawson 1995, 1999). Feminists are demonstrating how neoliberal discourses and policies rely on women's unpaid labour to take up the burdens of social reproduction (raising children, maintaining affordable homes, schooling, health care, food provision; Elson 1990; Scarpaci 1988; Lawson 1995). Geographic research has focused on how neoliberal policies redefine the positions/roles of individuals within the national and the global contexts (Katz 2001; Lawson 1995; Lawson and Klak 1990; Hays-Mitchell 1993; Kelly 1999), and structural adjustment programmes represent an example of this neoliberal rescaling of state functions under arguments about fiscal austerity. Vulnerable households and women take on increased work and expenses for previously state-provided or state-subsidised services, and this has contributed to the feminisation of poverty across the global South. For example, Jacquelyn Chase's (2002b) work in the Brazilian town of Itabira traces the impacts of the privatisation of a state-run mining company. She examines the downsizing of the company, the loss of family wage jobs and the rise of women working in home-based crafts, childcare provision and food preparation. As economic pressures on households increase in this town, Chase demonstrates how deeply neoliberal restructuring reaches into homes and private lives as women have reduced their fertility to very low levels in response to sharp drops in standards of living and their desperate need for additional incomes.

These rescalings of social reproduction both empower and disempower women as they are increasingly integrated into globalised processes of production, reproduction and consumption. Safa's (2002) work in the Dominican Republic examines how neoliberal restructuring of both work and social reproduction has contradictory effects on women's lives. On one hand, as more women enter the workforce they are gaining greater control over financial and other household decisions. At the same time, as men are laid off from family wage jobs, families face increasing stress, which is leading to the formation of more female-headed households. In response to these shifts in work and home lives, women are engaging in new forms of political activism, both at work and within labour unions (Van Eyck 2002; Safa 2002; Cravey 1998), and organising for social services (Nagar et al. 2002; Lind 2005; Radcliffe and Westwood 1993; Pearson 2000), thus challenging the idea of women as mere victims of structural adjustment programmes. Starting from the rescaling of social reproduction and its reverberations in households informs a trenchant critique of the social effects of neoliberal adjustments.

Marxist-feminist work on the social construction of scale makes important contributions to development studies. First, their work foregrounds the material bases for a politics of scale, rooted in the contradictory processes of capitalist economic systems. This research reveals both how states and international institutions have sought to retain power over development dollars and policies, and how political, economic and cultural processes are rescaling around them. Second, attention to the social construction of scales reveals the ways in which development processes occurring at specific scales (national, local, international) often exclude key social groups whose practices do not correspond with development priorities articulated by those in power. Third, by looking critically through the lens of scale, this Marxist-feminist work reveals not only how scale is constructed by elites, but also the counter-productions of scale produced by various subaltern groups in creative responses to capitalist and patriarchal restructuring. This research provides the materialist ground on which much of the post-structural analysis (discussed in chapter 5) builds to examine how discourses and cultural productions of scale also shape development processes and the political influence of various social groups.

4.4 Classed and gendered subjects

For Marxist and Marxist-feminist scholars, people experience D/development as subjects situated within social relations of production and gender that define and condition their agency. Nonetheless, they are theorised as active agents who shape the geo-historical specificities of development. The early Marxist work and the feminist-inflected Marxian work we have discussed in this chapter differ in their approach to the subjects of development and I discuss each briefly below. As you read this, compare Marxian conceptualisations of people in development – their differential power and their relations to economic, political and cultural systems – with the universal modern subject who acts with 'free will' constructed in mainstream theory in chapter 3. Marxist-feminist geographers understand the subjects of development in terms of their differential relations to economic resources and political power in the spaces of globalised capitalism; the ways in which economic restructuring reconfigures the economic and political power of various social groups; and the gendering of production and reproduction.

As I noted at the outset of this chapter, the divisions between Marxian and post-structural development geography are blurry. In many important respects, the work reviewed in this chapter provides the groundwork for the post-structural research we discuss in chapter 5. Indeed, many of the authors who began arguing for Marxist analyses of development now note the limits of these conceptualisations and have extended their thinking by drawing on post-structural theory (Slater 1993, 2004; Pred and Watts 1992). I want you to note this continuity, and then think here about the distinctions between mainstream and early radical thinking about the subjects of development.

Marxist theory constructs a class subject, rooted in European class politics of the nineteenth century. This collective subject is constituted through social relations of production and was initially conceived in terms of a division between capitalists and workers, who are differentiated in terms of their access to economic resources and their politics. As Marxist theory was initially brought to bear on development geography, analysis was largely framed in terms of abstract, structural processes of imperialism and colonial exploitation. People in the global South were ignored or implicitly understood in terms of these broad class divisions, and '...as objects of capitalist exploitation and restructuring' (Silvey and Lawson 1999: 126).

As Marxian development geography matured, scholars differentiated global South societies in terms of a range of social classes who have unequal power and who struggle over access to resources. Much Marxian development geography has focused on understanding poverty and marginalisation as systematic processes, situating classes in relation to capitalist processes of exploitation and uneven development. Agency in this work is conceptualised through class collectivities and diverse relations of production. For example, Ben Wisner's (1989) work on 'strong basic needs' starts from Marxian concepts of exploitation, inequality and collective political struggle to think about effective responses to poverty and disempowerment in Africa. He argues that poverty must be addressed through the reorganisation of social relations of power, including those of class, gender and sexuality. He argues that participatory politics are critical: a politics which identifies exploitation and concrete actions to challenge injustice in access to land and productive resources. Wisner argues that change comes from the formation of collective identities through which social subjects produce a shared vision of their goals and the actions they will take to achieve them.

Much early radical development geography viewed people in the global South as objects of theorisation rather than as interpretive and informative subjects. Marxist migration work, for example, often viewed migrants as the victims of capitalist transformation as they became disenfranchised in terms of land and labour (Gregory and Piche 1978; Shrestha 1988). Early radical migration research posed important questions about how capitalist resource extraction prompted migration (Taylor 1980; Omvedt 1980), about the ways in which the colonial state displaced peasants into migration streams (Jarosz 1990), and examined how the penetration of commercial agriculture displaced peasant producers (Breman 1979; Murray 1981). In the majority of this work, however, emphasis remains on broader shifts in capitalist political and economic relations, rather than on the migrants themselves (Silvey and Lawson 1999). Marxist work on informal production adopted a similar analytical stance. Much of this work focused on the exploitive connections between formal economy and 'self-employed' or subcontracted producers (Portes, Castells and Benton 1989; Lawson 1995; Bromley and Gerry 1979; Teltscher 1993). Bromley and Gerry's influential volume *Casual Work and Poverty in Third World Cities* (1979) frames poverty in terms of how people are situated within relations of production and employment, and in terms of structural transformations of capitalism. This edited collection provides rich case studies of the urban poor, including the autobiography of a bottle buyer. However, the overall tenor of this collection is about situating the poor in broader political-economic relations and transformations, focusing on poverty-in-employment and workers' structural position in relation to the capitalist economy.

Peasant studies research in geography moved early to problematise Western class categories and to theorise the different social structures in the global South. In contrast to the urban/industrial or national economy focus of Eurocentric Marxist theory, this work differentiates global South societies in terms of distinct economies, particularly within the rural sector. Researchers examine how peasant households respond to processes of agricultural intensification and the penetration of mechanised and commercialised farming practices. They pose questions about how these shifts rework peasant labour systems, gendered power within household divisions of labour and the sustainability of peasant livelihoods. Similar to the migration and informal economy research above, much peasant studies work analyses the relations between capitalist and peasant economies. Peasants are conceptualised in terms of their contested relations to, and differences from, capitalist social relations. For example, Watts (1989) reviews the range of work examining the agrarian question in Africa, focusing on the flexibility of households in adjusting to new conditions of accumulation; the ways in which ecological regulation is conditioned by property rights and social relations of production; how peasants resist the mobilisation of their labour as new production conditions arise; and the dynamics of famine in relation to the changing character of rural production and market systems.

While much of this work continues to emphasise the relations between capitalist and peasant economies, this research engaged early with feminist critiques and opened up the black box of the peasant household to think about the subjects within it, rather than assuming that male heads adequately represented the class position of all members. Geographers began to interrogate the power struggles, tensions, renegotiations of divisions of labour and access to resources taking place within households as they dealt with the structural forces noted above (Carney 1988; Carney and Watts 1990; Jarosz 1993; Hart 1986). The authors unpack the worker/capitalist class subject of Marxist thought and take seriously the ways in which gender and ethnicity inflect people's experiences of, and responses to, D/development processes.

For example, Judy Carney and Michael Watts' (1990) work on the Gambia examines domestic conflicts and struggles over the divisions of productive and reproductive labour that arise with a new irrigated rice project. In order to understand the consequences, costs and negotiations set in motion by this development project, they situate Mandinka households in relation to capitalist production, without reducing these peasant producers to Eurocentric class categories. They argue instead that '...as direct producers they hold direct access to their means of production, yet they may also buy and sell labour – but neither as workers (by virtue of their connections to property) nor as capitalist (since they labour)' (Carney and Watts 1990: 217). Through a detailed historical account of gendered landownership and divisions of paid and unpaid labour within production and the conjugal contract, the authors trace peasant resistance to agricultural modernisation. Their work demonstrates that women's resistance to reorganisations of production cannot be understood merely in class terms, but must also be understood in terms of household struggles over gendered access to land and women's ability to negotiate for remuneration for their labour in rice production. Carney and Watts also demonstrate that differences in ethnicity and cultural practices mediated the success with which women were able to negotiate for property rights, remuneration and a shift in the conjugal contract. Here the subjects of development are understood as people with agency, situated within the constraints and possibilities afforded by economic, cultural and ethnic relations (recall Schroeder's work discussed in chapter 1 as another example, and see also Hapke 2001; Elias and Carney 2005).

This Marxist-feminist work situates subjects within social relations of gender, as well as political-economic relations of power, and then examines the ways in which these positions differentiate experiences of D/development (this is extended to think of difference in terms of race/ethnicity, postcoloniality, sexuality and nationality; chapter 5). Feminist development geographers examine how gender subjectivities, ideologies and identities are employed and contested in capitalist economic restructuring, and how the construction of '... "work-production-public" and "home-reproduction-private" obscures and devalues activities defined as "women's work" wherever it is performed' (England and Lawson 2005: 86). A large literature within feminist development geography examines how these discourses of gender shape experiences, exclusions and possibilities within D/development processes.

For example, geographers have interrogated experiences and contestations around global economic restructuring and export-led manufacturing on the global assembly line. Beverly Mullings' (1999) work with Jamaican data-entry operators examines their strategies of survival and resistance against oppressive working conditions. The data-entry industry in Jamaica demands a docile, disciplined and hard-working labour force of low-paid women workers who are engaged in repetitive and boring work. Despite these difficult conditions, Mullings moves beyond the narrative of the exploited, victimised woman worker to explore how Jamaican women engage in everyday acts of resistance, such as refusal to work overtime, reporting irregularly for work and finger dragging (keying in data at a slower rate). Ironically, despite the ways in which household roles have devalued women's work, these resistance practices are made possible by households in Jamaica wherein practices of reciprocity and obligation, such as income pooling and exchange of unpaid services, provide support for women workers. Households are expansive (often including overseas members who send remittances) and supportive, and so provide a cushion that enables resistance to the harsh discipline of the workplace. Mullings' work reminds us of the complex interactions between social, economic and political dynamics in the different sites of women's lives. See also Altha Cravey's work on Mexican maquiladora workers' daily lives (1997, 1998, 2005) and Melissa Wright's (1997) work on how one woman resisted a representation of her as a 'typical Mexican woman' and was promoted into management in an export-processing factory on the US-Mexican border.

Marxist-feminist work also interrogates the ways in which gender inflects struggles for political voice within workplaces. Feminists have analysed how subjectivity is drawn upon and contested in the relations between 'globalised' capital and 'localised' labour (Nagar et al. 2002: 271). Globalised processes of capitalism tap into local gender identities and ideologies about the nature of work and workers. For example, Lawson's (1995, 1999) research on Ecuadorian garment workers reveals how struggles over narratives of women as 'unskilled seamstresses' rather than 'skilled tailors' contributed to their exclusion from male-dominated tailoring guilds and from political representation for better work conditions. This discourse of skill is deeply gendered in Ecuador. Despite the fact that both tailors and seamstresses are engaged in exactly the same activity (sewing), one business owner explained to me:

> Look, I hire men because, you see, tailoring has always been done by men... because tailoring work is a hard job...making a suit is hard work, you have to make the lapels, you have to have many skills, you see, it isn't like with a

seamstress who makes blouses or a dress, that is simple, that is light work. By contrast, a suit, making and finishing a suit, is extremely hard, it is a lot of work to press the suit properly, with a heavy iron, you have to use a lot of water and to press it very well, this is very hard... (personal interview)

While the speaker emphasises the specific tasks involved in making suits and blouses, he is working hard to construct a skill distinction between the work of male tailors and that of women garment producers, in order to valorise and protect historical privileges given to tailors by the Ecuadorian state. Kim Van Eyck (2002) builds a multi-scaled analysis of how global and national neoliberal restructuring transformed the political and economic security of bank workers in Colombia. She examined labour market restructuring within the banking sector to show how workplace reforms such as downsizing and outsourcing relied explicitly on the marginalisation and sexualisation of women workers. Van Eyck then traced the emergence of new political identities forged in the struggles of women unionists to get male-dominated unions to recognise the specific concerns facing women workers.

Despite many important theoretical advances over mainstream development, early Marxist-feminist work was silent on forms of subjectivity and agency that are constituted through relations of race/ethnicity, sexuality, nationality and the postcolonial status of development subjects. Through their very silence on these issues, these literatures construct a subject, conceptualised in Western class and, subsequently, gendered terms, that was normalised as a white citizen-subject, engaged in politics revolving around production and reproduction issues. We explore these limitations and build on these Marxist-feminist advances in radical development geography in chapter 5.

4.5 Continuities and breaks with post-structural theory

Marxist and Marxist-feminist work is a central intellectual and political strand within critical development geography. As we move to chapter 5, compare how geographers differ in their emphasis on material and cultural/discursive analyses of development and on their ideas about the subjects and terrains of action (for a range of positions see Peet (with Hartwick) 1999; Blaikie 2000; Schuurman 2000a; Bebbington 2000; Corbridge 1990, 1993; Watts 1993; Hart 2001, 2002).[viii] Many geographers are deeply inspired by Marxist theory and primarily motivated by grotesque inequalities across the globe; Peet and Hartwick (1999: 11) find '...still unrealised potentials in progress and modernity', and argue for what they term the fine principles of modernity: emancipation, development and progress, while critiquing their contemporary social form in neoliberalism. Arguments in this vein include Schuurman (2000a), Bebbington (2000) and Corbridge (1993), who emphasise the material experiences of inequality over a concern with the discursive power of development, and stress the ethical and moral imperative for those in development studies to act. For Schuurman (2000a: 9; emphasis in original):

> The very essence of development studies is a normative preoccupation with the poor, marginalised and exploited people in the South. In this sense, there should be in the first place *inequality* rather than *diversity* or *difference* that is the main focus for development studies: inequality of access to power, to resources, to a human existence – in short, inequality in emancipation.

These theorists stress inequality and embrace the potentials of economic growth, arguing that we must critically address the organisation of society and the distribution of the benefits of growth. In short, critical modernists argue that issues of poverty and inequality compel actions and policies that '... rescue modernity's beneficial aspects in new sociopolitical forms' (Peet with Hartwick 1999: 196). Beneficial aspects of modernity, for these theorists, include the social use of economic growth to benefit all people (Peet with Hartwick 1999: 208), or, more concretely, efforts towards universal human rights or technologies, such as those bringing gains in life expectancy (Corbridge 1998). For example, Corbridge (1990: 635) articulates a post-Marxism, not an ex-Marxism, which engages post-structural theory, but retains a

> ...materialist ontology and a commitment to causal analysis and a concept of dermination; it also accepts that people make history, but not under circum- stances of their own choosing, and that the 'economy' is structured by a system- atically uneven distribution of assets and powers that leads to contradictions in the process of accumulation...

In contrast, other geographers (previewing chapter 5) draw on post-struc- tural feminist, post-development and postcolonial theories to critique the truth- claims of modernism and to argue for attention to the vocabularies and narrations of development, as well as the imagery and particular uses of history, employed to construct the world as a terrain in need of intervention (Crush 1995; Watts 1993; Slater 2004). This work attends to the cultural construction of difference, subjectivity and identity, analysing the ways in which the reworking of meanings is central to capitalist and postcolonial restructuring and political transformations (Pred and Watts 1992; Gibson-Graham 1996; Nagar et al. 2002). Paraphrasing Peet (with Hartwick 1999: 124), the distinction between these bodies of thought is that structuralism employs economic language to criticise capitalism, whereas post-structuralism uses cultural language to criticise modernity.

As we see in chapter 5, many post-development and postcolonial scholars do not prioritise social relations of capitalism, but rather emphasise the dominating and homogenising impacts of Western developmentalism, refusing its potentials and analysing instead the ways in which it establishes its authority. These scholars argue that mainstream, Marxist and Western feminist analyses of development have homogenised and simplified histories of development, objectified Third World subjects and silenced other voices and alternative possibilities. Geographers have taken up these ideas to argue that we need historical geographies of development that reveal '...the relations of power that order the world and the words and images that represent those worlds' (Crush 1995: 6).

Notes

[i] I am very grateful to Lucy Jarosz, Neil Smith, Richard Peet, Stuart Corbridge, David Harvey and David Slater for their willingness to share their personal insights on the story of Marxist development geography.

[ii] For insightful, personal accounts of this priod and its political potential, see Nancy Hartsock's introductory essay in *The Feminist Standpoint Revisited* (1998) and Todd Gitlin's *The Sixties: years of hope, days of rage* (1987).

[iii] This section is heavily indebted to research by Jennifer Devine.

[iv] I use this reluctantly as an available descriptive and comparative measure of poverty reported by the World Bank for Sub-Saharan Africa. This measure is extremely heavy-handed because it frames poverty as a singular problem that can be adequately captured by universalizing the US $ as a measure of well-being and development. This universal measure serves to obscure vast differences in access to basic needs by place, gender, ethnicity/race, as well as obscuring enormous issues of social justic and inequality. Diverse people have enormously divergent relationships to Western standards of wealth and consumption and this measure can be deployed to depoliticize and limit the scope of development debate.

[v] To flesh out my brief discussion, see Naila Kabeer's (1994) book *Reversed Realities* for a thorough overview of feminist development thought.

[vi] Students in my seminar (Caroline Faria, Melissa Poe, Dawn Couch, Heather Rule

Day and Steve Hide) are responsible for this creative discussion about the multiple meanings of the term 'fix' and how these various meanings illuminate our analysis of Marxian crisis.

[vii] Globalisation is a poorly specified, chaotic term that has been imprecisely (and voluminously) applied across the social sciences on the right and the left (Martin 2004). While there has been much hype about globalisation in the last two decades (at the time of writing), the processes it refers to are in no sense new – recall the nineteenth-century global expansion of capitalism and imperialism, global flows of trade and finance, and so on. Nonetheless, there are the contemporary globalisation boosters (Toffler and Toffler 1995; Ohmae 1995; Fukuyama 2001), who argue across political and corporate settings that globalisation is the inevitable rise of a borderless world and of reductions in state power as an integral part of the unfolding of capitalism and late modernity. Even critical analyses of globalisation have often served to reinforce a top-down focus on global corporate strategies, a 'global economy' and geopolitical discourses of globality, precisely through their willingness to engage the term and the ideological and political work it is doing to frame gloablisation as inevitable (Gibson-Graham 1996; Nagar et al. 2002).

[viii] Despite their differences, the various 'post-arguments' and critical modernist perspectives both start from a critique of neoliberal development, as represented by the Washington Consensus (discussed in chapter 3).

chapter 5

POST-STRUCTURAL TURNS: DISCOURSE, IDENTITY AND DIFFERENCE

5.1 Contexts I: global shifts in the 'time of the posts'___

According to many, we live in the time of the 'posts' – postindustrialism, postFordism, postMarxism, posthumanism, posthistory, and postmodernism (Best and Kellner 1997: 3)

Development geography is undergoing its own 'time of the posts' at present. Both intellectual and political work in development geography is deeply influenced by shifts towards post-development and postcolonialism. As we discussed in chapter 4, a series of global shifts and upheavals, beginning in the 1960s, transformed political, cultural and economic life across the globe. This tumultuous global context led scholars in diverse directions. As we saw in chapter 4, some moved towards Marxian critiques of mainstream development, whereas for other activists and scholars, these times created the matrix for a turn to 'post' thought in development studies. Recall that our discussion of the 1960s 'and all that' in chapter 4 also set the political, cultural and economic stage for the intellectual shifts we discuss here.

While the prefix 'post' has been attached to many key terms, such as post-Marxism, post-development and postcolonialism, these bodies of theory are not one and the same. There are important differences between these 'posts'. In this chapter I trace post-development thought, from its influential rise in the 1990s to current critiques of its overly romantic engagement with social movements and the local scale. Post-development thought is sceptical of Western development knowledge, its interventions, its constructions of hierarchies based on race, class, gender and postcolonial status. I also discuss postcolonial theory, informed by theorists such as Fanon, Minh-ha, Bhabha,

Mohanty, Spivak and Said, who '... speak to the violence towards, and the marginalisation of, post-colonial subjects and knowledges whose exclusion from metropolitan status is embedded in notions of cultural and racial difference' (Radcliffe 2005: 292). I take up the question of how geographers are building a post-foundational (post-structural) development geography that brings together Marxist-feminist and postcolonial ideas in the concluding chapter 6.

The time of the 'posts' is often broadly termed the postmodern turn in social theory. However, postmodernism is a fuzzy term that is loosely applied to the post-Second World War period, to late capitalism, artistic and architectural styles and to theorisation of cultural formations and debates about subjectivity, class, race, ethnicity, sexuality, postcoloniality, and so on. More generally, it is a wide-ranging movement of cultural critique that is sceptical of the ideals and scientific practices that have dominated Western science and society since the Enlightenment (Sim 1998: 339). Strong (or radical) versions of a postmodern philosophical position reject the search for truth, origins and the idea of progress, assume that meanings are unstable and argue that no one voice or answer is superior to another, but that all are equally relevant in our efforts to represent and interpret the world (Best and Kellner 1997; McDowell and Sharp 1999: 211–15; Hartsock 1998).

Within development geography, the turn to 'post' theory is more post-structural than radically postmodern. Post-structural theory, as its name suggests, moves beyond structural analyses of society and rigorously questions the limits, inclusions and exclusions in social theories. Post-structural development geography nonetheless continues to engage with (rather than refuse) structural processes as they work out in relation to concrete contexts, meanings, histories and cultural productions (Sim 1998; Sarup 1993; McDowell and Sharp 1999). In other words, the crucial difference between postmodern and post-structural theory is that the latter is socially and politically accountable and committed to building constructive practice. This distinction is important because postmodern research is often sceptical, nihilist and refuses to define firm ground from which to take a political stand, and, by contrast, most critical development geography is consciously, socially and politically engaged (Yapa (1996) also makes a similar distinction between sceptical and affirmative postmodernism).

Within geography, post-structural feminist research has taken up these intellectual challenges most fully, starting from the vantage point of those people and places that have been marginalised by development (Barndt 2002; Lawson 1999; Laurie 1997; Jarosz and Qazi 2000). Feminist development geography is raising a series of crucial questions about the possibilities of constructing alliances across difference, both to build theoretical understandings of the processes at work, and to build effective political moments and strategies. This research seeks to explain the paradoxes of development through analyses that focus on: the spaces and scales of development as multiple, intersecting and politically constructed; the cultural construction of multiple dimensions of difference; the exclusion, silencing or erasure of certain development subjects; a concern for justice; and intersecting and multiple axes of identity, including gender, race, nationality and sexuality (Marchand and Parpart 1995; Kabeer 1994). Feminist geographers have expanded the conceptual and analytical terrain of development, as Nagar et al. (2002: 271; emphasis in original) argue:

> ...[S]lowly but surely these feminist studies have reshaped the terrain of development – at both discursive and policy levels – by deeply politicising notions of work; by placing households, shop-floors, hospitals, schools, weekly markets, and diasporic networks in direct relationships with corporations, markets, banks, and development institutions; engaging with people's lived experiences...in all their contradictions; and revealing that these erased and neglected voices...are by no means passive or simply victimised, but actively engaged in struggles over access to resources and over the very definitions of 'development,' 'progress,' 'empowerment,' and 'justice.'

Feminist theorists of development geography are building a simultaneously discursive and material analysis of how inequality is produced through difference in order to engage it more effectively.

This chapter highlights the intellectual space opened up by post-development and postcolonial theory, and the intellectual and political challenges it presents to mainstream, structural Marxist and liberal feminist development geography discussed in previous chapters.[i] As I shall argue in chapter 6, development geography is bringing together theoretical arguments from both post-development and postcolonial thought and putting them in creative tension with Marxist-feminist and antiracist theory (McDowell and Sharp 1999; Longhurst 2002). The result is a development geography broadly characterised by concern with oppressive and unequal power relations; the historical and geographical contexts of privilege and marginalisation; a concern with 'discourse' – the structures of knowledge and power that construct and structure the social realms of everyday life and scientific knowledge; and a conceptual pluralism in which identities and subjectivities are understood as complex and fluid. Post-structural thought in development studies does not entail a complete leap into postmodern ahistoricism, relativism, chaos and pastiche, but rather retains an analysis of multiple oppressions and the possibilities of constructing alternative lives. Despite the moniker 'post', geographers have engaged this body of thought to build constructive and socially accountable analysis, critiquing the more oppressive features of modernist society and engaging with processes of nationality, class, race, sexuality and gender, arguing that these were selectively silenced in earlier development work.[ii]

How, then, are these global and intellectual shifts remaking development geography? As we shall see in this chapter, these shifts have animated a range of substantive questions about the politics and practices of D/development, concerning:

- the nature and role of civil society emerging from these new social, cultural and institutional forms. Geographers are currently grappling with the diverse politics embodied in these social movements; as Watts (2001a: 178) cautions, new forms of politics do *not necessarily entail a progressive politics* and many of these new institutional forms '...substitute market orientated individualism for the radical autonomy of community empowerment' (it is sobering to note that groups such as Aryan Nations and movements such as the Rwandan genocide are also social movements).
- the geographies of governance, including the reworking of relations between the state, labour, business, non-governmental organisations, international institutions and transnational social movements.
- scalar shifts in political organising – shifting emphasis from the national to incorporate the transnational, global and local. Much of this work is shifting spatial registers, not only away from a fixation on the national scale, but also in terms of the importance of networks, of actors and relations of power, complementing a concern with spaces and places in much development geography. For example, there is burgeoning research on multi-scalar political networks organised on issues of ethnic identity, global social justice, environmental activism, and so on.
- collaborating with and learning from actors and subjects across the globe (such as collective indigenous subject positions, transnational social movements) not previously heard in development debates.
- incisive critiques of the 'Development industry', its discourses and institutions. These critiques locate and exoticise Western development thought and argue that its claims to expert development knowledge are actually claims to power over other peoples and places.

In section 5.2 I introduce central elements of 'post' thought. In section 5.3 I discuss geographers' contributions to post-structural development through their theorisation of the range of places, scales and networks that have been excluded or ignored; critical analysis of particular representations of places within development discourse; and attention to the political construction of scales. Post-structural development geography also breaks down conceptual boundaries between 'first' and 'third' worlds and subjects, complementing feminist scholarship in the USA and Britain (see for example Grewal and Kaplan 1994; bell hooks 1990; and Anzaldua and Moraga 1981). This work has pointed to common experiences and political struggles across a range of places of oppression and privilege *within* the West and global South (Nagar et al. 2002; Anzaldua 1990; hooks 1990). In section 5.4, I discuss the contributions geographers are making to theorising the subjects of post-structural development. Building from the previous section, where boundaries between spaces of development in the First and Third Worlds are exploded, I draw on geographers who are reconceptualising the subjects of development and working to recover complexity, difference as well as possibilities for alliances/commonalities in theorisations of women, gender relations and masculinity and femininity, in their re-theorisation of the subjects of development.

5.2 Contexts II: intellectual shifts in the 'time of the posts'

The political, cultural and economic ferment described under 'Contexts I' in chapter 4 set the stage for a series of intellectual shifts that led many to question the certainty of Enlightenment thought and modernist development (discussed in chapters 2 and 3), and to become disillusioned with truth, certainty, rationalism, essence and universality. Best and Kellner suggest the links between political and theoretical upheaval, but take pains not to claim that one produced the other in a determinist fashion.

> During the 1960s, consequently, a general intellectual mood of change and the dissolution of old paradigms was joined by a spectacular political upheaval and struggle throughout the world, along with the emergence of new forms of thought, culture, technology, and life, which would produce the matrix for the postmodern turn... (Best and Kellner 1997: 9)

As you read this section, think about how post-development and postcolonial theory remake development, its substantive scope, its actors and subjects, and think about how and where these ideas circulate and to what effects.

Figure 5.1 'Encuentro in Chiapas, 2002'. Source: CIEPAC

There are several common elements running through post-development and postcolonial theory. First, this work attends to subjugated knowledges and excluded voices and actors, taking seriously their arguments for alternative analyses of socially and environmentally just development. Second, the 'posts' also critique metanarratives such as the inevitability of neo-liberalisation and globalisation, the universal pretensions of modernity and singular representations of development subjects. Post-development and postcolonial scholars and activists insist on more nuanced and complex theorisations of subjects and subjectivities in all their messiness and contradictions. As Slater (1993) argues, this provides a way out of thinking a Marxist, essentialised class subject which could never adequately account for Latin American informal homeworkers, or African peasant farmers, and so on. Rather, 'post' scholarship analyses the simultaneous forces of racialised, gendered and classed oppression that face, and also construct, hybrid subjects of development in postcolonial societies. This attention to complexity goes beyond theorising development subjects to include a broad emphasis on plurality and open questioning about the diverse ways 'Development' plays out in specific places and political-economic contexts, rather than theorising deterministic closure and essentialism (Slater 1993; Parpart and Marchand 1995). Third, they also engage a series of theoretical shifts, emerging from attention to discourse and a concern with the intimate connections between knowledge, truth and power. This work on discourse critiques representations of places and people in the global South as dependent 'other' to Western Development, analyses the vocabularies and imageries employed to construct a world in need of development interventions and examines the ways in which dominant development discourse operates through treaties, institutions, 'professional experts' and bureaucratic procedures to establish a regime of truth about the 'natural' state of the world. In short, post-development and postcolonial thought exoticises the West by demonstrating that powerful Western Development knowledge is culturally and historically specific rather than universally 'true'.

Despite important commonalities that distinguish these post-structural approaches to development from the work we discussed in earlier chapters, post-development and postcolonial theory differ in important ways. In this section, I trace the main contributions of each to critical development studies to set the stage for our discussion of contemporary development geography.

Post-development critics and activists do more than just critique Western Development. Indeed much post-development thinking emerges from political actors in social movements who argue for both the need and the real possibility of alternative ideas and actions that push beyond Western Developmentalism. Social movements in the global South exist in enormous numbers and include a range of actors, scales of mobilisation and political agendas. Diverse social movements include: urban popular movements, such as the widespread IMF food riots of the 1980s and 1990s in myriad places, including Peru, Egypt, Ghana, Philippines, Turkey and Ecuador (Walton and Seddon 1994: 39–40); indigenous and peasant movements organising in protest of neoliberal policies and in defense of cultural and land rights, such as CONAIE (Confederation of Indigenous Nationalities of Ecuador), CSUTBC (Union Confederation of Peasant Workers of Bolivia); the MST (Landless Workers' Movement) in Brazil, the FSSCA (Foundation for Self-Sufficiency in Central America) in El Salvador; the Zapatistas of Chiapas and the National Land Committee in South Africa; women's movements struggling for social justice and economic rights, such as SEWA in India and Grameen Bank in Bangladesh, and Madre, an international human rights organisation working on reproductive rights, violence against women and women against war; human rights movements, such as women organising around political disappearances and in transitions to democracy in Chile, Peru and Argentina (see Jaquette 1989), and the Treatment Action Campaign, organising for greater access to HIV/AIDS treatments in South Africa; and environmental groups, such as the famous Chipko in India, and global movements such as Friends of the Earth and Third World Network. Throughout the global South, groups are organising around identities and issues that have been ignored or discredited in much development theory (these arguments are gathered together in the collection by Rahnema and Bawtree 1997).

Alternative social movements occur in many forms that are not inherently emancipatory or left-leaning in their politics. Our post-9/11 world raises the spectre of political Islamism that is global in scope, anti-imperialist, rooted in historical and particular religious and nationalist commitments (Watts 2003). As Watts argues, Islamism presents a more fundamental (and indeed more violent) challenge than the social movements listed above in its decentring of secular nationalism and invocations of religious fundamentalist forms of governance as an alternative to contemporary postcolonial states. The key point here is that social movements are sometimes exclusionary and oppressive, producing ambivalent or ever violent forms of development alternatives. Alternative (post-)development movements, then, encompass a dizzying diversity of participants, positions and beliefs. While post-development research has overemphasised the emancipatory potential of social movements, there is no singular, unified position or engagement with states or with the Development establishment and this is precisely the point. In the very diversity of their analyses and politics, activists' work has influenced (some would say transformed) the ways in which intellectuals, teachers and development actors in the West understand the 'work of development' (in all its senses). Post-development work is examining both openings and closures around the polyvalent concept of development, investigating new political spaces that are opened up by the rise of new scales of governance (Newstead 2002) or 'private-public alliances' for development (Oglesby 2002).

The politics and identities of these diverse movements emerge from situated experiences with Development and so is it meaningless to generalise their analyses and messages. Rather, post-development theory is built from detailed engagements with specific actors in order to shift development debate and action. For example, the following declaration was produced by 25 participants of the Latin American Consultation of Women for the Construction of Peace, which brought together small farmers, indigenous groups, human rights activists, and womens organisations from 11 countries in Latin America.[iii] It provides one illustration of the sorts of voices and political movements from across the globe that are educating scholars to re-theorise development processes and agendas in this

Figure 5.2 Women in Oaxaca rallying for the Partido Revolcionario Democratica, (2004).
Source: Lise Nelson, University of Oregon

'time of the posts'. The purpose of the consultation was to reflect on the fundamental role of women in the search for peace and in defending life in high-conflict
social and political contexts, and to allow participants to share their own experiences and strategies for constructing a culture of peace. This Declaration was
disseminated across the Americas on 8 March 2003 – International Women's
Day. In similar gatherings across the continent, women discussed their struggles
to defend the human, economic, political and cultural rights of women as well
as their demands for full citizenship rights (Figure 5.2 depicts indigenous women
in Michoacán, Mexico, supporting Partido de la Revolución Democrática in 2004).

**Box 5.1 Declaration of Latin American Women
Constructing Peace**

BEWARE, FOR HERE WALK WOMEN WITH MEMORY AND LOVE
FOR LATIN AMERICA!

Women from Mexico, Guatemala, El Salvador, Venezuela, Colombia,
Ecuador, Peru, Bolivia, Brazil, Argentina and Uruguay. With support from
women from East Timor, Holland, Belgium and Canada.

One must undress memory in order to reconstruct true history and awaken those fireflies that sleep in the eyes of our sons and daughters. Nora Murillo (Guatemala)

As women struggling for life, constructing hope and resisting war, united in Quito, Ecuador from February 24–28 2003, we declare that peace is a permanent construction of respect, justice, inclusion, equity, and solidarity. Peace is that which promotes ethical consensus, and politicians who guarantee the enforcement of integral human rights for women and men, changing the power structures found in our homes and in public spaces.

Nevertheless, we declare that:

A historic regional tendency toward militarisation is becoming more pronounced by the American government's intervention in our countries through the presence of troops, economic coercion, military bases and training camps, and local police units, all of which is expressed in Plan Cabañas in Argentina, Plan Dignidad in Bolivia, Plan Colombia, etc.

In the spheres of economy and politics, Plan Puebla-Panamá, the Andean Regional Initiative, the Free Trade Area of the Americas (FTAA), and the Andean-Mesoamerican Plan are being thrust upon us. These plans are expressions of the interests of transnational corporations and multilateral institutions such as the IMF, WTO, and World Bank.

The neoliberal model has intensified exclusion and discrimination based on gender, ethnicity, race, and class. It has lead to increasing poverty and marginalisation, a growing number of refugees, and the displacement of women, children, young adults and the elderly. This model favours surrendering of our natural resources and biodiversity; and has intensified violations of integral human rights, with the consequences of increased social conflict and decreased security, and women have suffered from both public and domestic violence.

Faced with this situation, the women of Latin America and the Caribbean, as bearers of life, recognising ourselves as permanent builders of peace, in both the home and in society, with experience and dedication in the search for our disappeared loved ones and in the struggle for justice and participation in the peace process:

We declare our total repudiation of war, the processes of intervention in Latin America, militarisation, and all forms of violation of integral human rights, which provoke suffering in the lives of all people.

> We state our repudiation of the threats against human rights defenders in Latin America and the Caribbean who struggle against impunity, and we demand respect from the United States for our integrity and our lives.
>
> We recognise and appreciate the historical presence of African and indigenous peoples, who inspire the hope that a just and peaceful world is possible.
>
> We, female builders of peace, call on all people to show their solidarity with all people committed to free and sovereign Latin America.
>
> We are women who defend life, and we defend the right of self-determination as a means of transforming society.
>
> We want a world where everyone has the right to live in dignity, justice, peace, and liberty.
>
> This declaration was translated by Emily Dulcan for the Center for Economic and Political Investigations of Community Action (CIEPAC, ciepac@laneta.apc.org) and disseminated by CIEPAC in *Chiapas Today* Bulletin No. 335. It is quoted here with permission from CIEPAC.

This declaration is just one product of the myriad social movements, organised around diverse identities, issues, strategies and contexts, that are challenging dominant Development projects and nationalist states, and articulating alternative visions of social and environmental justice and alternative developments in the global South. Post-development scholarship brings into view the analyses of people situated in diverse locations who are challenging state and market formations and actively reworking the multiple meanings and processes of development. For example, Esteva and Prakash's (1998) book *Grassroots Post-Modernism* emerges from direct experiences of organising and activism. They argue for a fundamental shift in analysis and action, rooted in the local soil of cultures and people power. Their grass-roots postmodernism asserts the legitimacy of indigenous and other marginalised peoples as full citizens, demands attention to histories of disenfranchisement, emphasises human rights to land and livelihoods, emphasises alternative values and ecologies that can realise social and environmental justice for those who have been excluded, and demands rights to cultural survival. Their alternative theorisation and practice is produced through moments such as the 1996 'Intercontinental Encounter for

Humanity and Against Neoliberalism', where thousands of people from over 40 countries convened in Aguascalientes in the Lacandon jungle of Mexico to build solidarity, while also creating political visions and actions specific to the defence of their particular livelihoods and communities. The gathering included members of social movements representing

> ...feminists, gays and lesbians, blacks, workers, peasants, the unemployed, national liberation movements, leftist political parties or organisations and former guerilleros... *they did not attempt to think the globe, or even less to manage it.* They did not abandon their own cultural roots and backgrounds. They prevented each other from falling into nice-sounding abstractions or plastic works – aping their counterparts in the 'Global Project'... (Esteva and Prakash 1998: 177; emphasis mine).

These new voices and identities are struggled over at the grass roots and have also been brought into development studies by post-development scholars. These thinkers argue for an alternative *to* development, rejecting the ways of thinking, lifestyles and social values of modernist development. Scholars such as Majhid Rahnema, Wolfgang Sachs, Ivan Illich, Vandana Shiva and Arturo Escobar (see Box 5.2), among many others, emphasise the destructive forces of Western developmentalism, and argue instead for a plurality of visions and actions in the face of developmentalism and a reaffirmation of alternative spiritual, feminist, antiracist and ecological values and ways of living. The *Development Dictionary*, edited by Wolfgang Sachs (1992) and *The Post-Development Reader*, edited by Majhid Rahnema and Victoria Bawtree (1997), provide compilations of many post-development writings. The scholarship of these writers is intimately connected to their own and others' activism. In other words, the insights and arguments of post-development thought are located in the politics of diverse, situated social movements.

Box 5.2 Escobar on the discourse of Development

Arturo Escobar, in his 1995 book *Encountering Development*, is inspired by Foucault's ideas (Box 2.1). Escobar sought to make sense of how post-Second World War, mainstream Development, a failed project in terms of declining social and economic conditions for the majority, maintained its dominant position despite its dismal record. He argued that Foucault's theorisation of '...the dynamics of discourse and power

---

in the representation of social reality' (Escobar 1995: 5) can reveal how dominant Development discourses become hegemonic and how they disallow alternative arguments and understandings of development. Escobar analysed mainstream Development theories as part of a discursive regime of truth that claimed universal expertise (denying its own cultural and historical specificity), while at the same time situating alternative arguments about development as specific, subjective and inferior to scientific, technocratic analyses of both 'development problems' and 'development solutions'. Drawing from Foucault, Escobar works out the ways in which mainstream definitions of the 'problems of development', such as 'overpopulation', 'poverty' and 'famine', come to be understood as essential truths about the global South. He is interested in how these problems came to be defined as central for the Development project, and the ways that this focus limited what could be included as legitimate issues for action. He illustrates his arguments through close examination of the politics and practices of rural health and nutrition programmes in Latin America, and attends to representations of peasants, women and the environment in development writings and how these are resisted as people engage in alternative ways of living. Peet and Hartwick (1999: 149) argue that Escobar provides a key link between distinct elements of 'post' theory. He draws on Foucault to critique Development discourse and so clear the way for alternative visions and action. This commitment to making space for alternative understandings of (or radical alternatives to) development links Escobar's work to the arguments of post-development activists discussed above.

Post-development activism and scholarship has been a key intervention in development debates since the 1990s. Authors such as Escobar showed how the idea of development is deployed for both geopolitical and geo-economic purposes – foregrounding both state-centred political interests as well as globalising entrepreneurial concerns (see Sparke and Lawson 2003). This emphasis on the power of discourse shifts our analyses beyond the functionalist and materialist readings in dependency and Marxist thought (see for example Crush 1995). However, post-development work is limited by its constructing of an oppositional binary between Development and post-development. Critics argue that this binary misrepresents the contingent, multidirectional and ambivalent ways in which D/development plays out (Lehman 1997; Sivaramakrishnan and Agrawal 2003). This oppositional framing of Development constructs a homogeneous global South, as well as resistant subaltern Southern subjects set up in opposition to dominant Northerners and international Development institutions (Corbridge 1998; Radcliffe 2005; Gidwani 2002; Slater 2004; Gibson-Graham 2005). Post-development work also constructs a populist and reactionary reading of responses and engagements with D/development in the global South, ignoring the multidirectional exercises and entanglements of power flowing through NGOs (representing a range of politics and places), postcolonial governments and state–society relations, and new forms of governmentality produced by policies emanating from international development institutions. Finally, there is an emphasis in post-development work on a singular Western modernity which ignores the histories of colonialism, exchange and regulation with the rest of the world that actually constitute Western Enlightenment accounts of 'progress' and 'development', as well as the different modernities emerging in other parts of the world (Hall 1992; Gidwani 2002; Sivaramakrishnan and Agrawal 2003; Slater 2004).

Nonetheless, development debates have been indelibly changed by post-development and postcolonial thought (see Boxes 5.2 and 5.3). By historicising and deconstructing Western development discourse, postcolonial theorists argue that Western forms of knowledge about development are always tied up with Western power and influence (Power 1998). Postcolonial theory also critiques singular representations of the people and places of development, rigorously questioning the limits of theoretical arguments within development studies by analysing the politics of their inclusions and exclusions and attending to the cultural production of difference (McDowell and Sharp 1999: 214). Postcolonial thinkers argue that Western development theory is severely constrained by our Western cultural context, our education in modernist ideas about economic growth and the totalising character of modernist discourses (about colonialism, development, globalisation, and so on) that justify Western dominance and close down other ways of thinking about the world. Paraphrasing Nagar, Lawson, McDowell and Hanson (2002: 263), modernist development discourses construct capitalist economies and Western cultural forms as the only possible path and future for the globe. The result is a 'development myopia', where we as researchers or activists cannot even see or imagine alternatives.

Box 5.3 Postcolonial thought and development as situated knowledge

Postcolonial theory has radically rethought representations of the 'Third World' and the formation of social identities produced through the interactions of indigenous cultures and colonialism (and Western imperialism more broadly). Some influential authors include Edward Said, Gyatri Spivak, Homi Bhabha, Chandra Mohanty, Trinh Minh-ha and V. Y. Mudimbe (see Childs and Williams 1997 for an introduction to postcolonial theory). Overall, postcolonial scholars underscore the heterogeneity of colonial powers and the multiple subjectivities produced in colonial and postcolonial contexts. In their insistence on multiplicity and ambivalence, these theorists disrupt the possibility of thinking a universal subject, or history, of development and emphasise the importance of theorising situated, plural understandings and effects in development (see chapter 6 in Power 2003 for more detail). Summarising a rich literature, these scholars argue that colonial and imperialist encounters produce complex and ambivalent subject positions that are often homogenised and simplified in Western theorisations of colonialism, Development and globalisation. For example, Spivak critiqued the subaltern studies project that sought to reinsert the perspective of Indian peasants into historical analyses of colonialism on the subcontinent, and to link their erasure to the dynamics of contemporary Indian politics. In attempting to construct a unified subaltern voice, Spivak argued that subaltern studies scholars ignored the multiple and intersecting networks of gender, ethnicity, caste, class, and so on, through which particular subject positions (and hence interpretations and politics) are constructed in specific sites and moments. Postcolonial theorists have also highlighted the importance of discourse in constructing objects of colonial and Development intervention, such as colonial subjects and entire continents, as well as for understanding forms of resistance to those dominations. Bhabha analyses the complex and contradictory processes through which both colonial and colonised subjectivities are produced. He emphasises the ways in which the entry of colonised peoples into colonial (and, for us, development) projects could subvert as well as reinforce dominant power relations. Mohanty critiqued Western feminism for its blindness to varied subject positions and political agendas of women in the global South. She argued

> that feminist development work engaged in a 'colonialist move',
> constructing a caricature, a homogenised 'Third World Woman', with
> 'needs' and 'problems', but no ability to organise in her own interests.

Postcolonial theorists move beyond these limits by arguing that Western intervention does not look the same from other cultural and political locations that are situated in subordinate relations to the West. They deconstruct the singular or universal subject of development and open space for reconceptualising postcolonial subjectivities in all their aspects. For example, Chandra Mohanty's influential essay 'Cartographies of Struggle' (1991) challenges mainstream and liberal feminist development theory for conceptualising subjects on the basis of a singular cultural or economic characteristic, or a geographic location such as 'Indian', 'peasant' or 'third world woman'. These labels, produced in the political-historical context of mainstream development, construct 'peasants' and 'third world women' as apparently coherent 'groups', with 'needs' that justify development interventions due to their supposedly 'backward', 'ignorant' and 'less evolved' status.

Consider the *World Development Report 2000/2001* (World Bank 2000) that focuses on attacking poverty in the global South. The report presents an arbitrary and bureaucratic definition of 'poor people' as the 2.8 billion people who live on less that $2 per day. While the report goes on to point out differences in poverty by gender and geographic location, the emphasis remains on this singular economic definition as the unifying characteristic that justifies targeting 'poor people' with Development interventions. This institutional concept of 'poverty' turns a political problem within particular social relations into an abstract and universal measurement problem. The challenge becomes moving people from $2 a day to $5 a day, rather than the issue of redistribution and justice within particular societies (Mitchell 2004). Similarly, the label 'poor people' is not meaningful or coherent because it obscures diverse groups, processes and relationships to Western standards of wealth and consumption. By contrast, postcolonial theory argues that meaningful subject positions and political alliances are defined by people on their own terms and in relation to specific configurations of racism, sexism, colonialism and imperialism (Mohanty 1991).

Taking the fluidity of meanings and identity further, postcolonial scholars argue that a particular identity or symbol will itself have multiple meanings, depending on the context in which it is being deployed and interpreted, rather than a label having some universal and stable meaning. Consider the example of *subcomandante* Marcos of the Zapatistas of Southern Mexico, whose masked face is a symbol for diverse groups – but a symbol that takes on different meanings depending on the place and politics from which it is being interpreted.

> 'Marcos is gay in San Francisco, a black person in South Africa, Asian in Europe, a Chicano in San Isidro, an anarchist in Spain, a Palestinian in Israel, an indigenous person in the streets of San Cristóbal...a Jew in Germany, an ombudsman in the Department of Defense, a feminist in a political party... In other words, Marcos is a human being in this world. Marcos is every untolerated, oppressed, exploited minority that is beginning to speak and every majority that must shut up and listen. He is every untolerated group searching for a way to speak, their way to speak...' (Autonomedia 1994: 312–13, quoted in Esteva and Prakash 1998)

Building from this unstable symbol of Marcos, postcolonial scholarship also engages in a critique of meaning and analysis of discourse. This work is informed by philosophical debates among French post-structuralist theorists, including Derrida, Baudrillard and Lacan, but has been influenced most directly by Michel Foucault (see Best and Kellner 1997; Sarup 1993; Sim 1998, for useful summaries of their ideas; also refer back to Box 2.1). Postcolonial scholars view all knowledge about development as culturally and historically specific – even when particular theories claim universal applicability. Western Development discourse, for example, has been an important object of study (see Box 5.3), as I discussed in chapter 2. The term 'discourse' describes the structures of knowledge, truth and power that construct and shape the social realms of both everyday life and specialised development interventions. A postcolonial emphasis on discourse shifts the object of development studies from standardised categories such as 'Third World Woman' or 'traditional peasant society' to analysis of Western knowledge about, and power over, 'Development':

> [postcolonial scholars] have interrogated the language of development policies and planners, particularly the way they (re)present their Third World clients, the solutions proposed for those clients and the role of development specialists in this process (Parpart 1995: 226)

Consider the following three examples, which critique the dominating and homogenising impacts of discourses of the Western Development industry. Development discourse rests on a series of *enduring narratives* to construct and justify policy interventions. One of the most pervasive of these narratives is the idea that countries of the global South are poor, hungry and environmentally fragile because they are 'overpopulated'. In other words, they are bursting at the borders and filled with people of unbridled fertility. This simplistic equation of poverty with 'too many people' suggests that large numbers and high densities stand in the way of development. And yet, even the most cursory glance at global population statistics challenges this claim, since the United States, Japan and Russia are among the 10 most populous countries of the globe. This emphasis in Development circles on solving population growth diverts attention from Western materialism and high consumption, which are major causes of environmental decline and poverty. The focus on 'overpopulation' as the central problem allows consumption to still be almost universally seen as a desirable goal of development policies (Durning 1992: 21). Using the example of the Green Revolution, Yapa (1996) demonstrates incisively how discourse actively constructs problems, objects and solutions for development. Farmers were classified by Green Revolution agents as 'progressive' or 'backwards' entirely in terms of their response to new high-yielding seeds. This discourse not only constructs farmers exclusively within the logic of Green Revolution thought, but also quietly constructs the academics and practitioners who produce these labels as expert and knowing subjects who hold the 'solution' for poor farmers.

> In South Asia, capitalist farmers with access to large areas of irrigated land and to capital for expensive inputs were transformed into 'progressive farmers', while poor farmers who could not afford to respond and intelligent farmers who actively rejected new seeds for ecological reasons were transformed into 'backward farmers'... The description of farmers as 'progressive' or 'backward' had little to do with the characteristics of farmers themselves; these labels were mere names imposed on the farmers by the productivist logic of a technology discourse (Yapa 1996: 713)

Development discourse also constructs its *objects as existing outside of history* rather than as products of specific histories of colonisation and incorporation into external circuits of political and economic power. For example, James Ferguson (1990), in *The Anti-politics Machine: 'Development', Depoliticisation and Bureaucratic Power in Lesotho*, contrasts a World Bank representation of Lesotho as a 'traditional peasant subsistence society' with its colonial history of trade and labour relations with South Africa. The invocation of 'peasant subsistence society' implies a predominantly agricultural economy that is static and introverted. However, Ferguson's analysis of the political-economic history of the country reveals that farmers have long engaged in commercial trade and that the country has exported wage labourers to the capitalist economy of South Africa for decades, and that labour migration dates from the earliest contact with European settlers. Thus Western arguments about the need for external intervention to bring roads, markets and credit in order to 'Develop' the country rest on a representation that ignores the fact that these are already present and do not explain continuing poverty in the country.

Postcolonial scholarship also *deconstructs the notion of the Western 'development expert'* and development knowledge as apolitical expertise, building on Foucault's (1980a, 1980b) insights about the rise of a professional middle class in nineteenth-century Europe. Foucault argued that the privilege and status of the middle class were sustained by their claims to certain knowledge and expertise. In similar vein, 'development experts' maintain their own global or national position by reference to their superior technical and managerial knowledge about how to produce Development in the global South. Chris Tapscott (1995), for example, examines historical narratives of 'development professionals' in South Africa, tracking the ways in which particular development logics legitimated and also depoliticised apartheid. Tapscott (1995: 180) unearths '...the writing of a number of developmentalists who, under the guise of pseudoscientific theory, continued to affirm the inherent fatalism, communalism and traditionality of African society'. In the 1970s, scholars and policy-makers compared the economic development of the Bantustans to other countries in Africa, ignoring in the process '...their racist and unbreakable relations to the dominant South African economy' (Tapscott 1995: 180). In his essay, Tapscott traces development rhetoric forwards, examining the ways in which the language of development shifted (literally), from Afrikaans to English and from ministries of the state to universities and think tanks, as the South African economy and society fell into crisis. In this period, 'development experts' shifted their analysis and institutional positioning, while maintaining control of scientific development as it was deployed to restructure apartheid. Most interesting in Tapscott's analysis is his tracking of the ways in which development discourse is reworked and redeployed by different political actors over time – suggesting that these discourses can produce political openings as well as closures. Post-structural work on 'expert knowledge' can reveal both how Development theory is deployed to perpetuate elite 'expertise' and intervention, but also how critical, alternative perspectives on development can rework these very meanings and power moves (Marchand and Parpart 1995; Mitchell 2004).

Taken together, all these aspects of post-structural analysis have substantially expanded debate within development studies and development geography, as Marchand and Parpart (1995: 11) point out:

> [T]he critique of modernity and Western hegemony, the focus on difference and identity, the emphasis on the relationship between language and power, the attention to subjugated knowledge(s) and the deconstruction of colonial and postcolonial representations of the South as dependent 'other' have much to say to those involved in the development business...

The challenge to development geography from the 'posts' is not for Western scholars to move marginalised people from silence to voice, but rather it is to learn to listen. Feminist scholarship has laid out our challenge, as in bell hooks' (1990: 208) call to black women in the USA: '...our struggle has not been to emerge from silence into speech but to change the nature and direction of our speech, to make a speech that compels listeners, one that is heard'. The work of post-structural development thinking and practice challenges Western theorists to decentre, provincialise and exoticise the West, and in the process to open their ears and minds to other speaking subjects, producing different understandings and alternative projects. Rather than 'talk about' others who are the subjects of their progressive scholarship (Crush 1991: 408), Donna Haraway (2000) calls us to build 'worked knowledges' or radically new understandings, which require us to move into spaces where all have something at risk in order to really learn and construct alternative developments.

The post-structural challenge for those engaged in development work is similar to that described by Gloria Anzaldua for US theorists of colour. She sees the challenge as formulating new positions that are in between communities and academies, that construct borderland worlds of expression and analysis, that recover 'blanked out' realities and

> change the focus from whitewoman's exclusionary practices to address the quality of what has been included and the nature of this inclusion. If we have been gagged and disempowered by theories, we can also be loosened and empowered by theories. (Anzaldua 1990: xxvi)

In sections 5.3 and 5.4, I examine geographic research that contributes to this post-structural challenge with its emphases on difference, diversity and the discourses of development by articulating diverse geographies of development, and by highlighting how subjects of development are constituted, and act, in relation to the exercise of power through D/development.

5.3 Geographies of post-structural developments

This section addresses two questions. First, how have the ideas of post-structural development (specifically, insights from post-development and post-structural theory) contributed to the remaking of geographical analyses of development? Second, in what ways are geographers contributing to the interdisciplinary field of post-structural development studies? This field employs concepts of discourse, difference and postcolonial identities to read against the grain of development thinking. Geographers are extending this work through attention to '…the power-laden processes through which space and scale are produced and redefined' (Hart 2002b: 815). I do not present an exhaustive review of geographical work, but rather I focus on the problems being identified and new insights gained, drawing on selected examples. Also see Marcus Power's (2003: 6) *Rethinking Development Geographies* and David Slater's (2004) *Geopolitics and the Post-Colonial* for book-length re-examinations of geographies of development from a post-structural perspective.

5.3.1 Rethinking place/space

Post-structural geographers posit relational understandings of place and space as entry points for creating more nuanced and theoretically creative understandings of development discourses and practices. Post-structural geography is highly indebted to Marxist-feminist theorisations (discussed in chapter 4), extending their emphasis on how capitalist and patriarchal processes reconfigure place and space by attending to the historical and cultural construction of relations of race, coloniality and indigenousness. These conceptualisations disrupt mainstream constructions of places that rested on all-encompassing categories such as 'undeveloped', 'backwards' or 'failed'. Geographers are also critical of post-development's construction of a unified 'local' always in opposition, reaction and resistance to a 'global'. Post-structural development geography starts instead from fluid and relational concepts of place/space that build analyses of the failures of D/development by locating a particular place's experience in relation to its geopolitical context, and by building comparative analyses of the complex, and often contradictory, operations of development processes across places (in the context of historical geographies of colonisation and state formation; racial, gender and ethnic differences; civil society formations and struggles; and geo-histories of access to land and resources).

Geographers are building critical analyses of the ties between places within the West and global South that connect wealth and poverty, privilege and subordination across a range of networked places. For example, Freidburg's (2004) book *French Beans and Food Scares* engages in multi-sited ethnography to connect Zambia and the UK, as well as Burkina Faso and France, through an investigation of the transnational green bean commodity chain. Her work interrogates how transnational trade relations work out in the context of colonial histories, culturally specific ideas about good food and place-specific constructs of food safety. She traces how each particular commodity chain constructs labour conditions, pay rates and relations of inequality and opportunity between producers and consumers (Freidburg 2004). Lucy Jarosz (1996) compares similarities and differences in the situation of farm-workers in the globalised fresh fruit and vegetable industry in South Africa and the USA. Her comparative research sheds light on competitive practices which drive changes in gender divisions of labour, growing reliance upon contract and temporary labour, and ways workers reproduce livelihoods from specific locations within this shifting production system. Judy Carney (2001) examines how West African rice seeds and cultivation techniques were imported to the USA by Africans forced into slavery. She demonstrates the importance of not only slave labour, but also the importation of seeds and techniques, to the rise of industrial agriculture in the American South. These authors connect a Marxian political-economy of food production with a rich analysis of the cultural politics and forms of regulation that produce regimes of production and consumption, forged in the reworking of postcolonial relations between North and South.

These scholars, as well as Cindi Katz, Gillian Hart (discussed in chapter 4) and Tad Mutersbaugh (chapter 2), analyse the connections between apparently discrete events and places in order to articulate a politics of connection (but not simplistic sameness). Through conceptualising a 'local that is constitutively global' (Katz 2001: 1214), researchers are revealing connections between sweatshop production in London and export processing in Bangladesh, rice production in the Southern USA and the slave trade, and between modernised agriculture in Sudan, Burkina Faso, Zambia and Mexico and transforming cultures of food consumption in the North. Despite the material and historical differences between these places, scholars are demonstrating that while capitalist restructuring, processes of deskilling labour, the production of racialised and gendered difference, disinvestments in social reproduction and deindustrialisation, are not identical processes across all places, they are also *not separate or unconnected*. A new politics of connection is enabled by articulating crucial connections between places and processes: this reveals the ways in which globalised processes of capitalist restructuring are discursively separated as 'deindustrialisation' in Western societies and 'modernisation' in postcolonial contexts.

This geographical research complements and deepens the post-development work by Escobar, Rahnema and Bawtree, Sachs and Esteva and Prakash, which bears witness to the contradictions and violences of mainstream Development, articulates alternative visions of human-friendly development and builds solidarity that is respectful of difference. Development geography is certainly informed by the work of social movements, NGOs and postcolonial state–society relations, but also pushes beyond post-development's local-scale emphasis. Geographers are theorising globalised social relations of production, reproduction and state-building, which connect diverse sites in relations of unequal power. These analyses connect processes such as welfare reform in the United States (with its particular impacts in Harlem, for example) with structural adjustment policies in Sudan (Katz 2004). These post-structural geographies of place and connection analyse specific material processes, such as environmental change, economic restructuring and social disinvestment in their complex relations to each other within and across places.

In these ways, this geographical work advances and extends post-structural emphases on difference and situated knowledge. Rather than solely focusing on a particular knowing subject, geographers are literally locating this subject in the material histories and geographies that produces subjectivity and identity. As Katz (2001: 1230) explains:

> [S]ituatedness suggests location in abstract relation to others but not any specific geography, leading to a politics of 'sites' and 'spaces' from which materiality is largely evacuated... ignoring the difference that space makes diminishes those political responses by avoiding the ways specific historical geographies embody and help reproduce particular social relations of power and production.

Putting notions of situated knowledge in creative tension with the material specificities of places and their geopolitical locations makes possible the sorts of politics that trace how D/development processes are connected and reproduce social relations of power (see also Bondi 1993; Mitchell 1997; Hart 2002a; Katz 2004; Slater 2004).

In addition to highlighting geographies and politics of connection, post-structural analyses of place critique Western Development discourse. This takes several forms, such as revealing actually existing alternatives to mainstream Development, as in Gibson-Graham's detailed empirical engagements with place, which work against metanarratives of 'development' or 'antidevelopment' by producing detailed case studies in the USA, Australia and the Philippines that examine in detail diverse ecologies of productivity and '...discourse[s] of economic difference' (Gibson-Graham 2005: 6). For example, they work in Jagna Municipality in the Southern Philippines in collaboration with practitioners, planners and organisers to make credible a range of economic practices, shared traditions and knowledges. By seeing the legitimacy of these alternative economies, people in communities work against the monocultural logic of capitalist development to reveal the diverse economic practices and relations that actually exist in places (Gibson-Graham 1996, 2005). Similarly, Curry (2003) builds a cultural and historical analysis of the persistence of gift exchange in the context of industrial oil-palm production in Papua New Guinea. He illustrates that the persistent importance of non-market economic practices signals the multiple ways in which people construct livelihoods and communities, and suggests that these practices reveal that alternatives to capitalist development are already being enacted.

Post-structural theorists deconstruct mainstream development discourse by locating and 'provincialising' the West as a specific cultural context that achieved political and economic power through its histories of colonial and imperial relations with places of the global South (Power 2003; Crush 1995). Slater (1993) points to the geopolitical enframing of development theory, examining the ways in which mainstream 'Development' discourse and practices have been deployed to exercise spatial power over a postcolonial globe (see also Escobar 1995; Watts 2000). For example, US policy towards sub-Saharan Africa from the 1960s to the 1980s was shaped by competition with the former Soviet Union, with US assistance to the region reaching its high point in the mid-1980s. Once the second leading aid donor to Africa, today the USA has fallen into fourth place, behind France, Germany and Japan (Table 5.1 and www.foreignpolicy-infocus.org). Israel, despite being a high-income country (ranked 19th in the world), is the single largest recipient of US foreign aid (almost a quarter of the US foreign aid budget). On a per capita basis, each Israeli citizen received approximately $500 of US aid in 1997, while a citizen of sub-Saharan Africa received only $3 (Council for a Sustainable World 1997).

Table 5.1: The Geopolitics of USAID

Region	1999 population (1000s)	2000 population (1000s)	1999 USAID (1000s)	2000 USAID (1000s)	1999 USAID Per Capita (US Dollars)	2000 USAID Per Capita (US Dollars)
South & East Asia	1,715,660	1,751,030	499,360	550,971	.29	0.31
Israel	6,100	6,040	1,080,000	949,056	177.05	157.12
Middle East/N. Africa	125,800	122,900	1,074,849	1,439,442	8.54	11.71
Sub Saharan Africa	546,100	563,700	1,937,184	1,979,634	3.55	3.51
Europe & Eurasia	340,953	340,237	499,360	550,971	1.46	1.62
Latin Amer. & Carib.	417,155	422,222	145,654	42,799	0.35	0.11

Sources: USAID website, http://usaid.gov/pubs/, United Nations 2000 Statistical Yearbook and United Nations 1000 Demographic Yearbook

Regional Classification: USAID classifications with the exception of the Middle East/N. Africa and Israel as independent classifications.

Note: West Bank and Gaza Strip population estimated at 3 million

Neoliberal reforms, again framed as bringing Western-style economic growth and democracy to nations of the global South, are intimately tied to the maintenance of a global trade regime that is geared to strengthening corporate and trade relations for Western nations (refer back to Box 4.6 on the Latin American debt crisis). This work of making visible colonial histories and contemporary geopolitical and economic relations between the West and the global South is a crucial move in deconstructing mainstream claims to universal or expert knowledge, demonstrating that '...the production of Western forms of knowledge [about development] is inseparable from the exercise of Western power' (Power 1998: 577).

Postcolonial geography also entails thinking about connections between metropole and (post)colonial spaces and between formerly colonised spaces themselves (Hart 2001; Radcliffe 2005). As a result, postcolonial theory insists on attention to metropolitan spaces within the West as crucially important (although largely ignored) sites for development studies. We need more geographical research drawing theoretical inspiration from postcolonial studies analysing development in the West to deconstruct the categories 'developed North' and 'undeveloped South' (initial calls for this in Harvey 2003; Pred and Watts 1992; Jarosz 1996; Lawson and Jarosz 2005; Gidwani 2002; Marchand and Parpart 1995). One fruitful set of connections is emerging between postcolonial theory and scholars of indigenous geographies. Researchers are examining processes of colonisation, dispossession and resistance in indigenous claims to land and water rights, conceptualisations of nature that challenge hegemonic practices and struggles for sovereignty by indigenous peoples across the USA, Canada and Europe (see for example Fixico 1998; Winchell 1996; Rundstrom et al. 2003; Berry 1998, 2000, 2002; Sparke 2005; Willems-Braun 1997).

More broadly, Slater (1992a: 324) argues that close empirical readings of the shifting geopolitical relations between peripheral and Western societies can reveal the contradictions *within Western development projects*:

> ...the struggle against the exclusionary logic of racism in South Africa reveals the hidden forms of the same logic in our societies, and US aggression against the Sandinista regime exposed the ultimate limit of liberal regimes, just as tacit acceptance of the Israeli appropriation and illegal occupation of Arab land has revealed the duplicitous attitude of the West to international law. In this way, Managua, the 'occupied territories' and Soweto become the names of frontiers *through which our own political identities are constructed...* (emphasis mine)

5.3.2 Rethinking scale

Post-structural development geographers are heavily indebted to Marxist arguments about the social construction of scale (chapter 4). This work extends the Marxist focus on how scales are produced and transformed by capitalist accumulation and regulation to consider other non-economic power relations that fix '...the territorial scope of particular modalities of power' (Newstead, Reid and Sparke 2003: 486). Specifically, post-structural development geography examines how processes of gender, race/ethnicity, postcoloniality and cultural productions of ideology and resistance are at work in the production of scale and the working out of development processes. This work also extends mainstream and Marxian development's focus on Anglo formations of the national scale that overemphasise the public realm of politics and economic processes. Post-development and feminist scholars insist on the importance of community, household, transnational and bodily scales as important sites through which development processes are both made and resisted. This focus on multiple and intersecting scales reveals subjects and processes that have been obscured and so expands the terrain of development theorising.

Post-structural scholars argue for a rereading of the roles and meanings of the national scale, beginning from postcolonial settings. Take, for example, work on emerging forms of supranational regionalism, which have been interpreted by Marxist scholars as a strategy for regulating globalised capitalist relations (Swyngedouw 1997; Brenner 1999). Post-structural theorists argue that this interpretation neglects '...postcolonial experiences or the perspectives of marginalised groups such as women and indigenous peoples', which can shed light on alternative narratives and dynamics operating to produce the national scale (Newstead 2002: 2). For example, Newstead's work on the Caribbean reveals that supranational regionalism is more focused on cultural and political processes of building national cultural identity and independence than on economic regulation of globalised capital. Similarly, research by Sidaway (2002) on southern Africa examines the ways in which postcolonial societies are engaged in a cultural politics of independent nation-building which is *actually enacted through* regional integration. In postcolonial states, participation in regional communities can provide a platform for the articulation of distinctive national identities, forged through the participation of national officials in regional meetings and ceremonies, which reinforces the legitimacy of the nation state in ways that inscribe it into narratives/strategies of resistance to external domination. By starting from postcolonial locations, the meanings of scalar strategies shift in ways that reveal distinct readings of the meaning of particu-lar scales (such as supranational regionalism in these cases) and the content of the processes producing them.

Extending beyond the national, post-structural development geography inter-rogates the production of other scales: from community to transnational. This work is revealing diverse processes of cultural and political identity formation, enacted outside of formal arenas of state-sponsored national politics and/or international development institutions. Scholars are researching grass-roots social movements, and their conceptions of community solidarity and belong-ing, as integral to building a politics of negotiation, resistance or alternatives to globalised processes. These movements are simultaneously local and transna-tional. For example, Paul Routledge (2003) works with People's Global Action (PGA), a grass-roots network that respects a diversity of interests and politics while also building common political actions across scales. A central principle of their organising is: '[w]e reject all forms and systems of domination and discrimination including, but not limited to, patriarchy, racism and religious fundamentalism of all creeds. We embrace the full dignity of all human beings' (http://www.nadir.org/nadir/initiativ/agp/en/index.html). PGA unites 10 grass-roots groups, who are organising both transnationally and regionally, including the Brazilian Landless Workers' Movement and the Karnataka State Farmers'

Union of India (Routledge 2003: 338). They work to produce a collective politics resisting corporate, neoliberal globalisation. Routledge uncovers PGA's scalar strategies, in which they build transnational solidarity while also retaining a grounding in each group's particular struggles in places.

People's Global Action was formed in 1996 from the Zapatista movement, which itself speaks from a discourse of self-governance, rooted in the indigenous traditions of specific communities and cultures (Esteva and Prakash 1998), and yet simultaneously articulates a generalised discontent within Mexico for the social and economic costs of NAFTA that is heard around the globe (Hilbert 1997; Slater 2004). Social movements are also deploying strategies of localisation and territorialisation to ground their political claims by articulating the relations between place, culture and nature. Escobar (2001: 159) describes the ways in which the movement of black communities in the Colombian Pacific rainforest has developed '...a sophisticated political ecology framework that links identity, territory, and culture to alternative strategies for conservation and sustainable use of the biodiverse resources of the region'.

Development geographers are exploring the forms and politics of transnational movements of workers, environmental activists, women's movements and indigenous community groups. For example, Rachel Silvey's (2004b) work with activists representing migrant Indonesian women working in Saudi Arabia explores the ways in which activists employ social constructions of scale to push for greater protections of overseas domestic workers. Activists invoke arguments about the scales of the body (issues of sexual violence) and the household (issues of poverty and survival) in international meetings and on the internet to mobilise support for migrants. At the same time, feminist activists are ambivalent about the politics of invoking these very scales because of the political costs that arise from associating women solely with sexuality and domesticity, given that the Indonesian state constructs women's domestic roles in households as fundamental to the formation of national identity. Further, focusing on women's domestic roles is limiting when struggles for rights must also take account of other profoundly important axes of difference, such as religion, class, ethnicity/race, and so on.

Radcliffe (2001) examines transnational advocacy networks that connect farmers' groups across Central America or indigenous groups across the Andes region, as they organise in the context of rollbacks of the neoliberal state in social service provision and infrastructure investments across Latin America. Her work maps out new structures of governance that are emerging and shifting state–society relationships as social actors use international agreements and organisations to protect their interests or to find funding for development projects. She examines how new forms of transnational activism can shape state policy-making and rework state–civil society relations. She also raises questions about the ways in which identities are constructed as forces of transnational mobilisation, cautioning that despite the apparent coherence of social movements, they are inevitably fractured by differences in power and author-ity. Pratt and Yeoh (2003) also caution against overly celebratory readings of transnationalism, noting that there is nothing inherently emancipatory about this scale of work, daily life or politics. They argue that transnationalism can as readily be oppressive as emancipatory, especially for low-income women whose worlds remain domesticated, even in transnational circuits:

> ...men often feature as entrepreneurs, career-builders, adventurers and bread-winners who navigate transnational circuits with fluidity and ease, while women are alternatively taken to be truants from globalised economic webs, stereotyped as exotic, subservient or victimised, or relegated to playing supporting roles, usually in the domestic sphere... (Pratt and Yeoh 2003: 159)

Work on transnational mobility, citizenship and organising raises a series of questions about the shifting roles and meanings of the nation state in the context of globalised capital and intensified transnational flows. Development geography needs to engage more fully with these questions given the continuing hegemony of the national scale in development circles and circuits. Katherine Mitchell's (1997) special issue of *Antipode* brings geography back into transnational theoris-ing by drawing on detailed empirical research to reveal the tensions between the modernist Development discourse of a bounded and coherent nation state and actually existing transnational flows of people, identities, resources and activisms. For example, Hilbert (1997) raises questions about the shifting role of the Mexican nation state in the 1990s, as the fighters of the EZLN in Chiapas struggled against NAFTA and the racialised position of indigenous people in neoliberal discourses of the modern Mexican nation. Hyndman (1997) reveals the power relations involved in producing state borders by contrasting flows of refugee aid and the immobility of refugee peoples in the Horn of Africa. Her research critiques transnational discourses celebrating mobility and diaspora through a critical analy-sis of when, and for whom, state borders are open or closed.

Our challenge going forwards is to theorise how places and scales are produced in ways that hold difference and the potential for political solidarity in creative tension. Escobar (2001: 164) suggests that the theoretical and political potential of place and scale lies in activating '...local places, cultures, natures and knowledge against the imperialising tendencies of space, capitalism and modernity'. We must resist the tendency to romanticise the local, because these spaces are not free of domination, and instead theorise the ways in which local places are embedded in circuits of capital, patriarchy and modernity, even as they are simultaneously producing crucially different kinds of cultural, environmental and political spaces. Starting from the dual prisms of place and scale, geographers are beginning to work for what Slater (2004: 219) terms 'alternative spatialities of solidarity'. He argues that intellectuals and social movements around the globe are organising in ways that are respectful of differences, against neoliberal globalisation and for a democratisation of power. Slater draws on the Zapatista movement in Mexico and the rise of the World Social Forum – a movement of movements – to uncover new sites and spaces of politics that are working across scales and that articulate '[a] transnational project for global justice and participatory democracy which does not prioritise any one spatial level...[and] offers a real alternative to the current hegemony of neoliberalism' (Slater 2004: 221). There is a radical potential in post-structural development geography, rooted in our ability to identify and support alternative politics enacted through these alternative spatialities.

5.4 Subjects and politics

Geographers draw on post-structural theory to understand how multiple axes of difference combine to shape people's experiences, accommodations and resistances to D/development. This work views people's identities as constituted in places, by people embedded in geo-historically situated social relations of gender, class, sexuality, religion, caste, race/ethnicity and postcoloniality, as well as in multiple networks for coping, transforming or resisting development (Nagar et al. 2002: 269). People are conceptualised as inhabiting multiple and fragmented identities which are constituted through linguistic and cultural representations in specific times and places. Of course, this work does not study difference for its own sake, but rather identifies differences that matter politically. This research interrogates how complex subjects of development are formed, and act, in relation to the exercise of power through D/development.

Inspired by both post-development and postcolonial theory, geographers are learning from actors that have been discredited in much development work –

taking seriously their arguments about 'alternative developments'. This focus on multiple subjects and agents of development teaches us about the inclusions and exclusions exercised in theories and practices of Development and about alternative conceptualisations of development altogether. This work highlights the complexities and contradictions in actors' relationships to development, recognising that as some are marginalised, others are privileged. As Rebecca Klenk (2003: 101) reminds us, '...people constituted as the supposed "targets" of development creatively receive, negotiate and re-present development's categories to make sense of the day-to-day experiences'.

Some of the post-structural work reviewed in section 5.2 focused on abstracted subjectivities, to the neglect of contextualised power relations, and concrete actors and practices in their specific relations to discourse and power. As Watts (2000: 171) cautions, '[D]evelopment as...story-telling runs the risk of excluding politics, interest, institutionalised authority and legitimacy and putting in their place a naïve sense of sitting around the campfire telling each other stories'. We look here at empirical research by geographers who are examining people's experiences of globalised processes of capitalist restructuring and development interventions. As you read this section, think about how attention to these subjects and agents of development opens up our thinking in new ways, to understand alternative readings of development and how it is being transformed in diverse social and political contexts.

Within geography, post-structural feminist theory has advanced our understanding of the multiple subjects of development most fully. As we discussed in chapter 4, much feminist research started from the marginalisation of women within development theory and policy. Post-structural feminist research has expanded this inquiry to

> ...provide[d] grounded and contextual understandings of globalisation (and development) by highlighting the ways gender – as a social category that is thoroughly interwoven with race, class, religion and other axes of social difference – has been central to reworked forms of capitalism and resistance... (Nagar et al. 2002: 275)

This work has illuminated myriad ways in which racialised and classed constructions of femininity and masculinity constitute the everyday politics of development processes in all their forms. While Marxist-feminist work focuses on how gender subjectivities, ideologies and identities are employed and contested in capitalist economic restructuring, here I highlight two additional aspects of feminist research. First, how political subjectivities are being reformulated in state–civil society struggles and, second, how cultural struggles over gendered, racialised and classed practices have been set in motion by neoliberal development. It is impossible to do justice to the vast body of work ongoing in geography and so in what follows I provide some examples.

Post-structural feminist research is examining people's shifting political subjectivities in relation to neoliberal restructuring of states, governance and civil society. For example, Lise Nelson's (2000) work examines the changing parameters of gendered citizenship among indigenous communities in Michoacán, Mexico. She collected women's life histories to analyse relationships between globalisation and democratisation, looking at how mass action and civil disobedience against PRI (Institutional Revolutionary Party) local officials in 1988 and 1989 fostered the emergence of new political identities for women. Indigenous women in the community spoke of new understandings of their capacity for political participation at the local level and their ability to challenge the paternalistic, national-level dominance of the PRI and its project of neoliberal restructuring (Figure 5.3). Radcliffe and Westwood's (1996) book *Remaking the Nation* interrogates the ways in which the Ecuadorian state employs cultural productions (museums, educational curricula, sporting events, and so on) to construct national narratives of a geographically coherent nation in the face of deep ethnic

Figure 5.3 Oaxacan women at a political rally. Source: Lise Nelson, University of Oregon

and class differences. The state works to construct a sense of collective belonging to the Ecuadorian nation in an attempt to produce unified political subjectivities, supportive of neoliberal economic reforms, even as these reforms work against the identities and interests of indigenous peoples within this imagined 'Ecuadorian community'.

Shifting gender subjectivities have also set in motion a range of cultural struggles around processes of mobility, work and sexuality. Richa Nagar (1998) explores the ways in which South Asian women's subjectivity and agency are negotiated and redefined in struggles over migration, marriage practices, shifting ideologies of gender and across different class, religious and caste positions. She traces shifting material and cultural conditions in Tanzania, Europe and North America, through which upper- and middle-class South Asian women renegotiated their mobility and discourses of purity and sexuality. At the same time, Nagar traces how these cultural struggles arose in tandem with new ideologies of difference (between castes, Asian and African women, and so on) that maintained patriarchal ideologies and power hierarchies, shaping Asian women's experiences (see also Nagar and Leitner 1998). Rebecca Klenk's (2003) work on women educated in a Gandhian ashram in Northern India demonstrates how women reinterpreted their personal lives in ways that contradicted family expectations. Through this education, some women left village life entirely, becoming professionals in far-off places and rejecting arranged marriages. Further, the teachings of the ashram where women studied questioned the development project of the Indian state, leading many women to take on controversial roles that challenged the state's hegemonic version of nationalism through their work as teachers and social workers.

Radcliffe, Laurie and Andolina (2003) trace the hierarchies of femininities and masculinities that pervade development institutions, practices and discourses in Latin America. They trace the unmarked Western masculinities that frame neoliberal development agendas and counterpose this invisible norm with the feminisation of indigenous men within international development institutions and programmes. So, for example, programmes of international or national development institutions frequently assume Western or mestizo masculine attributes, such as familiarity with technologies and an emphasis on economic rationality. Indigenous men and women who bring other cultural expertise to the table are often devalued and disempowered in these settings. More nuanced understandings of ethnic-racial differences in the cultural construction of femininities and masculinities would move us towards development projects that do not marginalise indigenous men or essentialise indigenous women as bearers of tradition and domesticity. Gender and ethnicity are tangled up with 'ethnodevelopment' programmes across a range of scales, and analysing these differences would create the possibility for more empowering programmes.

In addition to this explicit focus on the differentiated subjects of D/development, postcolonial scholarship analyses the ways in which poor women and children have become recurring tropes (symbols) for all places and peoples of the global South (Parpart 1995; Kabeer 1994; Mohanty 1991). Researchers point out the pervasiveness and power of this image of 'third world woman' that constructs a feminised victim who is needy, weak, helpless, in need of saving by the Development Establishment (Mohanty 1991; Enloe 1992; Parpart 1995). Researchers are working to deconstruct these representations through empirical fieldwork with the very subjects of these discourses. Their empirical work reveals that these representations ignore more complex identities and political actions of women in the global South; for example, women in Peru advocating for peace against Sendero Luminoso and abuses by the Peruvian military in the 1980s and 1990s (Hays-Mitchell 2005); transnational networking by women environmental justice activists (Di Chiro 2005); indigenous women fighting for both communal and women's land rights against postcolonial states in Latin America (Deere and Leon 2002); women employed in masculinised, elite and leadership positions across Asia (Raghuram and Hardhill 1998; Yeoh et al. 2000); and middle-class women in Ecuador, Nigeria, India and elsewhere employing other women in their homes (England and Lawson 2005).

Postcolonial research also deconstructs boundaries in post-Second World War development studies between subjects in the global South and invisible Western bodies. As I discussed in chapter 1, regions of the West and Western subjects remain disturbingly invisible in contemporary development studies, reinforcing the discourse of the West as 'fully developed' (Sparks 2005, personal communication). We need to understand connections and commonalities in oppressions and political struggles across the globe (Spivak 1990, 1998). Development geography can learn from critical race theorists, who empower subjects to reveal deep inequalities and racialised fissures within the West and the operation of white privilege (Anzaldua 1990; hooks 1990; Gomez-Pena 1987). As bell hooks puts it:

> [M]oving from silence into speech is for the oppressed, the colonised, the exploited, and those who stand and struggle side by side a gesture of defiance that heals, that makes new life and new growth possible. It is that act of speech,

of 'talking back,' that is no mere gesture of empty words, that is the expression
of our movement from object to subject – the liberated voice. (hooks 1990: 211)

Similarly 'liberated voices' in development studies are disrupting claims of universal Western 'successes' and 'experts' within development thought and practice
and pointing to the importance of building understandings of development that
are grounded in the experiences of women from around the globe (Mohanty
1991; Parpart 1995; Mies and Shiva 1993; Lycklama et al. 1998; Pratt 2004).

In addition to identifying multiply constituted actors and agents, post-development and postcolonial scholarship also identifies collective subjects. For
example, Esteva and Prakash (1998: 179) point to the rising political importance
of collective political subjects as people organise their social life autonomously
from unresponsive or repressive states, exercising power in their commons or
communities. This contrasts with the myth of the universal, individual subject
of mainstream development who has free access to representative and democratic institutions of the state (Mitchell 2004). New political styles are being
created at the grass roots that point to the interweaving of individual and collective emancipatory subjectivities in the work of social movements as they connect
through gatherings like the World Social Forum (Slater 2004). These political
actors are simultaneously grounded (localised) in specific material struggles and
are also working across scales, learning the connections between the politics of
peace, ecological struggles, gender emancipation and radical democratisation
(Slater 2004: 200; Anderson 2003). Along these lines some social movements
are eschewing hierarchy, such as the Zapatistas and Bolivian peasants against
privatisation of water, who explicitly organise themselves horizontally and collectively in order to avoid any concentration of political power and to foster participatory and inclusive democracy within the movement. These movements are
self-consciously organising with

> ...a vision for an alternative kind of global politics based on redistribution and
> recognition – the drive towards greater equality together with a greater recog-
> nition of difference. This requires respect for the autonomy of different
> movements while seeking out what may be held in common and what might bring
> movements together in new forms of cooperation. Differences to be respected,
> but commonalities discovered... (Slater 2004: 220)

In summary, the 'time of the posts' includes actors and voices unheard in
much development theory; an emphasis on the complex subject positions from

which people understand or rework development; and an interrogation of the institutional and political-economic production of meanings and material differences, the ways in which these construct Western authority and power over the global South, and how these are resisted and reworked from other locations.

Critics of 'post' theorists, like Sachs, often suggest that emphasising failures will lead to political paralysis, and that global injustice demands action not deconstruction.

> The idea of development stands like a ruin in the intellectual landscape. Delusion and disappointment, failures and crimes have been the steady companions of development and they tell a common story: it did not work... It is time to dismantle this mental structure... (Sachs 1992: 1)

At their most shrill, critics view post-structural arguments as overly focused on the limits of discourse, arguing that their emphasis on the dominating and homogenising impacts of Western developmentalism, and on diversity and difference in the global South, leads to cultural relativism and an outright rejection of modern development (Peet 2002: 87; Schuurman 2000a: 15; Blaikie 2000: 1034).

This criticism ignores crucial continuities with modernist development in much 'post' thought. While articulated quite differently, the very ideas of freedom, social justice and democracy emerged from the modernist project, and this prior agenda makes these ideals and rearticulations possible. 'Post' thought, as it has come into development studies, may be usefully thought of as a radicalisation of the modern and a commitment to struggle and transformation rather than outright rejection of these debates. I have argued here that most post-structural geographers are 'disenchanted modernists', engaged in a project of critical and socially accountable reworking of development rather than being in outright opposition or disengagement. So for example, groups may work in direct opposition to neoliberal policies, but remain committed to the idea that social justice and human-friendly projects are possible.

Geographers are engaging the political potential of post-structural thought by focusing on the implications of recent global and intellectual shifts for producing more inclusive and accountable forms of knowledge and for articulating progressive, radical democratic practices going forwards. In 1999, Donna Haraway, Nancy Hartsock and David Harvey (2000) gave a joint presentation at the University of Washington, entitled *Knowledge and the Question of Alliances*.

These scholars have all influenced debates about the nature of evidence and knowledge construction, about the diverse forms of oppression that shape societies and geographies of difference, and they have all become very concerned about how to construct meaningful political alliances across difference. Taking seriously challenges from post-structural theories does not necessarily entail an apolitical relativism, but rather can lead development geography towards an engaged, accountable analysis that allows for a series of inclusions that are central to constructing a progressive and democratic development. Indeed, the stakes are too high *not to think* about the implications of struggles over meaning and the project of constructing political alliances around difference. We take up these ideas in the concluding chapter, considering seriously the possibility that

> ...postmodernisms, post-structuralisms, and post-developmentalisms...are...open to forms of criticism and political practice that might enhance or reform the project of critical modernism... (Pickles 2001: 387)

Notes

[i] For a review of the complexity and diversity of post-structural thought, see Best and Kellner (1997) and Rabinow (1984). For a discussion of post-structural thought in geography and development studies, see McDowell and Sharp (1999) and Crush (1995).

[ii] As you will see, my discussion of the 'posts' differs from earlier Marxist and feminist development geography; however, this is a fuzzy (even forced) distinction, because much of the post-structural development geography discussed here has deep roots in the work I have just reviewed.

[iii] The Latin American Consultation of Women for the Construction of Peace was organised by Programa de Mujeres Constructoras de Paz (The Programme for Women Building Peace), International Fellowship of Reconciliation (IFOR) and Servicio Paz y Justicia (SERPAJ, Peace and Justice Service) from Ecuador, under the auspices of the International Observatory for Peace and the Program of Human Rights from the Andean University Simón Bolívar, with the support of SIPAZ, International Service for Peace.

INTELLECTUAL AND POLITICAL DIRECTIONS

Development studies in this new century are inextricable from seismic global and intellectual shifts: globalisation and neo-liberalisation; reframing of the national scale; reconceptualisations of modernity, and new ways of doing politics around the globe. Our critical geographical approach positions us to respond creatively and constructively to the challenges of reframing D/development in the context of globalisation, connection and critique. This reframing must begin from interrogation of development processes and our roles within them, because understanding the limits and potentials of existing approaches to development is our path to building progressive alternative conceptualisations and politics. In this brief conclusion I think about our roles as researchers, teachers and political actors, and about the sorts of questions that geography opens up going forwards.

Critical development geography begins from D/development as situated knowledge, taking seriously the links between language (epistemology), power and material life. This approach reveals the ways in which mainstream, Marxian, feminist and post-structural (not mutually exclusive categories) development theory construct their central assumptions, relevant subjects and geographies. Each chapter traces how power/knowledge works through geographies (places/spaces, scales, contexts and situated subjects) to create discourses and interventions with the power to change lives, legitimate certain scales and places, and to include and exclude. From this vantage point, we can build the intellectual and political tools to pose complex, sometimes frustrating questions, with the goal of reimagining development.

Our critical geographical approach in development studies focuses on contexts of knowledge, scalar relations, conceptions of place/space and situated subjects. Interrogating D/development processes through these spatial prisms opens up crucial questions and contributes to democratising development. Thinking about processes producing poverty and inequality, and ecological change spatially (rather than only temporally), reveals the workings of power in discourses and practices of globalising capital, in systems of race/ethnic, gender and nationality that put people in competition across the globe, and the rise of new politics that are reframing political scales and alliances. Thinking through space, place, scale and situatedness (of ideas and people) our geographical work uncovers the implicit geographies of power constructed in development theory and so opens possibilities for change.

As we learned in chapter 5, many geographers bridge Marxist-feminist and post-structural theoretical positions to keep the material relations of political-economy analysis firmly in conversation with post-structural attention to discourse and subjectivity/identity. David Slater, in his book *Geopolitics and the Post-Colonial,* rereads dependency and Marxist development theory in relation to postcolonial theory, and argues that '...Marxist thought, especially in its Gramscian variant, still has relevance today, but that relevance has to be continually rethought in a critical manner, as part of a wider body of social and political theory' (2004: 22). His Gramscian reading of Marx moves away from the preordained centrality of class subjects and capital logics to recover concepts of hegemony, representation, agency and resistance as material for thinking more widely about collective political action. Radcliffe (2005) takes up the imperatives and the challenges of marrying postcolonial theory, focused on discourses, texts and histories, with the political-economy emphases of geography on places/spaces and people. Postcolonial thought contributes through its decentring of Western hegemony within development thought and practice, and through analyses of how global South subjects have been marginalised through particular renditions 'of cultural and racial difference' (Radcliffe 2005: 292). However, she points out that this marriage (between postcolonial theory and geography) is challenging because of the limited engagements between political-economy analyses of global capitalism and the cultural/textual concerns of many postcolonial writings. Indeed, the relationships between political-economy and postcolonial/post-structural thought remain contested within the discipline.

Most development geographers have engaged in a limited way with postcolonial theory, arguing against a singular emphasis on development discourses and on cultural diversity and difference. Watts (2000: 171) cautions that '...the danger of a turn to discourse is that development ideas become (and remain) narratives or stories', and in the process, political-economic relations and class differences that contribute to the constitution of power differences are downplayed. Blaikie (2000: 1034) expresses a more explicit frustration:

> [T]he realisation of the limits of discourse, and the risk of losing sight of the materiality of life and agency of nature haunt the authors of the more hostile exegesis of development texts. As the dust settles from yet another deconstruction, 'what now?' the battered modernist might be heard to mutter, and also 'so what?'

For Blaikie, this frustration stems from the pressing human concerns at issue and his position that the purpose of development studies is to make a difference. Geographers insist on the intimate connections between discourses, power relations and the gritty materiality of life as it is lived out through places and the political-economic connections between them. Development for these authors is not unambiguously negative and singularly imposed by the West on people across the globe. Development does not *necessarily* curtail freedoms, although it may in certain circumstances (Gidwani 2002).

These concerns have led many geographers to rescue political-economy analysis back from its position as '...a distant mirage on the horizon' and to construct a blend of Marxian and postcolonial theory (Hart 2001: 654). Current development geography contributes to larger debates in development studies by moving away from determinist and oppositional theoretical work (Marxism *or* postcolonial theory) and recuperating a nuanced and blended approach that refuses to reinstate a singular, globalising logic of capitalist accumulation. Rather, development geography

> ...focuses on processes of interconnection and mutual constitution... By the same token [contemporary critical geography] undermines claims about the inexorable logic of capital, encouraging instead attention to interrelations, constitutive processes, and forms of power – as well as slippages, openings and contradictions. From this perspective, sorting out capitalist from non-capitalist elements – or deconstructing 'the economy' to demonstrate its parasitic character – become far less interesting than the question of how multiple forces come together in practice to produce particular dynamics or trajectories, as well as possible alternatives... (Hart 2002: 97)

In chapter 5 we examined the work of geographers who are engaging relational and dialectical readings of Marxist theory to construct anti-essentialist analyses of development that do not assume either a singularly beneficial nor destructive Western modernity. Geographers are examining the ways in which systems of language, meaning and knowledge production circulate through concrete practices, institutions and political-economic contexts to produce regimes of truth and practice (Watts 1993; Crush 1995; Power 2003). For example, in *Reworking Modernity*, Pred and Watts (1992) demonstrate how cultural and political struggles in specific contexts give rise to a multiplicity of capitalisms. They argue for spatially and culturally nuanced analyses in which the restructuring of multiple identities, the local articulation of knowledges and practices, and the reworking of cultural meanings are all crucial in understanding the reworking of capitalist social relations. Gidwani extends these arguments to note that the actual outcomes of D/development '...should be interpreted as "counterwork": the syncretic product of interactions between dominant actors and those in positions of subalternity' (Gidwani 2002: 5).

Contemporary development geography brings together material and discursive analyses to trace these restless and uneven postcolonial landscapes and the ways in which their inhabitants reinterpret and appropriate D/development processes. Following the admonitions of Sivaramakrishnan and Agrawal (2003: 35), for '...an understanding of development [that]...recognise[s] the actions of literally countless of millions of those outside the West who constantly shape and produce development', geographic work must be sensitive to how local agents engage with, negotiate, accommodate and rework D/development processes in ways that are worked out in place and in the relations of places to each other.

In addition to this focus on the mutual production of development discourses and practices, postcolonial theory extends Marxist-feminist development geography through its arguments for political responsibility. I clearly distinguish this from discourses of personal freedom and responsibility, foregrounded in neoliberal theory and policy which construct individuals as solely responsible for their own health, education, security and for lifting themselves from poverty (discussed in chapters 2 and 3); government becomes self-government and dismantles national discourses of welfarism and social redistribution (Mitchell 2004). By contrast, political responsibility starts from an understanding of how power/knowledge is exercised through D/development. Spivak (1998) exhorts us to take responsibility for learning the histories of unequal power and the relations of difference, inequality and hierarchy that construct subjects and places across the globe in their relations to each other. She terms this work transnational literacy that entails '...learn[ing] to be responsible as we study to be political' (Spivak 1998: 337). This resonates with Massey's call for Anglo geography to rethink the nature of its responsibilities. She argues that in Western societies we frame responsibility as local and territorially based, as primarily rooted in those nearest to us, in our homes, our communities and our nation – before thinking about our responsibilities to those further away (Massey 2004: 9). Transnational literacy challenges us to understand our responsibility for historical events and the contemporary geographies of inequality, hierarchy and struggle that those histories have produced. From here we can construct a politics that understands the places we inhabit and the power we hold as depending upon these histories of connection.

For Spivak and Massey, these politics of responsibility are built through open dialogue. We are responsible for engaging with our interlocutors in new ways where all involved in the conversation are being heard, where all is being revealed. These exchanges require trust and a willingness to listen: what Haraway (2000) terms 'worked knowledges', where all participants have something at risk in the discussion. Learning transnational literacy and responsibility is hard work and reveals painful histories of privilege, racism and subordination. It calls us to learn our privilege, take responsibility for our historical blindness and to construct in its place an 'accountable positioning' (Visweswaran 1994: 104). Calls for 'learning together' are emerging from several quarters, as in Giles Mohan's calls for participatory research which pulls apart dualisms to argue for a radical intersubjectivity which breaks down hierarchies and reveals the power relations that sustain dualisms and our images of each other (Mohan 1999: 50). Similarly Sparke et al. (2005: 363) argue for a broad vision of collaboration and responsible scholarship, taking their lessons from participation in the 2003 World Social Forum in Porto Alegre, Brazil. Learning together through open dialogue moves us away from romanticised or flabby notions of local social movements and civil society and towards more ethical understandings of how power hierarchies, cultural productions of difference, processes of capital accumulation, the violence of development interventions, virulent forms of nationalism, and so on, have worked out in geo-historical moments and places.

This idea of 'accountable responsibility' must inform our approach to development studies. Critical development geography entails epistemological and ontological commitments to a relational approach, which brings wealth and privilege in relation with poverty and vulnerability, and works to denaturalise conceptual boundaries, such as those between well-fed/hungry, rich/poor and North/South. This work explodes the boundary between 'developing' spaces and 'modern' spaces and understands their active co-constitution. This relational approach compels us to attend to the 'North' in the 'South' and the 'South' in the 'North', so that we recognise the 'there' and 'here' of our work simultaneously. Visweswaran (1994) terms this homework, wherein '...a critical eye would necessarily be cast on a whole range of practices at "home" that authorised American intervention in the "Third World".'

These commitments to a relational approach suggest several directions for our theory and practice: building a critical spatiality; working with difference while maintaining a commitment to a '...materially engaged transformative politics' (Staeheli and Nagar 2002: 168); and refocusing our attention on the Western spaces and subjects in development studies. I have argued for a *critical spatiality* in our approach to development studies. Our radical rethinking of place/space, scale, contexts of knowledge production and situated subjects positions us to rethink development. For example, Gillian Hart's relational comparison critiques the view of places as either 'ideal types' (failed, successful) or as local expressions of a global phenomenon (neoliberal development). She argues instead for the mutual constitution of places, as in her comparative work on South Africa and East Asia, which reveals distinct forms of gendered, classed and racialised differences in these spaces, and the ways in which these shape possibilities for production, reproduction and political action (chapter 4). We have also explored at length the analytical potential in Marxist-feminist arguments about the politics of scale, which open up complex rescalings of capitalist processes around the globe, the changing scalar geographies of governance and the rescaling of political action and networks by diverse social groups (chapter 4). In chapter 5 we explored postcolonial geography's attention to the cultural and historical construction of multiple dimensions of difference; to situating and 'provincialising' Western knowledges and practices of development; a consideration of non-economic power relations that territorialise power at particular scales; and concerns with the situated production of identity, subjectivity and agency.

Feminist geographers grapple with the challenges of working with difference and accountable positioning through a consideration of our fieldwork practices (see Katz 1992; McDowell 1992; Nast's special issue of *Professional Geographer* 1994; Sundberg 2003). They are now posing questions about how we build transnational feminist praxis through which scholars and activists in very different circumstances can learn transnational literacy and strengthen political connections. A viewpoint section in *Gender, Place and Culture*, edited by Staeheli and Nagar (2002), takes up these questions and identifies a continuing set of material inequalities, as well as institutional, cultural, social and geographical limits to achieving transnational praxis. This set of essays is an important corrective to the idealism of theory, reminding us that efforts to build transnational political alliances are fraught with difficulty. In addition to serious material inequalities that prevent actors from travelling and exchanging ideas, both Raju and Nagar note the disconnect between Northern academics' focus on theoretical research and Indian scholars' and activists' concerns with more grounded work that focuses on pressing social problems. Rachel Silvey's (2000a) essay in this same collection points to power differences within institutions, universities, non-governmental organisations, and so on, that further limit the possibilities for alliance and open exchange. Working to build alliances across difference requires us to address serious material inequalities, to refocus priorities in our work, to address the accessibility of our language and our institutional politics both within places and across worlds.

Both 'critical spatiality' and 'accountable positioning' foreground the importance of analysing marginalised Western places and subjects, as well as privileged places and subjects in the global South. Clearly, such a focus runs the risk of recentring the West, which is not the goal. Rather, critical development studies should work to disrupt both the centrality and the invisibility of the West, through a variety of analytical strategies and questions that both reveal oppressions and failures of development in the West and interrogate the ways in which D/development processes are interconnected across the globe. Schrijvers (1995) proposes that we '...study up, down and sideways' (Mohan's 1999: 49 paraphrase), tracing power as it works across scales to reveal and disrupt the power relations of those with global reach. Similarly, Pred and Watts (1992) argue for more work on the rich and powerful across the globe rather than an endless focus on oppressions or naive versions of 'resistance'.

In closing, let me suggest some crucial questions for our work as we go forwards:

- How are discourses of Development and neo-liberalisation, terror, security, privatisation, and so on, related to the material interests of corporations, states, activists and communities?
- What is the relationship between Development discourses and institutions and neoliberal transformations of societies? How are Development actors and institutions implicated in the globalisation of Western intellectual property rights; the expansion of genetically engineered organisms; the shrinking role of states in social redistribution and support; in liberalising places to flows of investments and commodities; in the devaluation of alternative identities and livelihoods; in the perpetuation of hierarchies of difference and oppression?

■ What are the possible spaces for alternatives and what do they look like? What role for the state, for radical democracy of people power and social movements, and so on, in service of social justice? How might accountable positioning and transnational literacy contribute to the articulation and enactment of social and environmental justice goals?

What, then, is (and can be) the relationship between critical development geography and development studies/action more broadly? Development geography came late to development studies both within and beyond the mainstream. Since the 1970s, much development geography has been critical in nature and this is reflected in our under-representation in the powerful institutions of development (both by choice and lack of invitation!). Furthermore, by its very nature, development geography emphasises space as well as time, whereas much development thought has been time-focused by its emphasis on change. While this very spatial focus, and its under-appreciation in the academy and international development institutions, has made geographers less central to development studies, I argue that here lies our critical contribution. I have brought our critical spatiality into clearer focus by arguing for the analytical power of examining the politics of making places, scales and situated subjects. I argue that geographic questions, inspired by post-structural Marxist-feminist theory, are guiding us towards more progressive politics and informed actions. I am thinking of the grounded research and participation of geographers in specific social movements, in transnational organising for social and environmental justice and in policy changes within development institutions that you have read about throughout this volume. We have discussed examples of geographers collaborating for progressive change 'on the ground', even as they are not feted as the public figures of a dominant international development project. One of our challenges going forwards is to expand these practices while taking responsibility to engage in transnational, long-term, committed relationships of mutuality, involving respect, engagement and support for common goals as they are expressed and worked out in specific places and networks.

Notes

[i] I must end with a vital caveat. The field of development studies is interdisciplinary and vast, and so in this short volume I have focused on presenting an account of the shifting development debates within Anglo geography. In so doing, I have referred to their relationships to broader literatures in development economics, Marxian and feminist theory and in post-structural and postcolonial thought.

REFERENCES

Agnew, J. (1999) The new geopolitics of power, in **D. Massey, J. Allen and P. Sarre** (eds), *Human Geography Today*. Cambridge: Polity Press, 173–94.

Ambrogi, T. (1999) Goal for 2000: unchaining slaves of national debt. *National Catholic Reporter*, 26 March: 3–5.

Anderson, B. (2003) Porto Alegre: 'a worm's eye view'. *Global Networks* **3**(2): 197–200.

Anzaldua, G. (ed.) (1990) *Making Face, Making Soul = Haciendo Caras: Creative and Critical Perspectives by Women of Color*. San Francisco: Aunt Lute Foundation Books.

Anzaldua, G. and C. Moraga (1981) *This Bridge Called My Back: Writings by Radical Women of Color*. Watertown: Persephone Press.

Appignanesi, R. and C. Garratt (1995) *Postmodernism for Beginners*. Cambridge: Icon Books.

Arcayfio-Schandorf, E. (1993) Household energy supplies and women's work in Ghana, in **J. Momsen and V. Kinnaird** (eds), *Different Places, Different Voices. Gender and Development in Africa, Asia and Latin America*. London: Routledge, 15–29.

Armstrong, W. and T. McGee (1985). *Theatres of Accumulation: studies in Asian and Latin American urbanization*. London and New York: Methuen.

Arrighi, G. (1970). Labour Supplies in Historical Perspective: A Study of the Proletarianization of the African Peasantry in Rhodesia. *The Journal of Development Studies* **6**(3): 197–8.

Balogh, A. and Z. Imam (1988) *A Political History of National Liberation Movement in Asia and Africa 1914–1985*. New Delhi: ABC Publishing House.

Bambirra, V. (1972) Integración monopólico mundial e industrialización: sus contradicciones. *Sociedad y Desarrollo* No. 1.

Bandarage, A. (1984) Women in development: liberalism, marxism and marxist-feminism. *Development and Change* **15**: 495–515.

Barndt, D. (2002) *Tangled Routes: Women, Work and Globalization on the Tomato Trail.* Lanham, MD: Rowman and Littlefield.

Barnes, T. (2000) Universalism, in **R. Johnston, D. Gregory, G. Pratt** and **M. Watts** (eds), *The Dictionary of Human Geography.* Oxford: Blackwell, 869–70.

Barnes, T. and J. Duncan (eds.) (1992) *Writing Worlds: discourse, text, and metaphor in the representation of landscape.* London: Routledge.

Bassett, T. (1988) The political ecology of peasant herder conflicts. *Annals of the Association of American Geographers* **78**: 453–72.

Bauer, L. (1984) Remembrance of studies past: retracing first steps, in **G. Meier** and **D. Seers** (eds), *Pioneers in Development.* New York: Oxford University Press.

Bebbington, A. (2000) Reencountering development: livelihood transitions and place transformation in the Andes. *Annals of the Association of American Geographers* **90**(3): 495–520.

Bebbington, A. (2001) Globalized Andes? Livelihoods, landscapes and development. *Ecumene* **8**: 414–36.

Bebbington, A. (2002) Geographies of development in Latin America? *Conference of Latin Americanist Geographers' Yearbook* **27**: 105–48.

Bebbington, A. (2003) Global networks and local developments: agendas for development geography. *Tijdschrift Voor Economische en Sociale Geografie* **94**(3): 297–309.

Beneria, L. and M. Roldan (1987) *Crossroads of Class and Gender: Industrial Homework, Industrial Subcontracting and Household Dynamics in Mexico City.* Chicago: Chicago University Press.

Benton, L. (1990) *Invisible Factories: The Informal Economy and Industrial Development in Spain.* Albany: State University of New York Press.

Berry, B. J. L. (1961a) City size distribution and development. *Economic Development and Cultural Change* **9**: 673–87.

Berry, B. J. L. (1961b) Basic Patterns of Economic Development, in **N. Ginsberg**, *Atlas of Economic Development.* Chicago: University of Chicago Press.

Berry, K. (1998) Race for water? Native Americans, eurocentrism, and western water policy, in **D. Camacho** (ed.), *Environmental Injustices, Political Struggles: Race, Class and the Environment*. Durham, NC: Duke University Press.

Berry, K. (2000) Water use and cultural conflict in 19th-century northwestern New Spain and Mexico. *Natural Resources Journal* **40**: 759–81.

Berry, K. (2002) The *Ahupua'a* and water allocation in Hawai'i : a study of cultural values and water law, in University of Colorado Natural Resources Law Center (ed.) *Allocating and Managing Water for a Sustainable Future*, 11–14 June. Boulder, CO: University of Colorado School of Law (CD ROM). Available from Natural Resource Law Center (reference number CF27).

Best, S. and D. Kellner (1997) *The Postmodern Turn*. New York: The Guilford Press.

Bhabha, H. (1991) 'Race' and time and the revision of modernity. *Oxford Literary Review* **14**: 1–29.

Blaikie, P. (1981) *The Political Economy of Soil Erosion*. London: Longmans.

Blaikie, P. (2000) Development, post-, anti-, and populist: a critical review. *Environment and Planning A* **32**: 1033–50.

Blaikie, P. and H. Brookfield (eds) (1986) *Land Degradation and Society*. London: Methuen.

Blaut, J. (1970) Geographical models of imperialism. *Antipode* **2**: 65–85.

Blaut, J. (1973) The theory of development. *Antipode* **5**: 22–6.

Blaut, J. (1975) Imperialism: the Marxist theory and its evolution. *Antipode* **7**(1): 1–19.

Blunt, A. and G. Rose (eds) (1994) *Writing Women and Space: Colonial and Postcolonial Geographies*. New York: Guilford Press.

Bondi, L. (1993) Locating identity politics, in **M. Keith and S. Pile** (eds.), *Place and the Politics of Identity*. London and New York: Routledge, 34–5.

Boserup, E. (1970) *Woman's Role in Economic Development*. New York: St. Martin's Press and George Allen & Unwin.

Bottomore, T. (1991) *Classes in Modern Society*. London: Harper Collins.

Breman, J. (1979) Seasonal migration and cooperative capitalism – Part 2. *Journal of Peasant Studies* **6**(2): 168–209.

Brenner, N. (1998). Between fixity and motion: accumulation, territorial organization and the historical geography of spatial scales. *Environment and Planning D: Society and Space* **16**: 459–81.

Brenner, N. (1999) Beyond state-centrism? Space, territoriality and geographical scale in globalization studies. *Theory and Society* **28**: 39–78.

Brenner, N. (2001) The limits to scale? Methodological reflections on scalar construction. *Progress in Human Geography* **25**(4): 591–614.

Bridge, G. and A. Jonas (2002) Governing nature: the reregulation of resource access, production, and consumption. *Environment and Planning A* **34**: 759–66.

Brohman, J. (1996) *Popular Development: Rethinking the Theory and Practice of Development.* Oxford: Blackwell.

Brohman, J. (1997) Economism and critical silences in development studies: a theoretical critique of neoliberalism. *Third World Quarterly* **16(2)**: 297–318.

Bromley, R. and C. Gerry (eds) (1979) *Casual Work and Poverty in Third World Cities.* Chichester: John Wiley and Sons.

Brookfield, H. (1973) On one Geography and a Third World. *Transactions of the Institute of British Geographers* **58**: 1–10.

Browett, J. (1980) Development, the diffusionist paradigm and geography. *Progress in Human Geography* **4**(1): 57–79.

Brown, L. (1991) *Place, Migration and Development in the Third World. An Alternate View.* London: Routledge.

Brown, L. and V. Lawson (1985) Migration in Third World settings, uneven development, and conventional modeling: A case study of Costa Rica. *Annals of the Association of American Geographers* **75**: 29–47.

Brydon, L. and S. Chant (1989) *Women in the Third World: Gender Issues in Rural and Urban Areas.* New Brunswick, NJ: Rutgers University Press.

Camdessus, M. (1993) The International Monetary Fund. Key Problems, Opportunities and Guideposts for the Way Ahead. *Vital Speeches of the Day* **60**(2): 43–9.

Cardoso, F. and E. Faletto (1979) *Dependency and Development in Latin America.* Berkeley: University of California Press.

Carney, J. (1988) Struggles over crop rights within contract farming households in a Gambian irrigated rice project. *The Journal of Peasant Studies* **15**(3): 334–49.

Carney, J. (1991) Disciplining women? Rice, mechanization and the evolution of Mandinka gender relations in Senegambia. *Signs* **16**(4): 651–81.

Carney, J. (1992) Peasant women and economic transformation in The Gambia. *Development and Change* **23**(2): 67–90.

Carney, J. (2001) *Black Rice: the African Origins of Rice Cultivation in the Americas.* Cambridge, MA: Harvard University Press.

Carney, J. and M. Watts (1990) Manufacturing Dissent: Work, Gender and the Politics of Meaning in a Peasant Society. *Africa* **60**(2): 207–41.

Carson, R. (1962) *Silent Spring.* New York: Fawcett Crest.

Castells, M. (1983) *The City and the Grassroots: a Cross-cultural Theory of Urban Social Movements.* Berkeley: University of California Press.

Castells, M. (1996) *The Rise of the Network Society.* Oxford: Blackwell.

Chant, S. (ed.) (1992) *Gender and Migration in Developing Countries.* London: Belhaven Press.

Chant, S. (2004) Urban livelihoods, employment and gender, in **R. Gwynne and C. Kay** (eds.) *Latin America Transformed: Globalization and Modernity.* London: Arnold.

Chase, J. (ed.) (2002a) *The Spaces of Neoliberalism: Land, Place, and Family in Latin America.* Bloomfield, CT: Kumarian Press.

Chase, J. (2002b) Privatization and private lives: gender, reproduction and neoliberal reforms in a Brazilian company town, in **J. Chase** (ed.) *The Spaces of Neoliberalism: Land, Place, and Family in Latin America.* Bloomfield, CT: Kumarian Press.

Childs, P. and P. Williams (1997) *An Introduction to Post-colonial Theory.* London: Prentice Hall.

Christaller, L. (1966) *Central Places in Southern Germany.* New Jersey: Prentice Hall.

Clemetson, L. (2003) The Nation: A nation transformed; inspired by the speech, they, too, had a dream. *New York Times* (Late Edition – Final, 24 August, Section 4, p. 12 column 1.

Columbia Legal Services (1996) *Washington's Families: Poverty Despite Work.* Seattle: distributed by Washington State Access to Justice Network.

Connell, J. (1973) The geography of development or the development of geography. *Antipode* **5**(2): 27–39.

Connelly, M. and P. Kennedy (1994) Must it be the West Against the Rest. *Atlantic Monthly*, December: 61–84.

Cooper, F. and R. Packard (eds.) (1997) *International Development and the Social Sciences: the History and Politics of Knowledge.* Berkeley: University of California Press.

Corbridge, S. (1986) *Capitalist World Development.* Totowa, NJ: Rowman and Littlefield.

Corbridge, S. (1990) Post-Marxism and development studies: beyond the impasse. *World Development* **18**(5): 623–40.

Corbridge, S. (1993) Marxisms, modernities and moralities: development praxis and the claims of the distant strangers. *Society and Space* **11**: 449–72.

Corbridge, S. (1995) *Development Studies, a Reader.* New York: Edward Arnold.

Corbridge, S. (1997) Doctrines of development. *Journal of Development Studies* **33**(5): 729–32.

Corbridge, S. (1998) 'Beneath the pavement only soil': the poverty of post-development. *Journal of Development Studies* **34**(6): 138–48.

Corva, D. (2004) *Localization, Globalization and the World Social Forum: Towards a Process Geography of Counterhegemonic Mobilization.* MA Thesis, University of Washington.

Council for a Sustainable World (1997) *Foreign Aid and the Arms Trade: A Look at the Numbers.* Washington, DC: Council for a Sustainable World.

Cowen, M. P. and R. W. Shenton (1996) The invention of development. *Doctrines of Development.* London: Routledge, 3–56.

Cravey, A. (1997) The politics of reproduction: households in the Mexican industrial transition. *Economic Geography* **73**(2): 166–86.

Cravey, A. (1998) *Women and Work in Mexico's Maquiladoras.* Lanham, MD: Rowman and Littlefield.

Cravey, A. (2005) Working on the Global Assembly Line, in **L. Nelson and J. Seager** (eds.) *A Companion to Feminist Geography*. Oxford: Blackwell.

Crush, J. (1987) *The Struggle for Swazi labor, 1890–1920*. Kingston, ON: McGill-Queen's University Press.

Crush, J. (1991) The discourse of progressive human geography. *Progress in Human Geography* **15(4)**: 395–414.

Crush, J. (1995) *The Power of Development*. London: Routledge.

Curry, G. (2003) Moving beyond postdevelopment: facilitating indigenous alternatives for 'Development'. *Economic Geography* **79**(4): 405–23.

Dalla Costa, M. and G. F. Dalla Costa (eds.) (1993) *Paying the Price: Women and the Politics of Economic Development*. London: Zed Books.

Deere, D and M. Leon (2002) Individual versus collective land rights: tensions between women's and indigenous rights under neoliberalism, in **J. Chase** (ed.), *The Spaces of Neoliberalism: Land, Place, and Family in Latin America*. Bloomfield, CT: Kumarian Press, 53–86.

Desai, A. (1966). *Social Background of Indian Nationalism*. Bombay: Popular Prakashan.

Dezalay, Y. and B. Garth (2002) *The Internationalization of the Palace Wars: Lawyers, Economists and the Contest to Transform Latin American States*. Chicago: University of Chicago Press.

Di Chiro, G. (2005) Performing a 'global sense of place': women's actions for environmental justice, in **L. Nelson and J. Seager** (eds) *A Companion to Feminist Geography*. Oxford: Blackwell, 496–515.

Dicken, P. (2003) *Global Shift: Reshaping the Global Economic Map in the 21st Century*. New York: Guilford Press.

Dickenson, J., B. Gould, C. Clarke et al. (1996) *A Geography of the Third World*, 2nd edn. London: Routledge.

Dixon, D. and J. P. Jones (1998) My dinner with Derrida, or spatial analysis and post structuralism do lunch. *Environment and Planning A* **30**(2): 247–60.

Domar, E. (1946) Capital Expansion, Rate of Growth and Employment. *Econometrica* **14**(2): 137–47.

Driver, F. (1992) Geography's empire: histories of geographic knowledge. *Environment and Planning D: Society and Space* **10**: 23–40.

Durning, A. (1992) *How Much is Enough: the Consumer Society and the Future of the Earth.* New York: Norton.

Economist (1989) A Survey of the Third World: Poor man's burden. *The Economist*, 23 September (special supplement).

Economist (1993) Yes, we have no mañanas (economic and democratic reform). *The Economist: A Survey of Latin America*, 13 November (special supplement), 5.

Elias, M. and J. Carney (2005) Shea butter, globalization and women of Burkina Faso, in **L. Nelson and J. Seager** (eds.) *A Companion to Feminist Geography.* Oxford: Blackwell.

Elson, D. (ed.) (1990) *Male Bias in the Development Process.* Manchester: Manchester University Press.

Emeagwali, G. (1995) *Women Pay the Price: Structural Adjustment in Africa and the Caribbean.* Lawrenceville, NJ: Africa World Press.

England, K. and V. Lawson (2005) Feminist analyses of work: rethinking the boundaries, gendering and spatiality of work, in **L. Nelson and J. Seager** (eds) *A Companion to Feminist Geography.* Oxford: Blackwell, 77–92.

Enloe, C. (1992) The gendered Gulf, in **C. Peters** (ed.), *Collateral Damage: the New World Order at Home and Abroad.* Boston, MA: South End Press, 93–100.

Escobar, A. (1995) *Encountering Development.* Princeton NJ: Princeton University Press.

Escobar, A. (2001) Culture sits in places: reflections on globalism and subaltern strategies of localization. *Political Geography* **20**(2): 139–74.

Esteva, G. (1987) Regenerating People's Space. *Alternatives* **XII**(1): 125–52.

Esteva, G. (1992) Development, in **W. Sachs** (ed.), *The Development Dictionary.* London: Zed Books, 6–25.

Esteva, G. and S. Prakash (1998) *Grassroots Post-Modernism.* London: Zed Books.

Evans, P. (1979) *Dependent Development. The Alliance of Multinational, State and Local Capital in Brazil.* Princeton, NJ: Princeton University Press.

Fanon, F. (1965) *The Wretched of the Earth*. New York: Grove Press.

Farrington, J. and A. Bebbington (with K. Wellard and D. Lewis) (1993) *Reluctant Partners? Non-Governmental Organizations, the State and Sustainable Agricultural Development*. New York: Routledge.

Faulkner, A. and V. Lawson (1990) Employment versus empowerment: a case study of women's work in Ecuador. *Journal of Development Studies* **27**(4): 16–47.

Ferguson, J. (1990) *The Anti-politics Machine. 'Development', Depoliticization and Bureaucratic Power in Lesotho*. Cambridge: Cambridge University Press.

Fernandez-Kelly, P. and J. Nash (eds) (1983) *Women, Men, and the International Division of Labor*. Albany: State University of New York Press.

Fixico, D. (1998) *The Invasion of Indian Country in the Twentieth Century: American Capitalism and Tribal Natural Resources*. Boulder: University of Colorado Press.

Folke, S. (1973) First thoughts on the geography of imperialism. *Antipode* **5**(3): 16–20.

Foucault, M. (1980a) Two Lectures, in **C. Gordon** (ed), *Power/Knowledge: Selected interviews and other writings 1972–1977*, trans. C. Gordon, L. Marshall, J. Mepham and K. Soper. New York: Pantheon Books, 78–108.

Foucault, M. (1980b) Truth and Power, in **C. Gordon** (ed), *Power/Knowledge: Selected interviews and other writings 1972–1977*, trans. C. Gordon, L. Marshall, J. Mepham and K. Soper. New York: Pantheon Books, 109–33.

Foucault, M. (1980c) Questions on Geography, in **C. Gordon** (ed), *Power/ Knowledge: Selected interviews and other writings 1972–1977*, trans. C. Gordon, L. Marshall, J. Mepham and K. Soper. New York: Pantheon Books, 63–77.

Foucault, M. (1984a) Nietzsche, Genealogy, History, in **P. Rabinow** (ed),*The Foucault Reader*. New York: Pantheon Books, 76–100.

Foucault, M. (1984b) Space, Knowledge and Power, in **P. Rabinow** (ed),*The Foucault Reader*. New York: Pantheon Books, 239–56.

Frank, G. (1969) *Latin America: Underdevelopment or Revolution*. London: Monthly Review Press.

Freidberg, S. (2004) *French Beans and Food Scares: Culture and Commerce in an Anxious Age*. New York: Oxford University Press.

Freidmann, J. (1966) *Regional Development Policy: The Case of Venezuela.* Cambridge, MA: MIT Press.

Friedmann, J. (1992) *Empowerment. The Politics of Alternative Development.* Oxford: Blackwell.

Fukuyama, F. (2001) Social capital, civil society and development. *Third World Quarterly* **22**(1): 7–20.

Furtado, C. (1970) *Economic Development of Latin America.* New York: Cambridge University Press.

Gaile, G. (1980) The spread backwash concept. *Regional Studies* **14**: 15–25.

Gaile, G. and A. Ferguson (1997) Success in African social development: some positive indications. *Third World Quarterly* **17**(3): 557–72.

Gaile, G and C. Wilmott (2005) *Geography in America at the Dawn of the Twenty-first Century.* Oxford: Blackwell.

Galeano, E. (1997) *Open Veins of Latin America: Five Centuries of the Pillage of a Continent.* New York: Monthly Review Press.

Gallup, J., A. Gaviria and E. Lora (2003) *Is Geography Destiny? Lessons from Latin America.* Washington, DC: World Bank.

Gausch, J. L. (1999) *Labor Market Reform and Job Creation: the unfinished agenda in Latin American and Caribbean countries.* Washington, DC: The World Bank.

Gelvin, J. (2002) Developmentalism, revolution and freedom in the Arab east: the cases of Egypt, Syria and Iraq, in **R. Taylor** (ed.), *The Idea of Freedom in Asia and Africa.* Stanford, CA: Stanford University Press, 62–96.

George, S. (1977) *How the Other Half Dies.* New Jersey: Rowman and Allanheld.

George, S. (1999) *A Short History of Neo-Liberalism.* Paper presented at Conference on Economic Security in a Globalizing World. Bangkok: 24–6.

Gereffi, G. (2002) Outsourcing and changing patterns of international competition in the apparel commodity chain. Paper presented at *Responding to Globalization Conference,* Boulder, CO, 4–7 April.

Gereffi, G. and D. Wyman (eds) (1990) *Manufacturing miracles: paths of industrialization in Latin America and East Asia.* Princeton, NJ: Princeton University Press.

Gibson-Graham, J. K. (1996) *The End of Capitalism (as We Knew It): A Feminist Critique of Political Economy.* Oxford: Blackwell.

Gibson-Graham, J. K. (2005) Surplus possibilities: postdevelopment and community economies. *Singapore Journal of Tropical Geography* **26**(1): 4–26.

Gidwani, V. (2002) The Unbearable Modernity of Development? Canal Irrigation and Development Planning in Western India. *Progress in Planning* **58**: 1–80.

Gingrich, N. (1995) *To Renew America.* New York: HarperCollins.

Ginsberg, N. (1961) *Atlas of Economic Development.* Chicago: University of Chicago Press.

Gitlin, T. (1987) *The Sixties: years of hope, days of rage.* New York: Bantam Books.

Glassman, J. (1999) State power beyond the 'territorial trap': the internationalization of the state. *Political Geography* **18**: 669–96.

Glassman, J. (2001) Development theory in Geography, in **N. Smelser and P. Baltes** (eds), *International Encyclopedia of the Social and Behavioral Sciences.* Amsterdam, New York: Elsevier.

Glassman, J. and A. Samatar (1997) Development geography and the third-world state. *Progress in Human Geography* **21**(2): 164–98.

Gomez-Pena, G. (1987) The conflicts and culture of the borderlands. *Utne Reader,* 1 July.

Gonzales de la Rocha, M. (1994) *The Resources of Poverty.* Oxford: Blackwell.

Goodman, D. and M. Redclift (1991) *Refashioning Nature.* London: Routledge.

Gordon, C. (1980) Afterword, in **C. Gordon** (ed.), *Power/Knowledge: Selected interviews and other writings 1972–1977,* trans. C. Gordon, L. Marshall, J. Mepham and K. Soper. New York: Pantheon Books, 229–60.

Gore, C. (1984) *Regions in Question: Space, Development Theory and Regional Policy.* London: Methuen.

Green, D. (2003) *Silent Revolution.* London: Cassell.

Greenhalgh, S. (1996) The Social Construction of Population Science: An Intellectual, Institutional and Political History of Twentieth-Century Demography. *Comparative Studies in Society and History* **38**(1): 26–66.

Greenwood, M. J. (1975) Research on migration in the United States: a survey. *Journal of Economic Literature* **8**: 397–433.

Gregory, D. (1998) Power, Knowledge and Geography. *Geographische Zeitschrift*, **86**(2): 70–93.

Gregory, D. (2000) Epistemology, in **R. J. Johnston, D. Gregory, G. Pratt and M. Watts** (eds), *The Dictionary of Human Geography*. Oxford: Blackwell, 226–8.

Gregory, J. and V. Piche (1978) African Migration and Peripheral Capitalism, in **W. Van Bisbergen and H. Meilink** (eds.) *Migration and the Transformation of African Society*. Leiden: Afrika-Studiecentrum

Grewal, I. and C. Kaplan (1994) *Scattered Hegemonies: Postmodernity and Transnational Feminist Practices*. Minneapolis: University of Minnesota Press.

Griffin, K. (1969) *Underdevelopment in Spanish America*. London: Allen & Unwin.

Gupta, A. (1998) *Postcolonial Developments. Agriculture in the Making of Modern India*. Durham, NC: Duke University Press.

Gwynne, R. and C. Kay (eds) (2000) Views from the periphery: futures of neoliberalism in Latin America. *Third World Quarterly* **21**(1): 141–56.

Gwynne, R. and C. Kay (2004) *Latin America Transformed: Globalization and Modernity*. London: Arnold.

Hackenberg, R. A. (1980) New patterns of urbanization in Southeast Asia: an assessment. *Population and Development Review* **6**(3): 391–419.

Hall, S. (1992) The west and the rest: discourse and power, in **S. Hall and B. Gieben** (eds), *Formations of Modernity*. Trowbridge: Redwood Books, 275–332.

Hall, S. and B. Gieben (eds) (1992) *Formations of Modernity*. Oxford: Polity Press.

Hannah, M. (1993) Foucault on theorizing specificity. *Environment and Planning D: Society and Space* **11**(3): 349–63.

Hansen, N. (1981) A review and evaluation of attempts to direct migrants to smaller and intermediate size cities, in **G. Demko and R. Fuchs** (eds.), *Population Distribution Policies in Development Planning*. New York: United Nations, Department of International Economics and Social Affairs, Population Studies 75.

Hanson, S. (1992) Geography and feminism: worlds in collision? *Annals of the Association of American Geographers* **82**(4): 569–86.

Hapke, H. (2001) Petty traders, gender and development in a South Asian fishery. *Economic Geography* **77**(3): 225–49.

Haraway, D. (1988) Situated knowledges: the science question in feminism as a site of discourse on the privilege of partial perspective. *Feminist Studies* **14**(3): 575–99.

Haraway, D., N. Hartsock and D. Harvey (2000) *Knowledge and the Question of Alliances* (video recording). Department of Geography, University of Washington.

Harding, S. (1986) *The science question in feminism*. Ithaca, NY: Cornell University Press.

Harris, R. (2000) The Effects of Globalization and Neoliberalism in Latin America at the Beginning of the Millennium. *Journal of Developing Societies* **16**(1): 139–62.

Harriss, J. (2001) *Depoliticizing Development: The World Bank and Social Capital*. New Delhi: Leftword Books.

Harrod, R. (1948) *Toward a Dynamic Economics*. London: Macmillan.

Hart, G. (1986) *Power, Labor and Livelihood: Processes of Change in Rural Java*. Berkeley: University of California Press.

Hart, G. (2001) Development critiques in the 1990s: *culs de sac* and promising paths. *Progress in Human Geography* **25**(4): 649–58.

Hart, G. (2002a) *Disabling Globalization. Places of Power in Post-Apartheid South Africa*. Berkeley: University of California Press.

Hart, G. (2002b) Geography and development: developments beyond neoliberalism? Power, culture, political-economy. *Progress in Human Geography* **26**(6): 812–22.

Hart, G. (2003) Disabling globalization: places of power in post-apartheid South Africa. *Environment and Planning D: Society and Space* **21**(4): 505–7.

Hartmann, H. (1981) The unhappy marriage of marxism and feminism: towards a more progressive union, in **L. Sargent** (ed), *Women and Revolution: A Discussion of the Unhappy Marriage of Marxism and Feminism*. Cambridge, MA: South End Press.

Hartsock, N. (1983) *Money, Sex, and Power: Toward a Feminist Historical Materialism.* New York: Longman.

Hartsock, N. (1998) *The Feminist Standpoint Revisited and Other Essays.* Boulder, CO: Westview Press.

Harvey, D. (1973) *Social Justice and the City.* Baltimore, MD: Johns Hopkins University Press.

Harvey, D. (1982) *The Limits to Capital.* London: Verso.

Harvey, D. (1990) *The Condition of Postmodernity.* Oxford: Blackwell.

Harvey, D. (1993) Class relations, social justice and the politics of difference, in **M. Keith and S. Pile** (eds), *Place and the Politics of Identity.* New York: Routledge, 41–66.

Harvey, D. (1996) On the history and present condition of geography: An historical materialist manifesto, in **J. Agnew, D. Livingstone and A. Rogers** (eds), *Human Geography. An Essential Anthology.* Oxford: Blackwell, 95–107.

Harvey, D. (2000) Reinventing Geography. *New Left Review* **4**: 75–97.

Harvey, D. (2003) *The New Imperialism.* Oxford: Oxford University Press.

Hays-Mitchell, M. (1993) The ties that bind: informal and formal sector linkages in street vending: the case of Peru's ambulantes. *Environment and Planning A* **25**: 1085–102.

Hays-Mitchell, M. (2005) Women's struggles for sustainable peace in post-conflict Peru: a feminist analysis of violence and change, in **L. Nelson and J. Seager** (eds.), *A Companion to Feminist Geography.* Oxford: Blackwell.

Hecht, S. and A. Cockburn (1989) *The Fate of the Forest: Developers, Destroyers and Defenders of the Amazon.* London: Verso.

Hettne, B. (1995) *Development Theory and the Three Worlds: Towards an International Political Economy of Development.* Essex: Longman.

Heyman, R. (2004) Against a national research agenda: the AAG and American empire, past and present. Paper presented at the AAG Annual Meeting in Philadelphia, PA, 14–19 March.

Hickey, M. and V. Lawson (2005) Beyond Science: Human geography, interpretation and critique, in **N. Castree, A. Rodgers and D. Sherman** (eds) *Questioning Geography.* Oxford: Blackwell.

Hilbert, S. (1997) For whom the Nation? Internationalization, Zapatismo, and the struggle over Mexican Modernity. *Antipode* **29**(2): 115–148.

Hodder, R. (2000) *Development Geography.* New York: Routledge.

hooks, bell (1990) Talking back, in **G. Anzaldua** (ed.), *Making Face, Making Soul = Haciendo Caras: Creative and Critical Perspectives by Women of Color.* San Francisco: Aunt Lute Foundation Books.

Hudson, B. (1977) The new geography and the new imperialism. *Antipode* **9**(2): 12–19.

Hyndman, J. (1997) BorderCrossings. *Antipode* **29**(2): 149–76.

Illich, I. (1997) Development as planned poverty, in **M. Rahnema and V. Bawtree** (eds), *The Post-Development Reader.* London: Zed Books.

Isard, W. (1956) *Location and Space Economy.* New York: John Wiley.

Jaquette, J. (ed.) (1989) *The Women's Movement in Latin America.* Boston, MA: Unwin Human.

Jarosz, L. (1990) *Rice on Shares: Agrarian Change and the Development of Sharecropping in Alaotra, Madagascar.* Ph.D. Dissertation, University of California, Berkeley.

Jarosz, L. (1991) Women who sharecrop in Madagascar, *Society and Natural Resources* **4**(1): 53–63.

Jarosz, L. (1992) Constructing the Dark Continent: metaphor as geographic representation of Africa. *Geografiska Annaler Series B* **74**(2): 105–15.

Jarosz, L. (1993) Defining tropical deforestation: shifting cultivation and population growth in colonial Madagascar, *Economic Geography* **69**(4): 366–79.

Jarosz, L. (1996) Working in the Global Food System: a Framework for International Comparative Analysis. *Progress in Human Geography* **20**(1): 41–55.

Jarosz, L. (2003) Review of Disabling globalization: places of power in post-apartheid South Africa by Gilllian Hart, *Environment and Planning D: Society and Space* **21**(4): 505–7.

Jarosz, L. and V. Lawson (2002) Sophisticated people versus rednecks: economic restructuring and class difference in America's west. *Antipode* **34**(1): 8–27.

Jarosz, L. and J. Qazi (2000) The geography of Washington's world apple: global expressions in a local landscape. *Journal of Rural Studies* 16(1): 1–11.

Johnson, C. (1998) Cold War economics melt Asia. *The Nation.* 23 February, 16–19.

Johnston, R. (2000) Intellectual respectability and disciplinary transformation? Radical geography and the institutionalization of geography in the USA since 1945. *Environment and Planning A* **27**: 971–90.

Kabeer, N. (1994) *Reversed Realities. Gender Hierarchies in Development Thought.* London: Verso.

Kaplan, R. (1994) The Coming Anarchy. *Atlantic Monthly,* February: 44–76.

Katz, C. (1992) All the world is staged: intellectuals and the projects of ethnography. *Environment and Planning D: Society and Space* **10**: 495–510.

Katz, C. (2001) On the grounds of globalization: A topography for feminist political engagement. *Signs: Journal of Women in Culture and Society* **26**(4): 1213–34.

Katz, C. (2004) *Growing up Global: economic restructuring and children's everyday lives.* Minneapolis: University of Minnesota Press.

Kay, C. (1989) *Latin American Theories of Development and Underdevelopment.* London: Routledge.

Kelly, P. (1999) The geographies and politics of globalization. *Progress in Human Geography* **23**: 379–400.

Keynes, J. M. (1936) *The General Theory of Employment, Interest and Money.* New York: Harcourt.

Klak, T. (1998) *Globalization and Neoliberalism: The Caribbean Context.* Lanham, MA: Rowman and Littlefield.

Klenk, R. (2003) 'Difficult Work': Becoming Developed, in **K. Sivaramakrishnan**, and **A. Agrarwal**, (eds.) *Regional Modernities. The Cultural Politics of Development in India.* Stanford, CA: Stanford University Press.

Koedt, A. (1973) *Radical feminism.* New York: Quadrangle Books.

Kofman, E. (2005) Feminist political geographies, in **L. Nelson and J. Seager** (eds), *A Companion to Feminist Geography.* Oxford: Blackwell, 519–32.

Konadu-Agyemang, K. (2000) The best of times and the worst of times: structural adjustment programs and uneven development in Africa: the case of Ghana. *Professional Geographer* **52**(3): 469–83.

Kothari, U. and M. Minogue (2002) *Development theory and practice. Critical Perspectives.* Basingstoke: Palgrave.

Kristof, N. (1997) Tiger tales: Why Africa can thrive like Asia. *New York Times* Sunday, 25 May, Week in Review, Section 4, p. 1, column 1.

Krugman, P. (2002) For richer: how the permissive capitalism of the boom destroyed American equality. *New York Times Magazine.* 20 October, 62–72.

Laclau, E. (1971). Feudalism and Capitalism in Latin America. *New Left Review* **67**: 23.

Laclau, E. (1979) Feudalism and capitalism in Latin America, in **P. Klaren and T. Bosset** (eds), *Promise of Development: Theories of Change in Latin America.* Boulder, CO: Westview Press, 166–93.

Lansing, J. S. (1991) *Priests and Programmers: Technologies of Power in the Engineered Landscape of Bali.* Princeton, NJ: Princeton University Press.

Larner, W. (2003) Neoliberalism? *Environment and Planning D: Society and Space* **21**: 509–12.

Latour, B. (1987) *Science in Action: How to Follow Scientists and Engineers through Society.* Cambridge, MA: Harvard University Press.

Laurie, N. (1997) Negotiating femininity: women and representation in emergency employment in Peru. *Gender, Place and Culture* **4**(2): 235–51.

Lawson, V. (1986). National Economic Policies, Local Variations in Structure of Production, and Uneven Regional Development: The Case of Ecuador. *Studies on the Interrelationships Between Development and Migration in Third World Settings, Discussion Paper Series* 33: i–163. Department of Geography, Ohio State University. Also Ph.D. Dissertation, Department of Geography, Ohio State University.

Lawson, V. (1992) Institutional, research, and philosophical domains of concern, in **G. Elbow** (ed), *Future Directions in Latin Americanist Geography: Research Agendas for the Nineties and Beyond.* Auburn, AL: Conference of Latin Americanist Geographers, Special Publication No. 3.

Lawson, V. (1995) Beyond the firm: restructuring gender divisions of labor in Quito's garment industry under austerity. *Environment and Planning D: Society and Space* **13**(4): 415–44.

Lawson, V. (1998) Hierarchical households and gendered migration: a research agenda. *Progress in Human Geography* **22**(1): 32–53.

Lawson, V. (1999) Tailoring is a profession, seamstressing is work! Resiting work and reworking gender identities among artisanal garment workers in Quito. *Environment and Planning A* **31**: 209–27.

Lawson, V. (2002) Global governmentality and graduated sovereignty; national belonging among poor migrants in Ecuador. *Scottish Geographical Magazine* **118**(3): 235–55.

Lawson, V. and Jarosz, J. (2005) *Locating Poverty Studies.* Paper presented at the Association of Pacific Coast Geographers Meeting, Phoenix, AZ.

Lawson, V. and Klak, T. (1990) Conceptual linkages in the study of production and reproduction in Latin American cities. *Economic Geography* **66**(4): 305–9.

Leach, M. (1994) *Rainforest Relations: Gender and Resource Use Among the Mende of Gola, Sierra Leone.* Washington, DC: Smithsonian Institution Press.

Lefebvre, H. (1990) *The Production of Space.* Oxford: Blackwell.

Lehman, D. (1997) An Opportunity Lost: Escobar's Deconstruction of Development. *Journal of Development Studies* **33**(4): 568–78.

Lenin, V. (1965 [1917]) *Imperialism: the highest stage of capitalism, a popular outline.* Peking: Foreign Language Press.

Lewis, A. (1955) *The Theory of Economic Growth.* London: Allen & Unwin.

Lind, A. (2000) Negotiating boundaries: women's organizing and the politics of restructuring in Ecuador, in **M. Marchand and A. Runyan** (eds), *Gender and Global Restructuring.* London: Routledge, 161–75.

Lind, A. (2005) *Gendered Paradoxes. Women's Movements, State Restructuring, and Global Development in Ecuador.* University Park, PA: Penn State University Press.

Lipset, S. M. and A. Solari (1967) *Elites in Latin America.* New York: Oxford University Press.

Lipton, M. (1977) *Why Poor People Stay Poor. Urban Bias in World Development.* Cambridge, MA: Harvard University Press.

Livingstone, D. and C. W. J. Withers (1999) *Geography and Enlightenment.* Chicago: Chicago University Press.

Logan, M. (1972) The development process in the less developed countries. *The Australian Geographer* **XII**(2): 146–53.

Longhurst, R. (2002) Geography and gender: a 'critical' time? *Progress in Human Geography* **26**(4): 544–52.

Losch, A. (1954) *The Economics of Location.* New Haven, CT: Yale University Press.

Luxemburg, R. and N. Bukharin (1972) *Imperialism and the accumulation of capital.* London: Penguin Press.

Lycklama, G., A. Nijeholt, V. Vargas and S. Wieringa (eds) (1998) *Women's Movements and Public Policy in Europe, Latin America and the Caribbean.* New York: Garland.

Marchand, M. and J. Parpart (1995) *Feminism, Postmodernism, Development.* London: Routledge.

Marini, R. (1969) *Subdesarrollo y revolución.* Mexico: Siglo Veintiuno Editores.

Marston, S. (2000) The social construction of scale. *Progress in Human Geography* **24**(2) 219–42.

Martin, R. (2004) Editorial: Geography: making a difference in a globalizing world. *Transactions of the Institute of British Geographers* **29**(2): 147–50.

Massey, D. (1984) *Spatial Divisions of Labor: Social Structures and the Geography of Production.* New York: Routledge.

Massey, D. (1994) *Space, Place and Gender.* Minneapolis: University of Minnesota Press.

Massey, D. (1999). Space-time, 'science' and the relationship between physical geography and human geography. *Transactions of the Institute of British Geographers* **24**: 261–76.

Massey, D. (2004) Geographies of responsibility. *Geografiska Annaler* **86B**: 5–18.

Massey, D. (2005) *For Space.* London: Sage.

Massey, D. and R. Meegan (1982) *The Anatomy of Job Loss: The How, Where and Why of Employment Decline.* London: Methuen.

Mathewson, K. and B. Wisner (2005) The Geographical and Political Vision of J.M. Blaut. *Antipode* **37**(5): 900–10.

Matless, D. (1992) An occasion for geography: landscape, representation, and Foucault's corpus. *Environment and Planning D: Society and Space,* **10**(1): 41–56.

McClelland, D. (1961) *The Achieving Society.* Princeton, NJ: Van Nostrand.

McDowell, L. (1992) Doing gender: feminism, feminists and research methods in human geography. *Transactions of the Institute of British Geographers* **17**(4): 399–416.

McDowell, L. and J. Sharp (1999) *A Feminist Glossary of Human Geography.* New York: Oxford University Press.

McGeary, J. and M. Michaels (1998) Africa Rising. *Time* **151**(12): 35–46.

McGee, T. (1974) In praise of tradition: towards a geography of anti-development. *Antipode* **6**(3): 30–49.

Meier, G. and D. Seers (eds) (1984) *Pioneers in Development.* Washington, DC: World Bank and Oxford University Press.

Mies, M. and V. Shiva (1993) *Ecofeminism.* London: Zed Books.

Mitchell, K. (1997) Transnational discourse: bringing geography back in. *Antipode* **29**(2): 101–14.

Mitchell, K. (2004) *Crossing the Neoliberal Line. Pacific Rim Migration and the Metropolis.* Philadelphia: Temple University Press.

Mitchell, T. (1991a) America's Egypt. Discourse of the Development Industry, *Middle East Report,* March–April.

Mitchell, T. (1991b) *Colonising Egypt.* Berkeley: University of California Press.

Mitchell, T. (2002) *Rule of Experts.* Berkeley: University of California Press.

Mohan, G. (1999) Not so distant, not so strange: the personal and the political in participatory research. *Ethics, Place and Environment* **2**(1): 41–54.

Mohanty, C. (1991) Cartographies of struggle: third world women and the politics of feminism, in **C. Mohanty, A. Russo and L. Torres** (eds.), *Third World Women and the Politics of Feminism.* Bloomington: Indiana University Press.

Mohanty, C., A. Russo and L. Torres (eds) (1991) *Third World Women and the Politics of Feminism.* Bloomington: Indiana University Press.

Momsen, J. and V. Kinnaird (1993) *Different Places, Different Voices: Gender and Development in Africa, Asia and Latin America.* New York: Routledge.

Momsen, J. and J. Townsend (1987) *Geography of Gender in the Third World.* London: Hutchinson.

Moser, C. (1987) The experience of poor women in Guayaquil, in **E. Archetti, P. Cammack and B. Roberts** (eds), *Sociology of Developing Societies: Latin America.* London: Monthly Review Press.

Mullings, B. (1999) Sides of the same coin?: Coping and resistance among Jamaican data-entry operators. *Annals of the Association of American Geographers* **89**(2): 290–311.

Multinational Monitor (2003) Grotesque inequality: corporate globalization and the global gap between rich and poor, byline Robert Weissman, 1 July.

Munck, R. and D. O'Hearn (eds) (1999) *Critical Development Theory: Contributions to a New Paradigm.* London: Zed Books.

Murray, C. (1981) Families Divided. *The Impact of Migrant Labor in Lesotho.* Cambridge: Cambridge University Press.

Mutersbaugh, T. (2002) The number is the beast: a political-economy of organic-coffee certification and producer unionism. *Environment and Planning A* **34**(7): 1165–84.

Myrdal, G. (1957) *Economic Theory and Underdeveloped Regions.* London: Duckworth.

Nagar, R. (1998) Communal Discourses, Marriage, and the Politics of Gendered Social Boundaries among South Asian Immigrants in Tanzania. *Gender, Place and Culture* **5**(2): 117–39.

Nagar, R. and H. Leitner (1998) Contesting social relations in communal spaces. Identity politics among Asian communities in Dar Es Salaam, in **R. Fincher and J. Jacobs** (eds.) *Cities of Difference.* New York: Guilford Press.

Nagar, R., V. Lawson, L. McDowell and S. Hanson (2002) Locating Globalization: feminist (re)readings of the subjects and spaces of globalization. *Economic Geography* **78**(3): 285–306.

Narayan, D. (2000) *Voices of the Poor. Can Anyone Hear Us?* New York: Oxford University Press for the World Bank.

Nast, H. (1994) Women in the field. *Professional Geographer* **46**(1): 54–66.

N'Dione, E., J. P. De Leener, M. Ndiaye and P. Jackolin (1997) Reinventing the Present: the Chodak Experience in Senegal, in **M. Rahmena and V. Bawtree** (eds), *The Post-Development Reader*. London: Zed Books.

Nelson, L. (2000) *Remaking gender and citizenship in a Mexican Indigenous Community*. Ph.D. Dissertation, Department of Geography, University of Washington.

Nelson, L. (2003) Decentering 'the movement': collective action, place and the 'sedimentation' of radical political discourses. *Environment and Planning D: Society and Space* **21**: 559–81.

Neumann, R. (2005) *Making Political Ecology*. London: Hodder Arnold.

Nevins, J. (2001) *Operation Gatekeeper: The Rise of the 'Illegal Alien' and the Remaking of the US-Mexico Boundary*. New York: Routledge.

Newstead, C. (2002) *(Dis)entangling the politics of regional possibility in the post-colonial Caribbean*. Ph.D. Thesis, University of Washington.

Newstead, C. (2005) Scaling Caribbean (in)dependence. *Geoforum* **36**: 45–58.

Newstead, C., C. Reid and M. Sparke (2003) The Cultural Geography of Scale, in **K. Anderson, M. Domosh, S. Pile and N. Thrift** (eds) *The Handbook of Cultural Geography*. London: Sage.

Nguyen, S. (2004). www.adamsmith.org/blog/(weblog entry), 15 December.

Oglesby, E. (2002) *Politics at Work: Elites, Labor and Agrarian Modernization in Guatemala, 1980–2000*. Ph.D. Thesis, University of California, Berkeley.

Ohlin, B. (1933) *Interregional and International Trade*. Cambridge, MA: Harvard University Press.

Ohmae, K. (1995) *The End of the Nation-State: The Rise of Regional Economies*. New York: Free Press.

Omvedt, G. (1980) Migration in colonial India. The articulation of feudalism and capitalism by the colonial state. *Journal of Peasant Studies* **7**: 185–212.

Ong, A. (1987) *Spirits of Resistance and Capitalist Discipline: Factory Women in Malaysia*. Albany: State University of New York Press.

Ould-Mey, M. (1996) *Global Restructuring and Peripheral States: The Carrot and the Stick in Mauritania*. Lanham, MD : Littlefield Adams Books.

Ould-Mey, M. (1997) Alternatives to neoliberalism in Latin America *Latin American Perspectives* **24**(1): 80–91.

Pacione, M. (ed.) (1988). *The Geography of the Third World: progress and prospect.* London and New York: Routledge.

Parpart, J. (1995) Deconstructing the development 'expert': gender, development and 'vulnerable groups', in **M. Marchand and J. Parpart** (eds.) *Feminism, Postmodernism, Development.* London: Routledge, 221–43.

Parreñas, R. (2001) *Servants of Globalization. Women, Migration and Domestic Work.* Stanford, CA: Stanford University Press.

Peake, L. and A. Trotz (1999) *Gender, Ethnicity and Place: Women and Identities in Guyana.* London: Routledge.

Pearlstein, S. (1998) Tropical and landlocked make a poor combination. *The Washington Post*, Thursday 23 April, C1, C12.

Pearson, R. (2000) Moving the Goalposts: Gender and Globalization in the Twenty-first Century. *Gender and Development* **8**(1): 10–19.

Peck, J. (2001) Neoliberalizing states: thin policies/hard outcomes. *Progress in Human Geography* **25**(3): 445–55.

Peck, J. (2002) Political economies of scale: fast policy, interscalar relations, and neoliberal workfare. *Economic Geography* **78**(3): 331–60.

Peck, J. and A. Tickell (2002) Neoliberalizing space. *Antipode* **34**(4): 380–404.

Peet, R. (1979) Societal Contradictions and Marxist Geography. *Annals of the Association of American Geographers* **69**(1): 164–9.

Peet, R. (2000) Celebrating thirty years of radical geography. *Environment and Planning A* **32**: 951–3.

Peet, R. (2002) Poststructural thought policing. *Economic Geography* **78**(1): 87–8.

Peet, R. (with E. Hartwick) (1999) *Theories of Development.* New York: Guilford Press.

Peet, R., B. Borne, M. Davis et al. (2003) *Unholy Trinity: The I.M.F., World Bank and W.T.O.* London: Zed Books.

Peet, R. and M. Watts (2004) *Liberation ecologies: environment, development, social movements.* London: Routledge.

Perrault, T. (2003a) Changing places: transnational networks, ethnic politics, and community development in the Ecuadorian Amazon. *Political Geography* **22**(1): 61–88.

Perrault, T. (2003b) Making space. Community organization, agrarian change and the politics of scale in the Ecuadorian Amazon. *Latin American Perspectives* **30**(1): 96–121.

Perrault, T. (2005) State restructuring and the scale politics of rural water governance in Bolivia. *Environment and Planning A* **37**: 263–84.

Perrault, T. (2006) From the *Guerra del Agua* to the *Guerra del Gas*: resource governance, neoliberalism and popular protest in Bolivia. *Antipode* **38**(1): 150–72.

Perrault, T. and P. Martin (2005) Geographies of neoliberalism in Latin America. *Environment and Planning A* **37**: 191–201.

Perrons, D. (1999) Reintegrating production and consumption or why political economy still matters, in **R. Munck and D. O'Hearn** (eds), *Critical Development Theory.* London: Zed Books, 91–112.

Petras, J. and H. Veltmeyer, (2001) *Globalization Unmasked: Imperialism in the 21st Century.* New York: Zed Books.

Petras, J. and H. Veltmeyer, (2003) *Cardoso's Brazil: A Land for Sale.* Lanham, MD: Rowman and Littlefield.

Philo, C. (1992) Foucault's geography. *Environment and Planning D: Society and Space* **10**(2): 137–61.

Pickles, J. (2001) Development 'deferred': poststructuralism, postdevelopment, and the defense of critical modernism. *Economic Geography* **77**(4): 383–8.

Pickles, J. (2002) Reading development. *Economic Geography* **78**(1): 89–90.

Porter, P. (1987) Wholes and fragments: reflections on the economy of affection, capitalism and the human costs of development. *Geografiska Annaler* **69**(B): 1–14.

Portes, A., M. Castells and L. Benton (1989) *The Informal Economy: Studies in Advanced and Less Developed Countries.* Baltimore, MD: Johns Hopkins University Press.

Potter, R. (1999) *Geographies of Development.* Harlow: Prentice Hall.

Potter, R. (2001) Geography and development: 'core and periphery'? *Area* **33**(4): 422–39.

Potter, R., T. Binns, J. Elliott and D. Smith (2004) *Geographies of Development*, 2nd edn. London: Prentice Hall.

Power, M. (1998) The dissemination of development. *Environment and Planning D: Society and Space* **16**: 577–98.

Power, M. (2003) *Rethinking Development Geographies.* London: Routledge.

Pratt, G. (2004) *Working Feminism.* Philadelphia: Temple University Press.

Pratt, G. and B. Yeoh (2003) Transnational (Counter) Topographies. *Gender, Place and Culture* **10**(2): 159–66.

Prebisch, R. (1959) Commercial policy in the underdeveloped countries. *American Economic Review* **49**(2): 251–73.

Prebisch, R. (1962) The economic development of Latin America and its principal problems. *Economic Bulletin for Latin America* **7**(1): 1–22.

Pred, A. and M. Watts (1992) *Reworking Modernity: Capitalisms and Symbolic Discontent.* New Brunswick, NJ: Rutgers University Press.

Price, P. (2004) *Dry Place. Landscapes of belonging and exclusion.* Minneapolis: University of Minnesota Press.

Quijano, A. (1971) *Nationalism and Capitalism in Peru: A Study in Neo-Imperialism.* New York: Monthly Review Press.

Rabinow, P. (1984) Introduction, in **P. Rabinow** (ed.), *The Foucault Reader*, New York: Pantheon Books, 3–30.

Radcliffe, S. (1986) Gender relations, peasant livelihood strategies and mobility: a case study from Cuzco, Peru. *Bulletin of Latin American Research* **5**(2): 29–47.

Radcliffe, S. (1990) Ethnicity, patriarchy and incorporation into the nation: female migrants as domestic servants in Peru. *Environment and Planning D: Society and Space* **8**: 379–93.

Radcliffe, S. (2001) Development, the state and transnational political connections: state and subject formation in Latin America. *Global Networks* **1**(1): 19–36.

Radcliffe, S. (2004) Geography of development: development, civil society and inequality – social capital is (almost) dead? *Progress in Human Geography* **28**(4): 517–27.

Radcliffe, S. (2005) Development and geography: towards a postcolonial development geography? *Progress in Human Geography* **29**(3): 291–8.

Radcliffe, S. and S. Westwood (eds) (1993) *'Viva' Women and Popular Protest in Latin America*. London: Routledge.

Radcliffe, S. and S. Westwood (1996) *Remaking the Nation. Place, identity and politics in Latin America*. London: Routledge.

Radcliffe, S., N. Laurie and R. Andolina (2003) The transnationalization of gender and reimagining Andean indigenous development. *Signs* **29**(2): 387–416.

Raghuram, P. (1993) Invisible female agricultural labour in India, in **J. Momsen and V. Kinnaird** (eds), *Different Places, Different Voices. Gender and Development in Africa, Asia and Latin America*. London: Routledge, 109–19.

Raghuram, P. and I. Hardhill (1998) Negotiating a market: a case study of Asian women in business. *Women Studies International Forum* **21**(5): 475–84.

Rahnema, M. and V. Bawtree (eds) (1997) *The Post-Development Reader*. Atlantic Highlands, NJ: Zed Books; Dhaka: University Press; Halifax, NS: Fernwood Publishing; Cape Town: David Philip.

Raju, S. (1982) Regional patterns of female participation in the labor force in India. *Professional Geographer* **34**: 42–9.

Rankin, K. (2002) Social Capital, Microfinance, and the Politics of Development. *Feminist Economics* **8**(1): 1–24.

Richardson, H. W. (1978) *Regional Economics*. Chicago: University of Illinois Press.

Richardson, H. W. (1980) Polarization Reversal in Developing Countries. *Papers of the Regional Science Association* **45**: 67–85.

Richardson, H. W. and M. Richardson (1975) The Relevance of Growth Center Strategies to Latin America. *Economic Geography* **51**: 163–78.

Riddell, J. B. (1970) *The Spatial Dynamics of Modernization in Sierra Leone: Structure, Diffusion and Response*. Evanston, IL: Northwestern University Press.

Rivkin, M. D. (1976) *Land Use and the Intermediate Size City in Developing Countries with Case Studies of Turkey, Brazil and Malaysia*. New York: Praeger.

Rocheleau, D. (1991) Gender, ecology and the science of survival: stories and lessons from Kenya. *Agriculture and Human Values* **8**(1/2): 156–65.

Rodney, W. (1972) *How Europe Underdeveloped Africa*. London: Bogle-L'Ouverture Publications.

Rohter, L. (2003) New global trade lineup: haves, have-nots, have-somes. *New York Times*, 2 November, Section 4, p. 3.

Rondinelli, D. (1979) Applied policy analysis for integrated regional development planning in the Philippines.' *Third World Planning Review* **1**(2): 150–78.

Rondinelli, D. (1983) *Secondary Cities in Developing Countries: Policies for Diffusing Urbanization*. Beverly Hills, CA: Sage.

Rondinelli, D. and K. Ruddle (1978) *Urbanization and Rural Development: A Spatial Policy for Equitable Growth*. New York: Praeger.

Rose, G. (1993) *Feminism and Geography*. Minneapolis: University of Minnesota Press.

Rosset, P., J. Collins and M. Lappe (2000) Lessons from the Green Revolution. *Tikkun Magazine*, http://www.foodfirst.org/media/printformat.php?id=148 (accessed 20 June 2006).

Rostow, W. W. (1960) *The Stages of Economic Growth: A Non-communist Manifesto*. Cambridge: Cambridge University Press.

Routledge, P. (2003) Convergence space: process geographies of grassroots globalization networks. *Transactions of the Institute of British Geographers* **28**: 333–49.

Rundstrom, R., D. Deur, K. Berry and D. Winchell (2003) American Indian geography, in **G. Gaile and C. Wilmott** (eds.), *Geography in America at the Dawn of the 21st Century.* Oxford: Oxford University Press.

Sachs, W. (1992) *Development Dictionary: a Guide to Knowledge as Power.* London: Zed Books.

Sack, R. (1974) The spatial separatist theme in geography. *Economic Geography* **50**: 1–19.

Safa, H. (2002) Women and globalization: lessons from the Dominican Republic, in **J. Chase** (ed.), *The Spaces of Neoliberalism: Land, Place, and Family in Latin America.* Bloomfield, CT: Kumarian Press.

Sage, C. (1993) Deconstructing the household: women's roles under commodity relations in highland Bolivia, in **J. Momsen and V. Kinnaird** (eds), *Different Places, Different Voices. Gender and Development in Africa, Asia and Latin America.* London: Routledge, 243–55.

Said, E. (1979) *Orientalism.* New York: Vintage Books.

Samatar, A. I. (1989) *The State and Rural Transformation in Northern Somalia, 1884–1986.* Madison: University of Wisconsin Press.

Samatar, A. I. (1999) *An African Miracle: State and Class Leadership and Colonial Legacy in Botswana Development.* Portsmouth, NH: Heinemann.

Samatar, Abdi Ismail and Ahmed I. Samatar (2002) *The African State: Reconsiderations.* Portsmouth, NH: Heinemann.

Santos, M. (1974) Geography, marxism and underdevelopment. *Antipode* **6**(3): 1–9.

Sarup, M. (1993) *An Introductory Guide to Post-Structuralism and Postmodernism,* 2nd edn. New York: Harvester Wheatsheaf.

Sassen, S. (1998) *Globalization and its Discontents.* New York: New Press.

Scarpaci, J. (1988) *Primary Medical Care Under Military Rule.* Pittsburgh, PA: University of Pittsburgh Press.

Schrijvers, J. (1995) Participation and power: a transformative feminist research perspective, in **N. Nelson and S. Wright** (eds.), *Power and Participatory Development: Theory and Practice*. London: Intermediate Technology Publications, 19–29.

Schroeder, R. (1997) *Shady Practices. Agroforestry and Gender Politics in the Gambia*. Berkeley: University of California Press.

Schuurman, F. J. (1993) *Beyond the Impasse. New Directions in Development Theory*. London: Zed Books.

Schuurman, F. J. (2000a) Paradigms lost, paradigms regained? Development studies in the twenty-first century. *Third World Quarterly* **21**(1): 7–20.

Schuurman, F. J. (2000b) *Globalization and Development Studies*. Amsterdam: Thela Thesis.

Scott, J. (1992) Experience, in **J. Butler and J. Scott** (eds), New York: Routledge.

Seager, J. (1997) *The State of Women in the World Atlas*. New York: Viking.

Seager, J. (2003) *The Penguin Atlas of Women in the World: Completely Revised and Updated*. New York: Penguin Books.

Seager, J. (2005) *Atlas of Women in the World*. Sussex: Gardners Books.

Shaogong, H., H. Ping, L. Shaojun et al. (2004). Why must we talk about the environment? A summary of the Nanshan Seminar, trans. Y. Hairong. *Positions* **12**(1): 237–46.

Sheppard, E. (2002) The spaces and times of globalization, place, scale, networks and positionality. *Economic Geography* **78**(3): 307–30.

Shrestha, N. (1988) A Structural Perspective on Labor Migration in Underdeveloped Countries. *Progress in Human Geography* **12**: 179–207.

Shrestha, N. (1995) Becoming a development category, in **J. Crush** (ed), *The Power of Development*. London: Routledge, 266–77.

Sidaway, J. D. (2002) *Imagined Regional Communities: Integration and Sovereignty in the Global South*. New York: Routledge.

Silvey, R. (2000a) Stigmatized spaces: gender and mobility under crisis in South Sulawesi, Indonesia. *Gender, Place and Culture* **7**(2): 143–61.

Silvey, R. (2000b) Diasporic subjects: gender and mobility in South Sulawesi. *Women's Studies International Forum* **23**(4): 501–15.

Silvey, R. (2003) Spaces of Protest; Gendered Migration, Social Networks, and Labor Protest in West Java, Indonesia. *Political Geography* **22**(2): 129–57.

Silvey, R. (2004a) Transnational migration and the gender politics of scale: Indonesian domestic workers in Saudi Arabia, 1997–2000. *Singapore Journal of Tropical Geography*, **25**(2): 141–55.

Silvey, R. (2004b) Transnational Domestication: Indonesian Domestic Workers in Saudi Arabia. *Political Geography*, **23**(3): 245–64.

Silvey, R. and V. Lawson, (1999) Placing the migrant. *Annals of the Association of American Geographers* **89**(1): 121–32.

Sim, S. (1998) *The Icon Critical Dictionary of Postmodern Thought.* Cambridge: Icon Books.

Sivaramakrishnan, K. and A. Agrawal (eds). (2003) *Regional Modernities. The Cultural Politics of Development in India.* Stanford, CA: Stanford University Press.

Slater, D. (1973) Geography and Underdevelopment – I. *Antipode* **5**(3): 21–32.

Slater, D. (1977) Geography and Underdevelopment – II. *Antipode* **9**(3): 1–31.

Slater, D. (1992a) On the borders of social theory: learning from other regions. *Environment and Planning D: Society and Space* **10**: 307–27.

Slater, D. (1992b) Theories of Development and Politics of the Post-Modern: Exploring a Border Zone. *Development and Change* **23**(3): 283–319.

Slater, D. (1993) The geopolitical imagination and the enframing of development theory. *Transactions of the Institute of British Geographers* **18**: 419–37.

Slater, D. (2004) *Geopolitics and the Post-Colonial. Rethinking North–South Relations.* Oxford: Blackwell.

Smith, A. (1976) *An Inquiry into the Nature and Causes of the Wealth of Nations.* London: A. Strahan and T. Cadelt.

Smith, N. (1984) *Uneven Development: nature, capital and the production of space.* Oxford: Blackwell.

Smith, N. (1986) On the necessity of uneven development. *International Journal of Urban and Regional Research* **10**(1): 87–104.

Smith, N. (1993) Homeless/global: scaling places, in **J. Bird, B. Curtis, T. Putnam et al.** (eds), *Mapping the Futures*. London: Routledge.

Soja, E. (1968) *The Geography of Modernization in Kenya*. Syracuse, NY: Syracuse University Press.

Sokoloff, N. (1980) *Between Money and Love. The dialectics of women's home and market work*. New York: Praeger.

Sparke, M. (2005) *In the Space of Theory: Postfoundational Geographies of the Nation-State*. Minneapolis: University of Minnesota Press.

Sparke, M. (2006a) Acknowledging Responsibility For Space. *Progress in Human Geography* (forthcoming).

Sparke, M. (2006b) Everywhere, But Always Somewhere: Critical Geographies of the Global South. *Global South* 1(1).

Sparke, M. (2006c) Political Geographies of Globalization (2): Governance. *Progress in Human Geography* **30**(2): 1–16.

Sparke, M. and V. Lawson (2003) Entrepreneurial political geographies of the global-local nexus, in **J. Agnew, K. Mitchell and G. O'Tuathail** (eds.) *A Companion to Political Geography*. Oxford: Blackwell, 315–34.

Sparke, M., E. Brown, D. Corva et al. (2005) The World Social Forum and the Lessons for Economic Geography. *Economic Geography* **81**(4): 359–80.

Spivak, G. (1990) Gayatri Spivak speaks on the politics of the postcolonial subject. *Socialist Review* **20**: 81–90.

Spivak, G. (1998) Cultural talks in the hot peace: revisiting the 'Global Village', in **P. Cheah and B. Robbins** (eds) *Cosmopolitics: thinking and feeling beyond the nation*. Minneapolis: University of Minnesota Press.

Sridharan, K. (1998) G-15 and South-South cooperation: promise and performance. *Third World Quarterly* **19**(3): 357–73.

Staeheli, L. and R. Nagar (2002) Feminists talking across worlds. *Gender, Place and Culture* **9**(2): 167–72.

Stallings, B. and R. Kaufman (1989) *Debt and Democracy in Latin America*. Boulder, CO: Westview Press.

Stiell, B. and K. England Domestic distinctions: constructing difference among paid domestic workers in Toronto. *Gender, Place and Culture* **4**(3): 339–59.

Sundberg, J. (2003) Masculinist epistemologies and the politics of fieldwork in Latin Americanist geography. *Professional Geographer* **55**(2): 180–90.

Susman, P. (1974) Cuban development: from dualism to integration. *Antipode* **6**(3): 10–29.

Swyngedouw, E. (1997) Neither global nor local: 'glocalization' and the politics of scale, in **K. Cox** (ed), *Spaces of Globalization*. New York: Guilford Press.

Taafe, E. J., R. Morrill and P. Gould (1963) Transport expansion in underdeveloped countries: a comparative analysis. *Geographical Review* **53**(4): 503–29.

Tapscott, C. (1995) Changing discourses of development in South Africa, in **J. Crush** (ed.), *The Power of Development*. London: Routledge, 176–92.

Taylor, J. (1980) Peripheral capitalism and rural-to-urban migration in Costa Rica. *Latin American Perspectives* **7**: 75–90.

Taylor, R. (2002) *The Idea of Freedom in Asia and Africa*. Stanford, CA: Stanford University Press.

Teltscher, S. (1993) *Informal Trading in Quito, Ecuador*. Saarbruken: Verlag Breitenbach Publishers.

Tinker, I. (1976) *Women and World Development*. Washington, DC: Overseas Development Council.

Toffler, A. and H. Toffler (1995) *Creating a New Civilization: the politics of the Third Wave*. Atlanta: Turner Publications.

Townsend, J. (1993) Housewifisation and colonisation in the Colombian Rainforest, in **J. Momsen and V. Kinnaird** (eds), *Different places, Different Voices. Gender and Development in Africa, Asia and Latin America*. London: Routledge, 270–7.

Townsend, J. (1995) *Women's Voices from the Rainforest*. New York: Routledge.

Tsirgi, N. (1999) The paradox of development, in **D. Morales-Gomez, N. Tschirgi and J. Moher** (eds) *Reforming Social Policy: Changing Perspectives in Human Development*. Ontario: International Development Research Centre.

Turnbull, D. (1997) Reframing science and other local knowledge traditions. *Futures* **29**(6): 551–62.

Tyner, J. (1994) The social construction of gendered migration for the Philippines. *Asian and Pacific Migration Journal* **3**: 589–617.

UNCTAD (2002) Least Developed Countries Report. Geneva: UNCTAD.

United Nations Development Program (1999) *United Nations Human Development Report 1999: Globalization with a Human Face.* New York: Oxford University Press.

United Nations Development Program (2003) *United Nations Human Development Report.* New York: Oxford University Press.

Van Eyck, K. (2002) *Neoliberalism and democracy? The gendered restructuring of work, unions and the Colombian public sphere.* Ph.D. Thesis, University of Washington.

Visweswaran, K. (1994) *Fictions of Feminist Ethnography.* Minneapolis: University of Minnesota Press.

Walker, R. (1989) Socialist geography, in **G. Gaile and C. Willmott** (eds.), *Geography in America.* Columbus, OH: Merrill.

Wallerstein, I. (1974) *The Modern World-System: capitalist agriculture and the origins of the European world-economy in the sixteenth century.* New York: Academic Press.

Walton, J. and D. Seddon (1994) *Free Markets and Food Riots. The Politics of Global Adjustment.* Oxford: Blackwell.

Watts, M. (1983) *Silent Violence. Food, Famine and Peasantry in Northern Nigeria.* Berkeley: University of California Press.

Watts, M. (1988) Deconstructing determinism: Marxism's development theory and a comradely critique of capitalist world development by S. Corbridge. *Antipode* **20**(2): 142–68.

Watts, M. (1989) The agrarian question in Africa: debating the crisis. *Progress in Human Geography* **13**(1): 1–41.

Watts, M. (1991) Mapping meaning, denoting difference, imagining identity: dialectical images and postmodern geographies. *Geografisker Annaler, Series B, Human Geography* **73**(1): 7–16.

Watts, M. (1993) Development I: power, knowledge, discursive practice. *Progress in Human Geography* **17**(2): 257–72.

Watts, M. (1995) 'A New Deal in Emotions'. Theory and practice and the crisis of development, in **J. Crush** (ed.), *Power of Development*. London: Routledge.

Watts, M. (2000) Development, in **R. Johnston et al.** (eds), *The Dictionary of Human Geography*. Oxford: Blackwell.

Watts, M. (2001a) 1968 and all that... *Progress in Human Geography* **25**(2): 157–88.

Watts, M. (2001b) *The Local Global Dialectic: A Geographer's Perspective. Conversations with History* (video recording), 26 July. Institute of International Studies, University of California, Berkeley.

Watts, M. (2003) Development and Governmentality. *Singapore Journal of Tropical Geography*, **24**(1): 6–34.

Watts, M. and T. Bassett (1986) Politics, the state and agrarian development: a comparative study of Nigeria and the Ivory Coast. *Political Geography Quarterly* **5**: 103–25.

Wheen, F. (2000). *Karl Marx: a life*. New York: Norton.

Whelehan, I. (1995) *Modern Feminist Thought. From the Second Wave to Post-Feminism*. New York: New York University Press.

Whitehead, A. (1979) Some preliminary notes on the subordination of women. *IDS Bulletin* **10**(3): 10–13.

Willems-Braun, B. (1997) Buried epistemologies: the politics of nature in (post)colonial British Columbia. *Annals of the Association of American Geographers* **87**: 3–31.

Williamson, J. (1990) *Latin American Adjustment. How Much Has Happened?* Washington, DC: Institute for International Economics.

Winchell, D. (1996) The consolidation of tribal planning in American Indian tribal government and culture, in **K. Frantz** (ed.), *Human Geography in North America: New Perspectives and Trends in Research*. Innsbruck: Department of Geography, University of Innsbruck, 209–24.

Wisner, B. (1989) *Power and Need in Africa*. Trenton, NJ: Africa World Press.

Wolf, D. (1992) *Factory Daughters: Gender, Household Dynamics, and Rural Industrialization in Java.* Berkeley: University of California Press.

Wolf, E. (1969) *Peasant Wars of the Twentieth Century.* New York: Harper and Row.

Wolpe, H. (1980) *The Articulation of Modes of Production: Essays from Economy and Society.* London: Routledge and Kegan Paul.

World Bank (1975) *World Bank Country Report, Lesotho.* Washington, DC: World Bank.

World Bank (1991) Integration with the global economy. *World Bank Development Report: The Challenge of Development.* Washington, DC: Oxford University Press, 88–108.

World Bank (1999) Overview and new directions in development thinking. *World Development Report – 1999/2000: Entering the 21st Century.* Washington, DC: Oxford University Press, 1–30.

World Bank (2000a) *Voices of the Poor. Can Anyone Hear Us?* Washington, DC: Oxford University Press.

World Bank (2000b) *World Development Report 2000/2001: Attacking Poverty.* Washington, DC: Oxford University Press.

Wright, M. (1997) Crossing the factory frontier: gender, place and power in the Mexican Maquiladora. *Antipode* **29**(3): 278–302.

Wright, M. (2004) From protests to politics: sex work, women's worth and Ciudad Juarez modernity. *Annals of the Association of American Geographers* **94**(2): 369–86.

Wright, S. (2004) *Harvesting Knowledge: the contested terrain of intellectual property rights in the Philippines.* Ph.D. Thesis, University of Washington.

Yapa, L. (1996) What Causes Poverty?: A Postmodern View. *Annals of the Association of American Geographers* **86**(4): 707–28.

Yeoh, B., S. Huang and K. Willis (2000) Global cities, transnational flows and gender dimensions, the view from Singapore. *Tijdschrift voor Economische en Sociale Geografie* **91**(2): 147–58.

Yotopoulos, P. and J. Nugent (1976) *Economics of Development. Empirical Investigations.* New York: Harper and Row.

Young, K., C. Wolkowitz, and C. McCullagh (1981) *Of Marriage and the Market. Women's Subordination in International Perspective.* London: CSE Books.

INDEX